d'Artagnan
Training Ltd.

THE HANDBOOK OF
SKILFUL
MANAGEMENT

The Institute of Management (IM) is at the forefront of management development and best management practice. The Institute embraces all levels of management from students to chief executives. It provides a unique portfolio of services for all managers, enabling them to develop skills and achieve management excellence.

If you would like to hear more about the benefits of membership, please write to Department P, Institute of Management, Cottingham Road, Corby NN17 1TT.

This series is commissioned by the Institute of Management Foundation.

THE HANDBOOK OF
SKILFUL
MANAGEMENT

**A Personal Programme to
Develop Your Portfolio of Skills
and Boost Your Employability**

SHEILA CANE

**PITMAN
PUBLISHING**

London · Hong Kong · Johannesburg
Melbourne · Singapore · Washington DC

PITMAN PUBLISHING
128 Long Acre, London WC2E 9AN
Tel: +44 (0) 171 447 2000
Fax: +44 (0) 171 240 5771

A Division of Pearson Professional Limited

First published in Great Britain 1996

British Library Cataloguing in Publication Data
A CIP catalogue record for this book can be obtained from the British Library.

ISBN 0 273 62343 5

10 9 8 7 6 5 4 3 2 1

Typeset by Northern Phototypesetting Co. Ltd.
Printed and bound in Great Britain by Biddles Ltd, Guildford and King's Lynn

The Publishers' policy is to use paper manufactured from sustainable forests.

ABOUT THE AUTHOR

Sheila Cane developed and practised her management skills in the film and television industry during a period of considerable change and reorganisation.

During the past ten years she has been a coach to many individuals and worked with organisations as varied as the Strategic Planning Society, the Institute of Management, the Virgin Group and Greenpeace International.

She is the author of *Ready Made Activities for Communication Skills*, *Ready Made Activities for Negotiation Skills* and *Kaizen: Winning Through People* (for Pitman Publishing) as well as co-author of *Putting Redundancy Behind You* (for Kogan Page).

She is also a regular contributor to TimeLife Books on Leadership and Personal Development issues.

CONTENTS

Contents

PREFACE

To be successful you need to take personal responsibility for your own career path. It is unlikely that your immediate manager is going to have either the time to devote to grooming you or the inclination to create a threat to their own position.

Your grandparent probably worked for one employer all his working life, your parent probably worked for several different employers in the same sector or industry while it is likely that you will have several changes of career in your working life.

Your grandparent probably had a paternalistic style of employer who would have been committed to looking after their staff in every way, trying to ensure that they had job security, would have known what they needed to do a good job and if they wanted advancement would have taken them under their patronage and guided them. In your parent's working life, it had changed a little. Education was the route to a good job, the economy was growing fast and there were many opportunities for advancement as new companies and industries were started up. If your parent was effective at work, it is quite likely that he/she would have been approached by other organisations in their field. Moving to another employer was a widely recognised route to advancement.

Today the work situation has changed again. The emphasis is on lean workforces, leaving perhaps less time for the paternalistic development of the workforce. Uncertainty about ongoing employment has resulted in both a reduction in the movement of staff between organisations for promotion and the forced change of careers as industries have dramatically reduced their headcount in a drive for efficiency and survival.

This book has been prepared, using the experience of managers in a wide variety of organisations, with the aim of detailing the most important aspects of development that are likely to lead to success in any field. It has been designed to be easy to use, learn from and create action plans from each topic. Such a broad range of topics has inevitably resulted in each section being restricted in length as well as depth and therefore a reading list has been added so that further sources for research are easily available.

We hope you will read through the whole book and then go back to work through each chapter in some detail so that you can pick up new ideas and learn from the experiences of others in your own personal development programme. Once you have done this, you will have an action plan that you can put into operation, using all the skills that you want to try out for yourself. The book itself can then remain on your shelf, always available as a resource for any new situations that arise.

The journey towards achieving your personal potential and success is often a lonely one; this book is intended to act as a travel guide, giving you the advice and information that you might require and acting as your own personal coach along the way.

Have a good journey.

INTRODUCTION

'*I really want to be successful in my career and believe that I am capable of a great deal more than my current position but I only get offered training in the skills I need in the short term, how can I get help in developing my potential for the future?'*

This book has been prepared to answer the cries of anguish that are all too often heard at external training courses and in social gatherings all over the world.

It is aimed to be both a self-managed programme of development for ambitious people at the beginning of their management or supervision careers as well as an opportunity for review and a source of revision for the more experienced. It has been designed to be easy to read, fun to work through and aims to be an inspiration and support to the reader to unlock his or her personal potential.

The material contained in this book is unique. It has been designed after lengthy research with successful managers from a very wide background of experience. For several years, the author asked hundreds of managers 'What do you wish you had known at the beginning of your career?' and 'What experiences that you have learned from would you like to pass on to others?' The results of this research have resulted in a programme that is balanced between core management skills and personal development skills. The feedback from the differing industries and organisations (ranging from financial institutions to charities) confirmed that the learning of new business skills and techniques needs to be balanced with an understanding of how to manage and develop yourself better.

Too often management development has been seen as teaching skills and techniques without considering that it is often how they are implemented that results in success or failure. This book includes material rarely found in conventional management training, such as creativity, developing emotional maturity and the role of power and influence.

Each chapter in this book stands alone and consists of:

- *simple self-tests, questionnaires and exercises* most of which will only take a few minutes to complete in order to identify areas for development
- *theories and techniques* relating to each skill as well as practical steps for learning and implementing them
- *bullet points* to provide check lists and signposts for each section of the stage
- *case studies and scenarios* to illustrate each skill and provide real life examples of some of the success stories and painful learning experiences of the sources for this book
- a *series of icons* (see opposite) to aid easy reading, identify cross references with other chapters and pull out key learning points
- a *further reading list* on each topic
- a *planning section* to help structure the implementation of new skills.

The self-managed programme of development takes the reader through a highly interactive planned journey of self-discovery and learning that opens with sections on self-assessment and career-life planning, and continues with an introduction to all the skills that have been identified as necessary for success as a manager at work.

For those readers who are more experienced as well as for those who have already worked their way once through the programme but want to revisit a particular skill, the index at the end of the book provides instant access to the relevant section and the check-lists within each chapter pinpoint the particular sub-section that may be required.

This book is designed to be written on, to become a personal handbook with individual notes and comments. So readers should use their highlighters and pens to help make this book as valuable a reference tool for the future as possible.

KEY TO MARGIN SYMBOLS

Interesting facts and figures

A book reference

An exercise / questionnaire

A reference to another relevant section of the book

Key thoughts or key words for the section

Example / case study

Checklist

Personal profile

Scenario

ONE STOP GUIDE TO CORE MANAGEMENT SKILLS

ACKNOWLEDGEMENTS

This book has taken me eight months to prepare and write and without the support, encouragement and input from the following, might never have seen the light of day.

Among the many hundreds of people who made a contribution, I would particularly like to thank:

Mike Burge, Ray Hodgkiss, Uta Bellion, Rachel Spence and Martin Stone who read drafts, gave constructive feedback (very effectively) and provided the encouragement to keep going when it seemed like an impossible task.

Leo Gough for stepping in and writing the chapter on finance when I discovered that I didn't know enough to be able to do it justice.

Margaret Ryan of the Thames Valley Management School who introduced me to many of the concepts of power and influence and helped me identify the sources for Stage 4.

Peter Russell who introduced me to many of the concepts of creativity and stress management over a period of years.

Christina Saunders of Catalyst with whom I developed many of the ideas in this book and who helped me refine the section on counselling skills for managers.

Patrick Forsyth who lent me books on a wide range of topics from his library.

All the people who responded to the plea for help in the Institute of Management newsletter and Katy Dowbiggin, Keith MacGregor, Desi Gillespie, Rebecca Dowbiggin, Jane Kelly, Linda Maytum Wilson, Richard Beavan, Mickey Kaufmann who all provided valuable comments on particular sections.

At Pitman, I would particularly like to thank Vicky Siddle for her neverending support and encouragement and Richard Stagg, Amelia Lakin, Sally Green, Linda Dhondy and Mark Allen for being such a great team to have on your side.

PREPARING YOURSELF FOR YOUR JOURNEY THROUGH THE WORLD OF WORK

A better understanding of your unique attributes is fundamental to any valid assessment of your true potential

In the separate stages of the book all the areas of management development have been identified and clarified into a programme that you can work through at your own speed to enable you to both identify which areas you want to develop and learn how you can do so.

Are you somewhat dissatisfied with your current levels of success?	*Yes/No*
Are you looking for ways to achieve your potential?	*Yes/No*
Do you want to be more motivated at work?	*Yes/No*
Do you want to make a greater contribution at work?	*Yes/No*
Are you concerned that you are not fulfilled or satisfied with your life?	*Yes/No*

If you answer 'yes' to one or more of the above questions, this book has been written for you.

The first stage involves getting to know yourself because, like any journey, it is always important to understand where you are starting from and what resources you already have. The exercises in this section will help you acknowledge your existing strengths and skills so that you can identify the areas you want to develop further, as well as considering whether you use all the resources you already have as effectively as possible.

This chapter will help you identify:
- your strengths and weaknesses
- your personality profile
- what motivates you
- your achievements and successes

If you are tempted to skip this chapter because it seems to be full of exercises and questionnaires, please read a little further before making up your mind. It became apparent in preparing this book, that all too often people *think* they understand themselves and their personalities but later in their careers they discover that many of the attributes they believed they owned were in fact delegated to them by other people. Think for yourself – how often at school did a teacher tell you that you had a gift for a subject that you really weren't interested in or your family decided at a very early stage that you were musical/sporty/academic when you *knew* you weren't?

This chapter is an opportunity to acknowledge for yourself who you really are. The first series of questionnaires are designed to be answered quickly and provide an objective framework for you to assess yourself while the second set of exercises (beginning on page 19) provides you with an opportunity to consider for yourself what your values, strengths, skills and qualities really are.

The purpose of this chapter is to enable you to create a genuine, up-to-date self-portrait so that you are clear about where you are beginning your journey from and what is truly important to you.

 If knowledge is power then increased self-knowledge can enable you to become truly awesome.

PROFILING YOUR PERSONALITY

There are many tests available to make a profile of your personality, some of which are currently used in recruitment processes. The following questionnaire is taken from the book *Know Your Own Personality* by G. Wilson and psychologist Hans J. Eysenck, Professor Emeritus at the University of London and is designed to measure three broad personality types:

- *extrovert/introvert* (whether you are typically outgoing, social and impulsive or introspective, thoughtful and ordered)
- *emotional/stable* (whether you are emotionally reactive and liable to stress or relatively calm and collected)
- *toughness/tenderness* (whether you tend to be aggressive and ambitious or modest and sympathetic to others)

Each of these three areas is broken down into five sub-areas so that you can gain a better overall understanding of your personality. Mark each question as honestly as you can with a 'yes' or 'no' answer. (Try not to fall into the trap of saying 'sometimes'; aim to find whether or not you tend towards the behaviour.) Don't think too hard about each answer, follow your instinct and don't worry about adding them up as you go along as an opportunity comes at the end of each section.

Obviously no one fits neatly into a pigeon hole. We all resemble tapestries of different traits, but each of us is unique in having our own patterns and shades. This questionnaire is designed to help you discover your own unique pattern so that you can understand yourself more clearly, find a role that complements it and identify aspects of your personality that perhaps you are not demonstrating or want to develop further.

Extrovert or introvert?

This questionnaire assesses traits related to extroversion or introversion.

I.	Do you often feel ill at ease with other people?	Yes/No
2.	In conversation, do you generally defend your own point of view?	Yes/No
3.	When you travel, do you leave nothing to chance in the arrangements?	Yes/No

4. Do you always read the labels on food products? — Yes/No

5. Do you often find yourself in trouble because you don't stop to consider the consequences? — Yes/No

6. When invited to a party, do you usually go? — Yes/No

7. Would you rather watch sports than play? — Yes/No

8. Do you read documents before you sign them? — Yes/No

9. Do you obey signals telling you to wait and not to cross the street? — Yes/No

10. Is it very important to you to be liked? — Yes/No

11. Do you hate rushing when you shower? — Yes/No

12. Do you usually make decisions very quickly? — Yes/No

13. In an unfamiliar situation, do you usually say as little as possible? — Yes/No

14. Do you usually finish your meals faster than other people finish theirs? — Yes/No

15. If a police officer told you to do something strange, would you do it? — Yes/No

16. Do you ever buy things impulsively and then regret wasting your money? — Yes/No

17. Do you mix easily with the opposite sex? — Yes/No

18. Do you always arrange travel insurance before you take a long trip? — Yes/No

19. Do you prefer to take a back seat at any formal meeting to minimise the possibility that you might have to speak? — Yes/No

20. Ordering from a menu, do you avoid exotic or unfamiliar dishes? — Yes/No

20. Rather than waiting a few minutes for an elevator, do you take the stairs? — Yes/No

22. If people are talking loudly in a cinema, do you ask them to be quiet? — Yes/No

23. Would you go up to talk to a complete stranger at a party?   *Yes/No*

24. Do you always organise your holidays well in advance?   *Yes/No*

25. Do you like to sleep late at weekends?   *Yes/No*

26. Would you rather do almost anything than wait in a
long queue?   *Yes/No*

27. Do you think it is unreasonable to expect a parent to keep watch
over an infant at all times?   *Yes/No*

28. Are you amazed at how much others seem to accomplish
in a day?   *Yes/No*

29. Do you find it hard to get rid of persistent sales people?   *Yes/No*

30. Do you enjoy being on your own?   *Yes/No*

31. Do you often become excited by a new interest, only to drop it
when you discover something else?   *Yes/No*

32. If you won six months' salary playing roulette, would you bet it
all on the next spin?   *Yes/No*

33. Do you find that there are never enough hours in the day?   *Yes/No*

34. Do you usually prefer to know people for a long time before
revealing personal details about yourself?   *Yes/No*

35. Do you often radically revise your first impression of people
when you get to know them better?   *Yes/No*

36. When you begin a task, are you often daunted by the
thought of the effort it will take to complete?   *Yes/No*

37. Are you better at taking orders than giving them to
other people?   *Yes/No*

38. Do you often get involved in things and later wish you hadn't?   *Yes/No*

39. If you are angry with someone, do you keep your feelings
to yourself?   *Yes/No*

40. Do you like to tell jokes and stories?   *Yes/No*

41. Do you often have to hurry to arrive at your destination
on time?   *Yes/No*

42. If you found out that someone was bad-mouthing you behind your back, would you confront them? *Yes/No*

43. When you arrive at a party, do you often feel apprehensive as you ring the doorbell? *Yes/No*

44. Are you annoyed by people who insist on driving at no more than the legal speed limit? *Yes/No*

45. On holiday, do you like to just laze around and relax all day? *Yes/No*

46. Would you do almost anything on a date? *Yes/No*

47. Before making a decision, do you carefully weigh all the advantages and disadvantages? *Yes/No*

48. Are you the person who organises the social activities in your group of friends? *Yes/No*

49. Do you often think you might be happier living by yourself in a log cabin far from civilisation? *Yes/No*

50. Do you hesitate to ask for directions from a stranger in the street? *Yes/No*

SCORING: the totals are out of 10 for each section.

Sociability: give yourself one point for each 'yes' to questions 6,10,17,23 and 40 as well as one for each 'no' to 1,30,34,43 and 49. TOTAL: _____

High scorers seek out the company of other people, enjoy social functions and meet people easily. Low scorers prefer to have only a few special friends, enjoy solo activities such as reading and are inclined to withdraw from acquaintances they find oppressive.

Impulsiveness: add one point for each 'yes' to questions 5,12, 16,26,31, 35 and 38 and each 'no' to questions 3,24 and 47. TOTAL: _____

High scorers are inclined to act on the spur of the moment, make quick, sometimes premature, decisions and are usually carefree, changeable and unpredictable. Low scorers consider matters very carefully, are systematic, orderly, cautious and plan their life well in advance.

Activity: give yourself one point for each 'yes' to questions 14,21,33 and 48 and for each 'no' to questions 7,11,25,28,36 and 45. TOTAL:

High scorers are generally lively and energetic and enjoy physical exercise and hard work. Low scorers tend to move about at a leisurely pace and enjoy sedentary pursuits and quiet, restful vacations.

Assertiveness: give yourself one point for each 'yes' to questions 2,22 and 42 and each 'no' to 9,15,19,29,37,39 and 50. TOTAL: _____

High scorers have what is sometimes called a 'strong' personality, they are more dominant and stand up for their rights. Low scorers are more laid-back, non-confrontational, disinclined to take the initiative in an interpersonal situation and may be easily imposed on.

Risk-taking: give yourself one point for each 'yes' to questions 27,32,41,44 and 46 and for each 'no' to questions 4,8,13,18 and 20. TOTAL: _____

High scorers seek rewards with little concern for the possible consequences. They are gamblers who believe that an element of risk adds spice to life. Low scorers prefer safety, security and familiarity, even if this means sacrificing excitement, variety and sometimes opportunity as well.

Emotional or stable?

The following 50 questions to assess where you stand on the broad scale from emotionality to stability should be answered as honestly as you can with a 'yes' or 'no'.

1.	Do you frequently feel ashamed of yourself for things you have done?	*Yes/No*
2.	Have you ever wondered whether anyone would notice if you disappeared off the face of the earth?	*Yes/No*
3.	Are other people unsympathetic if you tell them you are feeling unwell?	*Yes/No*

4. When you look in a mirror, are you pleased by what you see? *Yes/No*

5. Do you instinctively feel that your decisions are the right ones? *Yes/No*

6. If you make a social blunder, does it haunt you for days afterwards? *Yes/No*

7. Do you think that you do not deserve the affection of other people? *Yes/No*

8. Do your shoulders or face sometimes twitch? *Yes/No*

9. Is there at least one person in the world who really loves you? *Yes/No*

10. Do you feel intimidated by your siblings or other members of your family? *Yes/No*

11. Are you frequently embarrassed? *Yes/No*

12. Do you suspect that you must ultimately pay a price for your pleasures in this life? *Yes/No*

13. Are there a lot of things about yourself that you would change if it were somehow possible? *Yes/No*

14. Do you frequently wince inwardly at the sudden recollection of a humiliating experience? *Yes/No*

15. Are you pleased with the direction in which your life is headed? *Yes/No*

16. Do you often catch yourself apologising for something when you are not really at fault? *Yes/No*

17. Do you often think of yourself as a failure? *Yes/No*

18. Do you often feel tired even though you have done no physical work? *Yes/No*

19. Can you quite easily drop off to sleep when you go to bed at night? *Yes/No*

20. Can you readily shrug off any uneasiness about your behaviour? *Yes/No*

21. Do you tend to turn your back on people and pay no attention when they criticise you? *Yes/No*

22. Have you ever been worried by recurring pains in your chest? *Yes/No*

23. Do you often feel miserable when you wake in the morning? *Yes/No*

24. Would you rather do almost anything than speak before a group? *Yes/No*

25. Do you ever wish your conscience would leave you alone? *Yes/No*

26. Have you ever seriously considered committing suicide? *Yes/No*

27. Do you ever scold people for being overly concerned with matters you consider trivial? *Yes/No*

28. Do you suspect that people would look down on you if they knew the 'real you'? *Yes/No*

29. Do you usually have a good appetite? *Yes/No*

30. Do you feel a strong need to confess things as soon as possible? *Yes/No*

31. Do you suffer from loneliness? *Yes/No*

32. Do severe aches and pains all over your body often make it impossible to concentrate on your work? *Yes/No*

33. Does your voice get shaky if you are talking to someone you particularly want to impress? *Yes/No*

34. Are you confident that you could make some worthwhile contributions to virtually any project? *Yes/No*

35. Are you a happy person, or at least generally in good spirits? *Yes/No*

36. Is it rare for you to develop a headache? *Yes/No*

37. When you think about people, do you often wish you were like them? *Yes/No*

38. Do you frequently feel faint? *Yes/No*

39. Do you often fidget when you are sitting or lying down? *Yes/No*

40. When you review your life up to this point, do you feel you have little to be proud of? *Yes/No*

41. Are you sometimes disgusted by your sexual desires and fantasies? *Yes/No*

42. Would you stay cool in an emergency? *Yes/No*

43. On balance, do you feel you have been dealt a bad hand in life? *Yes/No*

44. Do you get wound up and tense just thinking about your problems? *Yes/No*

45. Do you usually feel healthy and strong? *Yes/No*

46. Do you look forward to the future? *Yes/No*

47. Do you sometimes think you have disappointed your parents by the life you have led? *Yes/No*

48. Do you ever think you need a tranquilliser to calm you down? *Yes/No*

49. Is your skin very sensitive and tender? *Yes/No*

50. Do you think you are leading a useful life and have contributed something positive to the world? *Yes/No*

SCORING:

Anxiety: give yourself one point for each 'yes' to questions 6,11,14,27, 33,39 and 44 and one point for each 'no' to questions 19 and 42. TOTAL: _____

High scorers are easily upset by things that go wrong and are inclined to worry unnecessarily about things that may or may not happen. Low scorers are placid, relaxed and resistant to unfounded fears and anxieties.

Guilt: give yourself one point for each 'yes' to questions 1,7,12,16,25,30,41 and 47 and one point for each 'no' to questions 20 and 21. TOTAL: _____

High scorers frequently have a strict religious background and are self-blaming and troubled by their consciences regardless of whether their behaviour is actually morally wrong. Low scorers are much less likely to torment themselves about their past behaviour.

Stress: give yourself one point for each 'yes' to questions 3,8,18,22,32,38 and 49 and each 'no' to questions 29,36 and 45. TOTAL: _____

Your score does not measure how much stress you are subjected to, but how you respond to the stress you experience. High scorers seek out sympathy and show a lot of concern about the state of their health. Low scorers are seldom ill and worry little about their health.

Inferiority: give yourself one point for each 'yes' to questions 10,13,17, 24,28,37 and 40 and each 'no' to questions 29,36 and 45. TOTAL: _____

High scorers feel that they have failed to measure up in life. At the extreme, this feeling amounts to what is called an inferiority complex. Low scorers see themselves as worthy, well-liked and successful, but they may be somewhat arrogant and conceited.

Depression: give yourself one point for each 'yes' to questions 2,23,26,31 and 45 and one point for each 'no' to questions 9,15,35,46 and 50. TOTAL: _____

High scorers are inclined to be gloomy, pessimistic, disappointed with their lives, miserable and at odds with the world. Low scorers are happy and optimistic with a feeling of well-being. They are satisfied with their existence and find life rewarding.

Tough or tender

These 50 questions to assess where you are on the tough/tender scale need to be answered as honestly as you can with a 'yes' or 'no'.

1.   Do you like to stick to the cooking of your own ethnic group?   *Yes/No*

2.   Have you ever felt a genuine impulse to kill someone?   *Yes/No*

3. Do you sometimes argue just for the sake of argument, even when you know you are wrong? **Yes/No**

4. Do you normally feel that you have achieved enough at the end of your working day? **Yes/No**

5. Would you make an effort to spend time with a friend who was suffering emotional hurt? **Yes/No**

6. Do you meet bright and not-so-bright people with equal courtesy? **Yes/No**

7. Would you ever consider going sky-diving? **Yes/No**

8. Do you grind your teeth, consciously or unconsciously? **Yes/No**

9. Do you give small change to street people? **Yes/No**

10. Once you have made up your mind, do you stick to your guns? **Yes/No**

11. Have you ever taken drugs for fun? **Yes/No**

12. Do you stand still and wait for the escalator to move you? **Yes/No**

13. Do you believe that tough measures are often necessary to deal with the world's problems? **Yes/No**

14. Do you find it difficult to enjoy holidays because you'd rather be doing something more productive? **Yes/No**

15. Before a meeting, do you often plan how you are going to get your way? **Yes/No**

16. Do you mix easily with people whose cultural customs and religion are different from yours? **Yes/No**

17. Have you tended to avoid experimentation in your sex life? **Yes/No**

18. If someone is rude to you, do you consciously hold back from retaliating? **Yes/No**

19. Do you dislike people who play practical jokes? **Yes/No**

20. Do you often find people naïve and gullible in their business dealings? **Yes/No**

21. Do you like to keep people guessing about you? **Yes/No**

22. Would you enjoy a roller-coaster ride at an amusement park? *Yes/No*

23. Do you believe that 'tried and true' ways are always the best? *Yes/No*

24. Do you tend to blame other people when things go wrong? *Yes/No*

25. Do you think there is some element of truth in nearly everyone's point of view? *Yes/No*

26. Do you ever set your aspirations low to avoid disappointment? *Yes/No*

27. Do you always think honesty is the best policy? *Yes/No*

28. Would you like to film sharks from an underwater cage? *Yes/No*

29. Do you rate love as more important than success in your career? *Yes/No*

30. Could you imagine yourself as a preacher, politician or campaigner? *Yes/No*

31. Do you work hard for success rather than just dreaming about it? *Yes/No*
32. At school, were you usually well prepared for tests? *Yes/No*
33. Do you think people who refuse to fight are cowards? *Yes/No*

34. Do other people tend to listen to music at higher levels than you find comfortable? *Yes/No*

35. Are you polite to people who irritate you? *Yes/No*

36. Have you ever wanted to go to bed with two other people at once? *Yes/No*

37. Are there are more important reasons for getting married than love? *Yes/No*

38. Can you usually see the other person's point of view in an argument? *Yes/No*

39. Are you satisfied with the amount of money you now earn? *Yes/No*

40. Do you sometimes feel like picking a fight? *Yes/No*

41. Do you prefer to mix with people who can help you make your way in the world? *Yes/No*

42. If someone is pompous or conceited, do you put them in their place? *Yes/No*

43. Are you prepared to use flattery to get what you want? *Yes/No*

44. Do you have a strong desire to be well known to the public? *Yes/No*

45. Are you appalled by the ignorance shown by most people on social or political matters? *Yes/No*

46. If you inadvertently hurt someone's feelings, would you regard that as their problem? *Yes/No*

47. Does the success of others bother you? *Yes/No*

48. Are you often uncertain about how to vote in an election? *Yes/No*

49. Do you readily forgive people who have let you down? *Yes/No*

50. Would you ever choose to go exploring in underground caves? *Yes/No*

SCORING:

Aggressiveness: give yourself one point for each 'yes' to questions 2,8, 24,33,40 and 42 and for each 'no' to questions 6,18,35 and 49. TOTAL: _____

High scorers don't shy away from confrontations, they are given to bursts of temper, violent arguments and sarcasm. They take no nonsense from anyone and feel compelled to redress every perceived slight. Low scorers are gentle, even-tempered and prefer to avoid personal conflict – even when the other person is clearly in the wrong.

Thrill-seeking: give yourself one point for each 'yes' to questions 7,11,22,28,36 and 50 and for each 'no' to questions 1,17,19 and 34. TOTAL: _____

High scorers are forever seeking excitement in life. They have an insatiable lust for new experiences. Fighting to stave off boredom they will accept moderate levels of danger to life and limb. Low scorers have less need for adventure, preferring the safety and security of home.

Dogmatism: give yourself one point for each 'yes' to questions 3,10,13, 23,30 and 45 and for each 'no' to questions 16,25,38 and 48. TOTAL: _____

High scorers have set, uncompromising views on most matters and are likely to defend their views vigorously. Low scorers are less rigid and less likely to see things in black and white. They are generally open to rational persuasion and tolerant of uncertainty.

Ambitiousness: give yourself one point for each 'yes' to questions 14,31, 32,41,44 and 47 and for each 'no' to questions 4,12,26 and 39. TOTAL: _____

High scorers are hard-working, achievement-orientated and eager to improve their social standing. Low scorers place little value on competitive performance and may be content to take life as it comes.

Manipulation: give yourself one point for each 'yes' to questions 15,20,21, 37,43 and 46 and for each 'no' to questions 5,9,27 and 29. TOTAL: _____

High scorers are detached, calculating, shrewd, worldly, expedient and self-interested. Low scorers are warm-hearted, trusting, straightforward and altruistic, though perhaps also a little naïve and gullible.

Results

Collate all your results onto the following tables:

Extrovert or introvert

Sociability	0	1	2	3	4	5	6	7	8	9	10
Impulsiveness	0	1	2	3	4	5	6	7	8	9	10
Activity	0	1	2	3	4	5	6	7	8	9	10
Assertiveness	0	1	2	3	4	5	6	7	8	9	10
Risk-taking	0	1	2	3	4	5	6	7	8	9	10

Emotional or stable

Anxiety	0	1	2	3	4	5	6	7	8	9	10
Guilt	0	1	2	3	4	5	6	7	8	9	10
Stress	0	1	2	3	4	5	6	7	8	9	10
Inferiority	0	1	2	3	4	5	6	7	8	9	10
Depression	0	1	2	3	4	5	6	7	8	9	10

Tough or tender

Aggressiveness	0	1	2	3	4	5	6	7	8	9	10
Thrill-seeking	0	1	2	3	4	5	6	7	8	9	10
Dogmatism	0	1	2	3	4	5	6	7	8	9	10
Ambitious	0	1	2	3	4	5	6	7	8	9	10
Manipulation	0	1	2	3	4	5	6	7	8	9	10

Do they confirm or contradict the view that you have of yourself? While you should not worry unduly over any single score, you may identify a general trend in your profile that suggests that a change would be beneficial. Keep in mind that there is no right or wrong position in these profiles. Each characteristic has advantages and disadvantages. A better understanding of your unique attributes is fundamental to any valid assessment of your true potential.

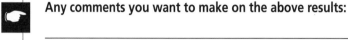

Any comments you want to make on the above results:

_____

_____

_____

_____

_____

IDENTIFYING YOUR STRENGTHS AND WEAKNESSES

Before you begin this process of self-understanding, it is important to recognise that there is no such thing as a weakness! It has been said that a 'weakness' is simply a strength applied at an inappropriate time or to an inappropriate degree. Consider for yourself how easily a strength such as tenacity can be seen by others at certain times as obstinacy.

Having put 'weaknesses' into this context, how can you begin to assess your own profile? Spend some time considering what your biggest supporter would say about you and also what your greatest enemy would say.

What my biggest supporter would say about me:

_____

_____

_____

_____

_____

_____

What my greatest enemy would say about me:

_____

_____

_____

_____

_____

_____

When you have completed these two extreme profiles, it is worth getting some genuine and specific feedback to add aspects you may not be so aware of. Make a list of at least five people who you think would be prepared to help you, including at least one from outside work (often we display strengths in the rest of our lives that we would do well to consider utilising more often at work).

Five people I could ask to help me:

_____

_____

_____

_____

_____

_____

Consider what exactly you want from them and then assertively (*see Stage 3*) ask them for their help, remembering to allow a period of time for them to prepare their answer. There is nothing worse than asking someone you respect to tell you what they think are your strengths and them not being able to think of anything. Then prepare yourself to deal constructively with the comments.

'I am working through a programme of self-development at the moment and wonder if you would be prepared to help me? I am currently doing a strengths and skills inventory and wonder if you would prepare an assessment of what you think mine are, then perhaps we could meet again next week for you to give me your views.'

When you meet the following week, it will be important to listen very carefully without, if possible, reacting too much to what they have to tell you. This is a mirroring exercise: by asking people you trust how they view you, you will be gaining a broader view of yourself than is normally possible and because you are asking for their opinion, disagreeing or exclaiming with shock will be unlikely to help the process. It is helpful to discover as much specific feedback as possible; it is wonderful to hear that someone thinks you are a good listener, but it is even more helpful for you to discover exactly what it is that you do that gives them the impression that you are a good listener. This might be called the evidence for the strengths and skills.

'Gosh – I have never thought of myself as being very good at listening. Can you tell me of any occasions where you thought I was listening well and what it was I was doing that led you to that conclusion?'

When you have begun to gather a list, break them down into strengths and skills. A strength is a trait that you were born with, often part of your personality such as being good at making friends, while a skill is generally something that you have learned such as being good with computers.

Both strengths and skills can be developed and this is one reason for doing this exercise because it is a perfect opportunity to assess whether you are utilising them effectively and whether there are some aspects of yourself that other people are not seeing because you are not displaying them at all. For example, if you value most about yourself that you are honest and open and none of your supporters comment on it, then you might need to consider whether you have

> *A strength is a trait that you were born with, often part of your personality such as being good at making friends, while a skill is generally something that you have learned such as being good with computers.*

become slightly complacent about it and plan to put it into action more consciously.

Put all the results onto a chart and consider how you might use them as effectively as possible, for example:

Strengths/Skills	Evidence	Future utilisation
Listening	When John didn't get the promotion he wanted, I spent a lot of time with him, saying little, just listening.	listen more, say less.
Being positive	Encouraged Jane when she was sitting her exams.	Look for more opportunities.

MY STRENGTHS AND SKILLS INVENTORY

Strengths/Skills	Evidence	Future utilisation

Examples of utilising all the items on your inventory more consciously include:

Jane, the managing director of a media company, consciously identifies all the positive feedback that she is given and makes an effort to practise it more. When a difficult situation arises, she is able to think 'John said that I can be inspirational and this situation certainly calls for it so I had better produce the goods now'. She finds the exercise valuable because she has added to her resources strengths and skills she didn't realise she had and the fact that others have commented on them gives her the confidence to use them when it is important. Eventually they become second nature.

Philip, production manager in a small manufacturing plant, found to his amazement that as he consciously put his strengths and skills into operation, the weaknesses he had been trying so hard to avoid minimised dramatically. 'It was extraordinary, all my life I had been trying hard to counteract what I considered my failings and it was only after I was encouraged to ignore them and concentrate on using my strengths that they seemed to resolve themselves. For example, I had always hated doing formal presentations and really wasn't very good at them but several colleagues gave me feedback that I was very good at speaking informally at meetings about my projects so I concentrated on speaking more off-the-cuff rather than trying to plan a complicated sort of lecture – and my boss began to congratulate me on my presentation skills!'

John, a sales manager, lists all his strengths and skills that he has been given by other people and chooses a new one each week to practise. 'It has helped me discover that I have qualities that I didn't know I had' he says.

23

Another process to discover skills and qualities is to list all the things you enjoy doing. Most of the time what we enjoy doing is what we are good at; it is unusual to become really good at something that we dislike.

What I like doing

What strengths/skills does it involve?

A final exercise in this section of self discovery is to list all your achievements (both inside and outside work) and what particular skills and strengths they required.

My achievements so far   **Strengths and skills required**

_____   _____

_____   _____

_____   _____

_____   _____

_____   _____

_____   _____

_____   _____

_____   _____

_____   _____

_____   _____

_____   _____

_____   _____

_____   _____

_____   _____

_____   _____

_____   _____

_____   _____

_____   _____

_____   _____

_____   _____

_____   _____

WHAT DRIVES YOU?

Another aspect to your personality that is helpful to understand more clearly is what might be seen as 'what drives you' – your values and how you see the world. These are founded on what is, and what is not, of real importance to you in life and they are central to the way you would like to live. Research by psychologists indicates that core or deep values revolve around the following six aspects:

- theoretical
- economic
- artistic
- social
- political
- spiritual

Theoretical: is the degree to which a person, group or society is concerned with the discovery of truth, assuming a cerebral or thinking attitude in pursuing this objective. It stems from interests that are rational, critical and ultimately based on observation and practical experience. A theoretical person is one who tends to question, likes discussion and continually wants to understand and make sense of everything. When on a training programme or in any group lecture situation, he/she will enjoy quizzing the tutor on a lot of the assertions and assumptions.

Economic: is the extent to which a person, group or society is interested in practicality and usefulness for the sake of economic self-preservation. To a large degree an economic person is motivated by success in the world of work, which results in the accumulation of wealth and material goods. In their relations with others, economic persons tend to be more interested in comparing and surpassing them in wealth, rather than satisfying any underlying social needs.

A good example of the emphasis on practicality and usefulness is their attitude to education and learning. For the economic type, its only real value is when it is practical and useful. Unapplied knowledge is regarded as waste. Ultimately, economic people get things done.

Artistic: is the degree to which a person, group or society is interested in and motivated by form and harmony in all things (not only the creative arts). In other words, their chief interest is in the artistic and creative episodes of life. The artistic person is one who looks at objects, people and language and whose first inclination is to reflect on their aesthetic beauty. For artistic people the sense of wonderment never diminishes when looking at objectively beautiful events such as sunsets. These people are also capable of finding beauty in even the most simple, mundane, things in life.

Social: is the degree to which a person, group or society is interested in and motivated towards drawing people together. Such people prize others for their human qualities and are themselves kind, sympathetic and unselfish. For the social person, life is all about people and everyday realities of social life. Nothing gives them greater pleasure than being in and with groups of people who are working in harmony with each other.

Political: is the degree to which a person, group or society is interested and motivated by the struggle for influence and power. Such people take the view that struggle is 'the stuff of life' and therefore yearn for personal power, influence and renown. The sort of person who holds this value is one who strives to be the leader when in any form of leaderless group discussion or activity. For such people usually the issue, whether it be political, work- or family-related, comes second to the fact that they have to influence others and be seen to be in charge.

Spiritual: is the degree to which a person, group or society struggles with understanding and experiencing the world as a united whole, consisting of some sort of higher meaning. Such people are orientated towards a search for the highest and most satisfying value experience – a sense of growth and inner calm. For such people this value orientation manifests itself in very different ways. Some may tend towards a spirituality that expresses itself within the context of everyday life and may involve caring for others or going to a religious institution regularly. Others, such as hermits and monks, choose to live apart from everyday life. Regardless of the particular type of expression, the spiritual person is one who believes in something that transcends the physical world: a faith that ultimately gives them inner calm and contentment.

Most of your values will be contained within these six themes. In order to bring them to life and make them clearer you may like to imagine the following scenario:

> Six individuals each representing one of the core value orientations are walking together through the woods on a sunny autumn afternoon. The theoretical individual is thinking about the growth and development of the trees and how the wood came about. The economic individual wonders about the viability of chopping down some of the trees and converting them to toothpicks to make some money. The artistic individual is happy to frolic in the leaves and take in the beauty of the surroundings. The social individual gains contentment from just from being in the company of five other friendly people. The political individual finds it hard to refrain from leading the group through a particular path, insisting that it is the right way. Finally, the spiritual person gets lost in thoughts concerning the ultimate reality of what these people and woods represent.

The theoretical, economic, artistic, social, political and spiritual are what may be called your 'core' values. Obviously no single individual holds only one of them; we are all a complex mix. In many ways they reflect who you are and why you do what you do. At a more specific level, various issues relating to these themes underpin your 'external' values – those closer to the surface and more recognisable to others.

Which three values do you think tend to drive you? Put them in order of importance:

I. _____

2. _____

3. _____

Any comments:

_____

_____

_____

_____

_____

_____

_____

_____

_____

_____

_____

_____

_____

_____

_____

What is important to you in life?

Another way to identify your values is to rate what is important for you in life. The following list (to which you may need to add) is prepared from many of the things that people find important.

Consider the importance to you of each in turn and rate it on the scale:

	LOW									HIGH
Achieving your goals	1	2	3	4	5	6	7	8	9	10
Adventure	1	2	3	4	5	6	7	8	9	10
Affection	1	2	3	4	5	6	7	8	9	10
Being creative	1	2	3	4	5	6	7	8	9	10
Competing with others	1	2	3	4	5	6	7	8	9	10
Co-operating with others	1	2	3	4	5	6	7	8	9	10
Financial security	1	2	3	4	5	6	7	8	9	10
Family happiness	1	2	3	4	5	6	7	8	9	10
Freedom	1	2	3	4	5	6	7	8	9	10
Friendship	1	2	3	4	5	6	7	8	9	10
Getting on/advancement	1	2	3	4	5	6	7	8	9	10
Having inner harmony	1	2	3	4	5	6	7	8	9	10
Health	1	2	3	4	5	6	7	8	9	10
Improving society	1	2	3	4	5	6	7	8	9	10
Integrity	1	2	3	4	5	6	7	8	9	10
Involvement	1	2	3	4	5	6	7	8	9	10
Loyalty	1	2	3	4	5	6	7	8	9	10
Order	1	2	3	4	5	6	7	8	9	10
Personal development	1	2	3	4	5	6	7	8	9	10
Recognition	1	2	3	4	5	6	7	8	9	10
Religion/Faith	1	2	3	4	5	6	7	8	9	10
Responsibility	1	2	3	4	5	6	7	8	9	10
Self-respect	1	2	3	4	5	6	7	8	9	10
Wealth	1	2	3	4	5	6	7	8	9	10
Wisdom	1	2	3	4	5	6	7	8	9	10

The reason for discovering your values in a self-development pro-gramme is to help you create a full and genuine self-portrait before moving on to the next chapter where you will be able to plan how to fulfil all the things that are important to you as an individual. You may have identified values that you hold that are not being fulfilled satisfactorily at present.

Any comments:

_____

_____

_____

_____

Now fill in your own personal self-portrait.

MY SELF-PORTRAIT as at: (date) _____

Strengths:

_____

_____

_____

Areas still to be developed:

_____

_____

_____

What I like doing:

_____

_____

_____

My achievements to date:

_____

_____

_____

Personality:

- Introvert/Extrovert:
  sociability/impulsiveness/activity/assertiveness/risk-taking

- Stable/Emotional:
  anxiety/guilt/stress/inferiority/depression

- Tough/Tender:
  aggressiveness/thrill-seeking/dogmatism/ambitious/manipulation

My core values are:

theoretical/economic/artistic/social/political/spiritual

(put in order and detail how they manifest themselves for you).

1 _____

2 _____

3 _____

4 _____

5 _____

The six aspects of life that are most important to me (*page 30*) **are:**

1 _____

2 _____

3 _____

4 _____

5 _____

6 _____

Any comments:

1 _____

2 _____

3 _____

4 _____

5 _____

Further reading

Know Your Own Personality (H.J.Eysenck/G. Wilson) (1991) Penguin

Signposts For Success: a guide to self-managed development (F. Dent, R. MacGregor, S. Wills) (1994) Pitman Publishing

IDENTIFYING YOUR CAREER GOALS

Career/Life planning provides a proven structure for making the whole of your life satisfying and supportive to what you want to achieve

Do you have a career/life plan?	*Yes/No*
Do you have a five-year plan?	*Yes/No*
Do you know what complete satisfaction would consist of for you?	*Yes/No*
Are you clear what the next two steps in your career will be?	*Yes/No*
Are you satisfied with your progress to date?	*Yes/No*

If you answered 'no' to any of these questions, you now need to prepare to enter the second stage in *The Handbook of Skilful Management*. This second stage is to understand what you are working towards, what you want from your life and how you are going to get it. It is, after all, your life; no one else is going to manage it for you and no one else is going to give you what you want. What else have you been learning and growing for than to make the most effective contribution you can in order to have what you require in return. If you don't know what it is that you want from your life, how will you know whether or not you are on course to get it. What you may have identified in the past as being what you wanted in your life may well have altered with time as you yourself have changed and it is worth undertaking a review of your long-term goals annually to check whether they are still appropriate or if they need adapting in light of current circumstances and experiences.

This chapter will include exercises and information on how to prepare:

- a long-term vision for your life
- a long-term career goal
- a career/life plan so that every area supports each other
- projects to create satisfaction in every area of your life
- a plan for the next two steps in your career

CREATING A LONG-TERM VISION FOR YOUR LIFE

You may think you have no idea about what you want out of your life and what your ambitions really are but it is likely that you do; it is simply that you do not allow yourself to think consciously about it.

One way to bring it out into your consciousness is to write your own obituary. Imagine that you are to die peacefully and satisfied at the age of 80 and consider what you would like your friends, supporters and family to write if they were publishing an obituary of you. Describe all the things that you would like to have achieved. Don't worry about whether or not you have begun any of them; the point of writing an obituary many years in advance is that you can include things that you haven't even begun to achieve.

MY OBITUARY

_____

_____

_____

_____

_____

_____

_____

_____

_____

_____

_____

Conditions of satisfaction

It may be that your obituary is based on achievements and tangible results so a second exercise is valuable to get in touch with all the aspects that would enable you to be completely satisfied at the end of your life.

Career/life planning includes both your working and personal life because one of the aspects that emerged very clearly from researching this book was that **success at work is helped enormously by a holistic approach**, that is that the whole of your life supports you getting what you want from work. It is obvious to most people that your health and fitness have a major impact on how effectively you perform at work, but after some consideration it is also likely that you will realise that every single aspect of your life can either support or hinder you from achieving the success you think you deserve. Having a home that works well for you, that helps you to relax, rewind and be creative at the end of the day as well as being on a good transport system can be enormously helpful as can supportive, encouraging friends and family, enjoyable holidays, fun and laughter and a powerful loving relationship.

Take a large sheet of paper headed 'What would be in my life in ten years' time if I were completely satisfied'. The important aspect to this exercise is that of *complete satisfaction*. So often we feel we have to compromise, that no one deserves to be completely happy and that life isn't fair. This exercise is quite different; forget all that pragmatic realism for a while and concentrate on what you would need in your life if you were completely satisfied. After all, if the aim is satisfaction and fulfilment, then it is vital to know what that would mean for you. Similarly to the previous exercise, a ten-year time-scale gives you the freedom to include aspects that do not exist at present.

You may find it helpful to add sub-headings to your large sheet of paper containing all the different aspects of your life:

- Career
- Money
- Health and Fitness
- Friends
- Family
- Loving relationship

- Home
- Fun
- Relaxation
- Creativity
- Personal development
- Spiritual development

Find a word to cover each category that is meaningful to you. 'Money' might become 'wealth', 'salary', 'nest egg', 'pension', 'fortune' or any one of numerous possibilities. The important thing is that the heading sums up for you what you want to include in the category.

In each category it is helpful to be as specific as possible. Under 'career' or 'work', for example, include what your working environment will look like, how many people you will be working with, what size the organisation will be, whether you will be office-based or travelling regularly, what you will be doing each day, who you will be reporting to and whether you want to be working in a team or on your own. Add everything you can think of that would give you complete satisfaction at work.

This particular exercise may take some time to complete as you think of different things that would mean satisfaction for you. Don't try to rush it. Find a place to put your list so that it catches your eye regularly and allows you to add to it whenever you think of something new.

Linda, a solicitor looking to change her career after beginning a family, thought this exercise was thoroughly suspect and doubted that anything of value would emerge. However, when she had pinned the list to her kitchen notice-board and found herself adding things regularly over a period of two weeks, she became very excited as a whole new possibility of how her life might progress emerged and she included her husband in the discussion. It gave her the freedom to identify what was truly important to her.

Conditions of satisfaction in my life in ten years' time:

What's missing?

If either of the previous exercises have been difficult to achieve, consider what is missing in each aspect of your life at the moment. Sometimes it is easier to work from a completely different point of view and identify what isn't satisfying before working on the positive aspects of what you want.

Linda, the solicitor mentioned previously, knew that she wanted to change her career but wasn't sure why. The money she earned was more than she needed, the work was interesting and she was good at it and she certainly wasn't sure what it was she wanted instead. When she considered what was missing from her life at that time, she immediately identified that having had a child, she wanted to make a bigger contribution to the world and to the future she was leaving her child. As soon as she had identified this, what she wanted instead became much easier to consider and discuss.

What's missing from my life at present?

_____

_____

_____

_____

_____

_____

_____

_____

_____

_____

You have now identified your long-term vision. Compile the results onto the following chart so that you can keep them easily available.

MY LONG-TERM VISION IS:

	Degree of importance	*Current level of satisfaction*
Career	_____	_____
Money	_____	_____
Health and fitness	_____	_____
Fun	_____	_____
Friends	_____	_____
Family	_____	_____
Loving relationship	_____	_____
Home	_____	_____
Relaxation	_____	_____
Creativity	_____	_____
Personal development	_____	_____
Spiritual development	_____	_____

Any other areas not covered

_____ _____ _____

_____ _____ _____

_____ _____ _____

_____ _____ _____

_____ _____ _____

_____ _____ _____

_____ _____ _____

CREATING AN INTEGRATED CAREER/LIFE PLAN

One of the things you are probably unused to doing is planning your life holistically. You have probably been encouraged to try to keep your home life and work completely separate. However, you will know that when things are not going well at home that it impacts on your performance at work and vice versa.

In a successful career/life plan, each aspect of your life will support the others. To perform effectively at work, you need to be fit and well, to have the support and relaxation offered by friends, family and a loving relationship, you need the break from routine offered by holidays, and laughter and fun will release pressures and encourage you to think positively about life.

 Also, it is unlikely that your work will be able to provide satisfaction for all the areas that you have identified as being most important in your life (*page 30*). For example, if the six areas that are the most important to you are: financial security, recognition, achieving your goals, integrity, responsibility and adventure, it may be that your work as, say, a financial director provides fulfilment for all of them except adventure. Rather than reacting by immediately deciding to change your career, it may be more appropriate to find an outlet outside work to satisfy the need for adventure – rock climbing, travelling to far-flung places on holiday, etc.

Career/Life planning provides a proven structure for making the whole of your life satisfying and supportive to what you want to achieve.

 Consider the results of your long-term goals for each area of your life (*page 43*) and mark out of ten how satisfied you are at present with each heading on the list (excluding Work and Money which we will return to shortly).

CREATING PROJECTS TO PRODUCE SATISFACTION IN EVERY AREA OF YOUR LIFE

When you have selected the areas you wish to work on, an important issue to bear in mind whether creating projects at work or home, is how to prioritise. Too many projects lead to a feeling of having too much to do and the chances are that you will do nothing! When you have got your first batch of projects underway successfully and feel that you want to take more on, you can always return to your list and create a second batch. (*See further advice on prioritising in Stage 10.*)

Choose the three areas that you feel most dissatisfied with and plan actions you can take to improve them. Some guidelines for project setting are:

- always clarify exactly what it is that you are aiming for. Be as specific as possible. What weight do you want to be? What would happen on the family holiday for it to be good? What does fun/relaxation/creativity mean to you exactly? Any aim to be 'better' will fail because it is non-specific, you need to clarify what 'better' would mean in measurable terms

- if the projects involve people, tell them what you have discovered and why you want to change the relationship. Help them identify what might be in it for them

- if the projects are activity based (fitness, fun, etc.) feel free to explore different routes to your goal. If you haven't done any physical exercise for some time, try different methods (after consulting with your doctor) and see which suits you best

- plan to take small steps. Suddenly running for five miles a day or transforming all your personal relationships overnight usually leads to disappointment. Start slowly and build on your successes

With these guidelines in mind, plan your three projects and prepare weekly plans as to:

- what you are going to do
- when you are going to do it
- how you are going to do it
- who or what is going to help you
- how you will measure your progress

Remember that you may have to make some additional time to implement your action plans. Often when we are short of time, we resent having to spend time doing new things, even when we know they are good for us.

Planning and re-evaluating your life will involve a short-term investment of time and effort for the long-term gain. For example, taking a small amount of exercise will give you more energy, improving personal relationships will save the time currently being spent on resolving misunderstandings and resentments.

How can you create time for your projects?

_____

_____

_____

_____

_____

_____

_____

_____

_____

_____

_____

LIFE PLANNING PROJECTS
Project 1:

Long-term goal with specific measurable criteria: _____

_____

_____

First step: _____

When: _____

How: _____

Who/what will help: _____

Next step:_____

Project 2:

Long-term goal with specific measurable criteria: _____

_____

_____

First step: _____

When: _____

How: _____

Who/what will help: _____

Next step:_____

Project 3:

Long-term goal with specific measurable criteria: _____

First step: _____

When: _____

How: _____

What/who will help: _____

Next step:_____

Reviewing

It is important to review regularly, preferably weekly but at least monthly, how your projects are going. Unless you plan to review regularly, the chances are that you will procrastinate and fail to start any of them! Find a time when you can sit down quietly on a regular basis: some examples quoted by the sources for this book include:

- travelling home on Friday night
- Saturday morning over breakfast
- a regular evening meeting with a friend who is acting as a coach

A weekly review gives you the opportunity to revise your projects if they are not going according to plan. You may find that you set yourself too many things to achieve in the first week and therefore find yourself in a position of not having finished anything. There is *no* failure in career/life planning – it is after all your plan and you can revise it as often as you like. If you find yourself avoiding one project, you may need to consider how important it is to you really. If the evidence is that you will do almost anything rather than starting this project, it is likely that it isn't important to you. Planning involves a continuing process of balancing how important projects are to you against how much time and energy you have available to you. For example, most of us could probably be considerably fitter than we are currently and are aware of the importance of fitness, but the only valid question is how important is it to you right now, at this stage of your life.

Don't allow yourself to be downhearted if you are not achieving all your weekly targets. Reassess how important the project is to you and re-plan the following week. Review everything you have achieved and learned during the process. Sometimes discovering what it is that you don't want is almost as important as achieving a goal.

Celebrate each success and build on it. Prepare yourself a list of treats for achieving each difficult step and allow yourself one for each success. Some examples include:

- buying the music/book/clothes that you want
- booking a massage/haircut/manicure/facial, etc.
- going out for a meal
- going to the cinema/theatre/concert/sports event

These treats can also act as bribes to yourself, for example 'I have booked tickets for the Albert Hall on Saturday on the basis that I will have finished the first goal of my project so I had better get on with it now'.

Getting support: a personal coach

You may find it useful to find yourself a coach to support you in your projects. A coach can be anyone you know; the only criteria is that they should be able to support you. This implies that they should have what the psychologists call 'positive unconditional regard' for you; they will respect you as an individual and believe that you are capable of even more than you have achieved to date.

You should tell them what it is you are intending to achieve and why. Declaring your plans out loud is the first step in ensuring that you actually do something about them. Your coach may even decide to join you in some of your projects, but their main role is to support you in your action plans and you will need to tell them what it is you want from them, which should include the following:

- encourage you by asking how the projects are going
- coach you when they are not going well
- help you reassess how important they are
- help you re-plan how to achieve them
- help you identify new learning each week
- help you celebrate each success

The role of a coach is not to tell you what you should be doing but help you work it out for yourself. Therefore, it involves questioning rather than giving advice:

- What are you finding difficult about ...?
- What is stopping you ...?
- What might make it easier?
- How could you do it differently?
- Are there any other routes you might consider?
- How would it be if it were perfect?

The role of a coach is one of the reasons why slimming clubs and exercise classes have proved to be so successful. Human beings are notoriously lazy about doing what we know we need to do. Having a formal structure where you have to check in on a regular basis is a powerful incentive to keeping yourself in check and on target. (*Further information on the role of a coach can be found in Stage 12.*)

Dick, a manager in an import/export business, found himself getting very tired and putting on weight in his office-bound job and decided that getting fit would help him feel better both about himself and be more effective at work. He had a friend who went jogging regularly and was talking about entering the London marathon so he went to talk to him. The friend agreed to take Dick jogging twice a week and plan out a schedule so that they could both enter the marathon in 18 months' time. Dick went to see his doctor for a check-up first and to ask advice about what he should be aiming for and a plan was created which the friend bullied, encouraged and helped carry him through. Dick completed the marathon 18 months later in five hours, raising money for charity and feeling triumphant about his achievement. Two years later he is still running regularly, is still a stone less than when he started his new regime and finds that he has more energy than he thought was possible in his thirties. Would he have managed it without his friend and coach? 'Almost certainly not. There were so many times when I wanted to give up but I couldn't take the loss of face – I am so grateful to him. He was a real friend just when I needed one.'

Who do you know who could help you with your projects?

_____

_____

_____

_____

_____

_____

CAREER PLANNING

It is likely that both your money and career goals are closely associated as most people are reliant on their careers for their incomes.

 Transfer from page 43 **your long-term career and money goals:**

_____

_____

_____

_____

_____

_____

Consider whether they are compatible and realistic. For example, if you are happy being a nurse or teacher and yet want to be earning £100,000 per annum, there is a reality gap! If there is a gulf between what you want and what is realistic, spend some time considering what is genuinely most important to you and how far you would be prepared to go to achieve it. Perhaps if you moved abroad or into the private sector, you might manage to bridge the gulf a little.

The next step is to ensure that this long-term goal is SMART. That is:

Simple/specific

Measurable

Achievable

Realistic

Timed

If a goal is not SMART, it is very unlikely that you will achieve it. For example, a long-term goal to be successful is very simple, but it isn't specific; it doesn't tell you what you will be doing to be successful, it isn't measurable so you won't know where you are on the path; it may or may not be achievable, you will never know; it isn't realistic because it has no definitions and there is no time frame to it. A goal to become chief executive by the year 2006 is much more likely to be achievable.

When you have a carefully considered SMART goal, it is time to consider it against where you are now.

TEN-YEAR GOAL   **PRESENT SITUATION**

_____

_____   _____

_____   _____

_____   _____

_____   _____

Does your long-term career plan satisfy all the requirements of what is really important to you (*page 30*) or have you found an alternative outlet for your needs?

_____

Will your long-term career goal really satisfy you? Will it fulfil your core values (*page 33*)?

_____

Does it fulfil what you wrote in your obituary (*page 38*)?

_____

Time taken now to consider carefully is important. After all, you will be spending the majority of your working hours on it, so it is important to think it through carefully.

You may want to do some research. Often our perception of the senior job is completely different to how it appears to those who are actually doing it. Read autobiographies and biographies of people doing similar jobs, talk to people who are actually doing the job you think you want or at least people around them. Researching like this is referred to as networking (*see Stage 4*) and it is generally easier than it sounds. Most people are flattered to be asked for help although because they are busy you may need to offer a motivator, a benefit to them.

You may find it helpful to compile a personality profile of the people doing similar jobs and consider, because the world is moving so fast, what profile might be appropriate in ten years' time. Then consider this personality profile against that which you have compiled for yourself (*page 32*) and add a personal development programme alongside your ten-year career plan.

Long-term planning

Long term career planning involves beginning at the ten-year goal and working back so that steps are produced leading you from where you are now to where you want to get to.

These steps may include:
- career steps on the way (promotions)
- experience
- training and developing skills
- personal development
- life-style changes

MY TEN-YEAR GOAL:

_____

What will I need to have done in year 9 to get there:

_____

What will I need to have done in year 8 to reach year 9:

_____

What will I need to have done in year 7 to reach year 8:

_____

What will I need to have done in year 6 to reach year 7:

_____

What will I need to have done in year 5 to reach year 6:

_____

What will I need to have done in year 4 to reach year 5:

_____

What will I need to have done in year 3 to reach year 4:

_____

What will I need to have done in year 2 to reach year 3:

_____

What will I need to have done this year to reach year 2:

_____

Short-term planning from a long-term perspective

'Keep your eyes on the hills and your feet on the ground'

It is only truly effective to plan for the short term if you know where you are intending to get to. A long-term vision gives you the freedom to adjust your short-term plans when you hit an obstruction rather than being completely blocked.

It is worth making the point here that plans and goals are not to be written on tablets of stone and regarded as sacrosanct. **All plans and goals that you create are yours and as such may be freely adapted as you progress**. There is no path already set out for you which it is imperative that you follow unless you allow it to be so. Any path only becomes yours when you take your first step on it. To take the analogy of a car journey, if you decide to travel by car from Dover to Edinburgh you will have a choice of motorways, 'A' roads or country routes. You make the decision as to which to take. However, if you take the motorway route and find roadworks and traffic jams, what do you do then? Get very angry because your route is blocked? Yes, you might but hopefully you would also take the next turning off the motorway and find an alternative route until the obstruction is well behind you. Similarly, as you approach Edinburgh, it is possible that you are having such a good time that you decide to continue to Inverness. Long-term goals can change as you get closer to achieving them as well as the route by which you decide to travel.

Justin began his career as an English teacher in a secondary school in Norfolk and his aim was to become head of the department. However, as he moved through positions of more responsibility within the department, it became clear to him that he felt he also had a contribution to make, not just to the English Department, but also to the school as a whole and has revised his long-term aim to become headteacher within another ten years.

Planning in the short term with a long-term perspective allows you to create considerable detail with a motivating vision to encourage you when the going gets tough.

Promotions or changes of job may be required for the first step on your journey to your ten-year goal. What are they? Do you know? How can you find out? Does your manager know your ambitions and long-term goals? How or when can you tell him/her? How can you gain their support? You might be able to enrol them in the process if you can show them how much better you could support them if you had the experience and training you have identified. It is always possible that they might see you as a threat if you declare that you want their position. Is there anyone else in your organisation who could support you? Quite often, simply declaring your long-term career goals can be the breakthrough that you need, because if your manager doesn't know where you want to progress to, how can they help you? What additional skills training and development will you require to become the obvious candidate for the promotion that you want? The more it is apparent that you have thought it through carefully, the more likely it is that you will be seen as being serious about promotion.

Experience is often a vital factor for promotion. What experience would you need to make you the obvious choice? How can you find out? How can you get it? You might find that you needn't necessarily change jobs to get the relevant experience. Sometimes volunteering for projects involving it or even voluntary work outside the organisation can supply it – so long as your managers and superiors know about it. Your local charities and organisations are probably desperate for professional help on their committees which meet in the evenings or weekends and offer opportunities for chairing meetings, financial controls and coaching. Many organisations encourage this sort of work within the local community (both for the PR value as well as the additional experience volunteers gain); research your local community and discuss it with your management.

Training and skills development should be an ongoing process in any working life. What skills have you identified that you could usefully develop?

Are others aware that you are consciously developing them? Often we have a 'picture' of each other that doesn't change until it is drawn to our attention. If you tell people that you are working on your presentation skills and ask for feedback after each session, your colleagues will probably be happy to make the effort to concentrate carefully on your performance and give you constructive comments. What training have you been doing and how well have you been implementing what you have learned? Perhaps you would benefit from a coach at work. Who could you ask to work with you, perhaps on a reciprocal basis?

 Personal development is an aspect to making yourself the ideal choice for promotion that is often overlooked. Review your personality profile and the qualities you already possess (*page 32*) and consider how they balance with what you have identified as the characteristics needed for your ten-year goal (*page 54*).

It is often not advisable to attempt to change your personality dramatically but it is certainly possible to balance how you are perceived. If, for example, you have identified that you score high on the tender side of the chart and that toughness is a quality that is admired and respected in your industry, you have two options. First, is it possible that over the next ten years the culture of your organisation will need to move towards a balance between tenderness and toughness? In other words, are you in a position to help change the culture? You may need to present your tenderness in a more pragmatic way – rather than being 'soft' on people you might counsel the need for negotiation in order to resolve the issue as quickly as possible. The second option involves balancing your inclinations carefully between your home and working life. It is highly desirable to be seen as tender and caring in a family environment (or even in charitable voluntary work) and you may be able to release all your feelings in those areas while remaining fair, but firm, at work.

Taking all four aspects listed above, create a plan to help you achieve this year all the things you need to do in order to be ready to begin year 2 at the identified position.

Remember to build in measurable stages that can help you review your progress.

Each section should include:
- **WHAT you are going to do**
- **WHEN you are going to do it**
- **WHAT the first step is**
- **HOW you will know when you've done it**

All too often people create plans that then come to nothing because the first step has been avoided. Take a deep breath and while the impetus is still strong – do it!

YEAR 1 PLAN TO ACHIEVE TEN YEAR GOAL:

Ten-year goal: _____

_____

Year 1 goal: _____

_____

Route (how are you going to get there):

_____

Promotions:

_____

Training and skills development:

_____

Experience:

_____

Personal development:

_____

Reviewing process:

_____

Who or what is going to help you?

_____

Further reading

What Colour is your Parachute? (R. Nelson Bolles) Ten Speed Press

[Reprinted each year and full of exercises to help you identify what you want from a career]

COMMUNICATION – THE VEHICLE TO ACHIEVE YOUR GOALS

I have a dream, brothers and sisters, I have a dream that one day...

(Martin Luther King)

Do you find it easy to make yourself understood?	*Yes/No*
Do you ever find yourself explaining things more than once?	*Yes/No*
Do you find it easy to receive or give criticism?	*Yes/No*
Do you ever find yourself tongue-tied with difficult people?	*Yes/No*
Do you often get angry when you want to remain calm?	*Yes/No*
Are there some people you find it difficult to talk to?	*Yes/No*
Do people sometimes ignore your ideas and opinions?	*Yes/No*

This chapter will explore:

- **why good communication skills are so important**
- **the conditions for effective communication**
- **the difference between talking and communicating**
- **how to avoid passive and aggressive behaviour**
- **a structure for effective communication**
- **how to create genuine two-way dynamic communication**
- **how to develop good listening skills and practices**
- **how to give and receive feedback constructively**
- **how to say 'no' without feeling guilty or selfish**
- **how to communicate effectively in difficult situations**

WHY EFFECTIVE COMMUNICATION SKILLS ARE SO IMPORTANT

Communication is the vehicle by which virtually every project or dream may be translated into reality. If Martin Luther King hadn't communicated his dream to others, it would have remained as a delightful fantasy in his head. He might have continued his personal mission, but would it have resulted in the movement that changed attitudes so profoundly in the 1960s? – almost certainly not.

> In the 1970s, Steve Jobs of Apple shared his vision of a range of personal computers that were small, user-friendly and had very little in common with the large room-sized machines that businesses were using. Now in the 1990s it is almost impossible to imagine what life would be like without them. Currently, Bill Gates of Microsoft and others are spreading their vision of the Information Super-Highway and it would be a brave person who could predict what the results will be.

Similarly at work, since the role of a manager is to achieve results through people, unless goals are communicated well, it is most unlikely they will be realised. People need to know exactly what is expected of them, be able to make a contribution and understand what they are aiming for. All of these are reliant on communication. If projects are stuck inside your head, nothing much will happen. When you write them down, they become more powerful for you but until you begin to communicate them to others the likelihood of them being realised is limited. It is the way in which they are communicated to others that provides the magic formula. Communication is the key to creating motivation to enable others to contribute, either by taking part themselves or supporting you in your progress. So it is fair to say that every single conversation is an opportunity to help you achieve your goals.

communication is the key to achieving almost any goal or objective

Communication is defined in the dictionary as 'the means by which information, opinions and ideas are transferred', which sounds easier to achieve than we know it is. It also doesn't quite match up to what we all instinctively know, that communication is the key to achieving almost any goal or objective because it can, when it is going well:

- produce genuine understanding
- build and develop relationships
- give clarity to the task required
- allow others to contribute
- save time
- avoid problems
- enable you to say difficult things with grace
- make working with others a joy as synergy is created

We all have situations and individuals with whom we communicate where the above is achieved and where we might be genuinely perceived as a good communicator. But there are also occasions where, despite all our best efforts, it fails to reach the heights of understanding that we aim for and problems arise.

Since effective communication is so important to the fulfilment of our objectives, it is helpful to reassess the basic skills and how we use them, as well as exploring what might have gone wrong when communication has broken down. Incidentally, it is worthwhile noting at this point that most of the inquiries into major tragedies over the past few years (the Lockerbie air crash, the Kings Cross fire, the death of vulnerable people in care) have concluded that a lack of communication was the root cause. The importance of effective communication cannot be overemphasised.

Communication is essentially a two-way dynamic process and may be seen in a flow-chart form as:

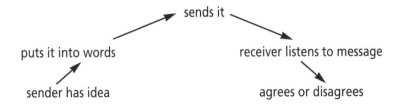

This process will be repeated many times in a conversation and the difference between talking and communicating generally comes in the process of listening and attempting to understand. Depending on the relationship and the way in which the message is sent, it will either be received as the sender intended or not.

THE CORE CONDITIONS FOR EFFECTIVE COMMUNICATION

There are three core conditions necessary before effective communication can take place:

- equality
- empathy
- congruence

The first condition is **equality and genuine respect for others as human beings**. When either party in the communication is feeling uncomfortable with either the situation or the other person, they are liable to talk 'up' or 'down'. For example, when meeting the chief executive of your organisation, if you find yourself feeling inadequate or nervous, you will be likely to talk 'up' to them and communication will become impossible. Similarly when talking to a junior member of staff, if you talk 'down' to them, communication will not exist.

Of course, people all play different roles in our lives but if you attempt to communicate with their role, you will fail. It is important to acknowledge the role, but communication can only exist between two equal human beings and both the chief executive and the junior member of staff fall into this category. This is a key area where talking often exists when the intention is communication.

Think for yourself, how often have you attempted to communicate and been disappointed with the results? Consider whether there might have been a element of talking 'up' or 'down' involved.

How can you create this element of equality in communication? First, by checking that you are not attempting to communicate with a 'box'! If you have already decided that this person is a problem, difficult, doesn't like you, etc., you will not achieve your goal. It is important to shift the prejudices you hold about them and don't try to fool yourself that you never hold preconceived judgements about anyone – we all do about everyone and everything! He or she has perhaps let you down in the past, but recognising that you have prejudices, put them on one side and ask yourself what might be interesting or valuable about the person to you, talk to that aspect and you will be amazed how they respond.

You will never be able to rid yourself of your prejudices but the important thing is to put them on one side whenever they pop into your consciousness and find a positive aspect with which to communicate. The more you treat the individuals around you as potential contributors to your 'purpose' in life, the more likely it is that they will do exactly that as the self-fulfilling prophecy takes effect. The way we behave reflects the way we are treated. If you want supportive, helpful people in your life, treat people as if they have these attributes, sit back and be amazed!

DEALING WITH DIFFICULT INDIVIDUALS

Name of individual I find difficulty in communicating with: _____

What I think about them:

_____

_____

_____

What I think that they think about me:

_____

_____

_____

Despite all that –

What have they got that could be useful to me:

_____

_____

_____

What would I be prepared to offer them in return:

_____

_____

_____

If you cannot find any items for the last two sections, you will be unable to communicate. Either try again or give up pretending that it is possible (they might not want to) and save yourself a lot of time and wasted effort!

The second condition of communication is **empathy**, which is defined as the ability to put yourself in another's shoes, to see and feel the world as they do without making a judgement as to whether they are right or wrong to feel the way they do. An impossible task? Yes, it is but it is important to continually try to achieve it. The key to transforming talking into communication is to demonstrate empathy. Genuine empathy involves getting to know the person so that you can understand what their background to the situation is, where they might be coming from. How often have you disliked or distrusted someone until you learned more about them and discovered that, in fact, you liked them a great deal? Empathy builds bridges and understanding between people, a crucial element in working together effectively.

If someone is trying to tell you something that you don't agree with, the tendency is to put them down which immediately destroys any possibility of communication. Demonstrating empathy will often involve acknowledging that you understand why they are feeling the way they are and that it is important for them. This process may often be all that is required for communication.

For example, a member of your staff is having difficulties achieving what you think is a simple task. If you tell them that they should just get on with it because it isn't very hard, you will have destroyed any possibility of communication and may have damaged the relationship. You will also be unlikely to get the task done well! If you say 'I can see that you are having some difficulties with this, what could we do differently to make it more achievable?', there is the possibility of an improved relationship and a task achieved correctly.

The third and final condition to effective communication is **congruence** which means that everything you say and do is appropriate to what you are trying to get across. The word 'incongruence' is more widely used and means something at odds with everything else. For example, a colleague shouting 'I am NOT upset' when you sympathise with them after they have been carpeted, is clearly behaving incongruently, the way the words are transmitted are at odds with the words being used.

Research in the USA conducted after the Second World War and still regarded as valid indicates that a message is received:

Visually	55%
By tone of voice	37%
By words	8%

This accounts for the fact that so often we find it easier to remember things if we see them in a visual form and that when you turn on the news and see a foreign leader talking in their own language before the subtitles come in, you have a pretty good idea what is going on. It explains why we understand that the colleague referred to above is very angry, the complete opposite of the words they are using.

The lesson to be taken from this is that you simply cannot be anything other than completely honest if you want to communicate effectively. If you are being false in any way, for example telling a subordinate that you have confidence in them when you do not, your body language and tone of voice will give you away. Always attempt to communicate only what is completely genuine.

If it is important to give some positive feedback to a member of staff, consider carefully what you can compliment that is genuine – there is always something so make the effort to find it.

Assertive/responsive behaviour

The three core conditions of equality, empathy and congruence will be present in all the situations where effective communication exists and may be called **assertive/responsive** behaviour. In the past, assertiveness has sometimes been seen as very strong, powerful and intimidating and it may indeed appear as such if it is not linked to a responsive attitude to the receiver. For the purpose of this book, assertive/responsive behaviour will be characterised as:

- being able to speak clearly about what you want
- treating the receiver with equality and respect
- showing empathy and understanding for the receiver
- being open and honest in all communications
- demonstrating high self-esteem

At this stage it is important to remember that out of all the communication possibilities that exist each day, you may never want to to be effective in each and every one of them. You may decide that the ticket collector, newsagent, etc. are simply not important enough to you each day to make the effort to communicate effectively and that is fine. This section of the book is about how to manage the situations where it is important to you that effective communication takes place and will explore some of the behaviour that inhibits effective communication.

Often a situation arises where it is important to you that an effective communication takes place (for example, you want a promotion or to delegate a task) and if it breaks down, you need to know how you can diagnose what might have happened and what you can do to resolve it.

UNDERSTANDING PASSIVE AND AGGRESSIVE BEHAVIOUR

At this point, we need to consider the unconscious workings of our minds briefly. When individuals in early civilisations met a threat, for example a sabre-tooth tiger, they reacted in one of two ways – fight or flight. Their bodies and brains instantly produced the necessary chemicals to allow them to run away as fast as possible or to attack the threat. Even in our modern society, the same reactions take place. Although it is no longer regarded as appropriate behaviour to run away from the boss or to hit the poor achiever over the head, all the chemical reactions in the body are encouraging us to behave that way!

Each of us has a preferred position from which we operate when we feel threatened – are you more likely to be passive or aggressive?

SELF-PERCEPTION QUESTIONNAIRE

Answer 'yes' or 'no' to the following:

1.	I have a tendency to think that others are better than me	Yes/No
2.	I am often suspicious of others' motives	Yes/No
3.	I usually rely on others to make decisions for me	Yes/No
4.	I often feel angry towards others	Yes/No
5.	I have a tendency to let others take responsibility for me	Yes/No
6.	I generally have a sense of well-being	Yes/No
7.	I often have a difficulty in getting close to people	Yes/No
8.	I have a tendency to mistrust other people	Yes/No
9.	I have a tendency to keep myself to myself	Yes/No
10.	I prefer others to take the lead and for me to follow	Yes/No
11.	I usually express my feelings openly towards others	Yes/No
12.	I often assume I won't get what I want	Yes/No
13.	I often think others are after something when they thank me	Yes/No
14.	I often feel miserable	Yes/No
15.	When I ask for what I want I generally give people no choice	Yes/No
16.	I usually tell people rather than ask them to do things	Yes/No
17.	I have a tendency to blame others when things go wrong	Yes/No
18.	I seek others' views when making decisions which affect them	Yes/No
19.	I have a tendency to put myself down	Yes/No
20.	When asked I often don't know what I want	Yes/No

21.	I am usually cautious about what I say to others about myself	Yes/No
22.	I usually listen to and take account of others' views	Yes/No
23.	I generally enjoy getting on with my work	Yes/No
24.	I usually deal with conflict situations directly	Yes/No
25.	I rarely say 'no' when asked to do something	Yes/No
26.	I have a tendency to be sarcastic	Yes/No
27.	I often have difficulty in delegating tasks to others	Yes/No
28.	I generally have creative solutions to problems	Yes/No
29.	When I refuse a request I usually feel guilty	Yes/No
30.	I have a tendency to be anxious about what people think about me	Yes/No
31.	I generally avoid taking on responsibility	Yes/No
32.	I have a tendency to see others as more important than me	Yes/No
33.	I am generally quick to feel criticised	Yes/No
34.	I often think I am the only one who can do the job correctly	Yes/No
35.	I generally deal with conflict situations indirectly	Yes/No
36.	I usually enjoy discussing ideas with people	Yes/No
37.	I rarely give praise to others	Yes/No
38.	I usually find it difficult to sort out my problems	Yes/No
39.	I rarely receive feedback about my behaviour	Yes/No
40.	I regularly appreciate others for what they have done	Yes/No
41.	I am often acknowledged by others for what I do	Yes/No
42.	I have a tendency to be inconsistent about what I tell people	Yes/No
43.	I am generally quick to criticise others	Yes/No
44.	I am often easily hurt by others	Yes/No
45.	I usually let others make decisions for me	Yes/No

46.	I am often hostile towards people	Yes/No
47.	I am often short-tempered with people	Yes/No
48.	I usually enjoy getting involved with and committed to tasks	Yes/No
49.	I generally take account of others' needs and wants	Yes/No
50.	I have a tendency to avoid eye contact	Yes/No
51.	I often feel resentful towards others	Yes/No
52.	I rarely ask for what I want	Yes/No
53.	I usually assume that I won't get what I want	Yes/No
54.	I have a tendency to feel lonely	Yes/No
55.	I often feel that others have let me down	Yes/No
56.	I usually ask questions in order to gather information	Yes/No
57.	I generally check out my assumptions with the people concerned	Yes/No
58.	I try not to offend other people	Yes/No
59.	I often fantasise about ways of getting my own back on people	Yes/No
60.	I usually tell people what I think	Yes/No
61.	I generally say sorry when I have made a mistake	Yes/No
62.	I readily accept that people will say 'no' to me sometimes	Yes/No
63.	I have a tendency to jump to conclusions	Yes/No
64.	I rarely tell others what I really think of them	Yes/No
65.	I usually want to go along with what other people want	Yes/No
66.	I usually feel inferior to others	Yes/No
67.	I am frequently demotivated in my work	Yes/No
68.	I am often despondent about things in general	Yes/No
69.	I have a tendency to dismiss others' wants and needs	Yes/No

70.	I usually respect other people, irrespective of their views	*Yes/No*
71.	I readily take on responsibility	*Yes/No*
72.	I am quick to put other people's ideas down	*Yes/No*
73.	I am usually anxious about upsetting other people	*Yes/No*
74.	I regularly seek feedback from other people	*Yes/No*
75.	I am usually keen to spot the flaws in others' arguments	*Yes/No*
76.	I often have negative thoughts about myself and others	*Yes/No*
77.	I usually feel equal to others	*Yes/No*
78.	I often expect that people will dislike me	*Yes/No*
79.	I have a tendency to be put on by others	*Yes/No*
80.	I usually assume that others will not get on with me	*Yes/No*

(Source: *Developing Assertiveness* (A. Townsend) (1993) Routledge)

Scoring chart: Count up your 'yes' scores in the relevant groups:

Assertive: 6,11,18,22,23,24,28,36,40,41,48,49,56,57,61,62,70,71,74,77

= _____

Passive: 1,3,5,10,19,20,25,29,30,32,44,45,52,53,58,65,66,73,78,79

= _____

Manipulative: 2,7,8,13,14,21,26,31,35,38,42,46,50,54,59,64,67,68,76,80

= _____

Aggressive: 4,9,12,15,16,17,27,33,34,37,39,43,47,51,55,60,63,69,72,75

= _____

Interpreting your scores:

14–20 suggest that this is how you *regularly* think and feel about yourself and others, and behave towards them.

7–13 suggest that this is how you *frequently* think and feel about yourself and others, and behave towards them.

0–6 suggest that is how you *rarely* think and feel about yourself and others, and behave towards them.

The fight reaction can be seen in **aggressive behaviour** which may include:

- raised tone of voice
- clipped use of words
- clenched muscles in face and body
- flushed skin
- fists banging on table or raised
- standing up or making body look larger
- staring eye contact
- moving close to invade other's body space
- allowing little response from other
- talking 'down'

The flight reaction can be seen in **passive behaviour** which may include:

- downcast eyes
- pale or flushed skin
- low voice, little response, often silence
- agreeing with everything and apologising
- body turned away from other
- body appearing smaller than normal
- being late and taking sick leave
- talking 'up'

Less obvious forms of this behaviour may be seen in manipulative and passive/aggressive behaviour. Someone whose preferred position when under threat is passive may feel aggressive in certain situations, but find it difficult to do so openly.

The result is likely to be a covert form of aggression such as:

- leaving the room, slamming the door, only to return a moment later saying 'sorry' very sweetly (as if they hadn't meant to – they had).

Manipulative behaviour is based in aggression but without being clear, for example:

> 'My manager only ever praises or compliments me when he wants me to do something so now I don't even listen to the nice things, I just wait quietly until I hear about the job that I probably don't want to do. I just wish he would tell me what it is he wants me to do without trying to soften me up first – it doesn't work, I don't believe the compliments any more.'

Manipulation is always covert and leaves the receiver feeling as if they have been misled; what is actually said is not what is received. It is highly damaging to relationships and can cause lasting resentment and lack of trust.

HOW TO AVOID UNASSERTIVE BEHAVIOUR

When communication breaks down, we are unable to transfer our ideas, opinions and information as effectively as we should, and the outcome is often misunderstandings, mistakes and muddles. So how can we avoid being ruled by our primeval feelings and react with passive or aggressive behaviours?

The first and most important key to learning how to avoid the 'fight' or 'flight' reactions turning into unhelpful behaviour is to **recognise the feelings of threat** as they arise in you. Getting in touch with your feelings is something that needs to be developed and taking a moment to think about what they are before you speak is crucial. If you are feeling threatened in any way, it is likely that you will be unable to communicate effectively unless you can resolve the emotion. Where appropriate, declaring how you are feeling is a highly effective way of releasing uncomfortable emotions so that you are free to move back into communication. 'I am worried about this approach', 'I am upset that we are thinking about redundancies', etc. can help you let go of emotions that otherwise might trap you into aggressive or passive behaviour. (*Stage 11* gives more detail on managing emotions.)

The second key to learning how to remain assertive is to **prepare for all important communications**. Take time to think. If you are initiating the conversation, it will be easy to make the time before you ask for a meeting.

If someone else has asked you for your opinion, take at least a few moments to gather your thoughts or, if appropriate, ask whether you can take some time to consider the matter and respond fully later on.

- **Preparation is crucial.**
- **Engage brain before opening mouth.**
- **Failing to prepare is preparing to fail.**

Think through the structure for effective communication (*see page 81*) and where possible rehearse the really important conversations with a friend or coach (*see page 85 for example*). Ask them to take on the role of the person with whom you intend to communicate, tell them a little about the personality, position and how you think they might respond and then go through what you have prepared to say as realistically as you can. Your coach will be able to give you feedback on how they felt as you said each section and you may find some valuable pointers to areas for improvement. Role play is often feared for all sorts of reasons, but the really important conversations need as much rehearsal as possible. It is not appropriate to tell your boss half-way through an appraisal that you have got it all wrong, can you go out, come back and start from the beginning again! Preparation will pay dividends – use it.

The third key to learning how to remain assertive is to take on board for yourself and to allow to the people with whom you intend to communicate a number of **personal rights**. These were developed for assertiveness training workshops after the Second World War and have been known to transform people's lives! Read them carefully for yourself and note any that you feel you would have difficulty allowing for yourself.

PERSONAL RIGHTS

I give myself the right to:

- be treated with respect
- have and express feelings and opinions
- be listened to and taken seriously
- set my own priorities
- say 'no' without feeling guilty or selfish
- ask for what I want
- ask for information from others
- make mistakes and be wrong
- choose *not* to assert myself
- consider my needs to be as important as those of others

(Source: *A Woman in Your Own Right* (A. Dickson) (1982) Quartet)

Now go through them again, reading them with a view to giving them to everyone you wish to communicate with because they are two-way rights and responsibilities and will demonstrate the responsive aspect of good communication.

The right **to be treated with respect** is the key to creating the equality that encourages genuine communication. If you give yourself the right to be treated with respect and give it to others, it will be impossible to talk up or down to another person.

The right **to have and express feelings and opinions** and the right **to be listened to and taken seriously** are the keys to having the confidence necessary to make a contribution to the communication. Be clear about what your opinions are, think them through carefully so that you can justify them if necessary and you will earn the respect of others and build a reputation of being someone it is worth listening to. By giving others these rights, you will also encourage them to engage in two-way communication.

The right **to set one's own priorities** is one that is often ignored at work. Every right carries with it a responsibility to own the consequences and this is particularly apt in this case. For example, if you choose not to start work before midday, you may have to pay the consequences of not finding the sort of job you want. You might, however, be able to find a job where these hours are quite acceptable. It is your choice to set your own priorities *so long as* you own the consequences.

The right **to say 'no' without feeling guilty or selfish** is based on the level of your self-esteem and is one that many people find difficult to accept. It is often easier to give this right to others than to accept it for yourself. It involves a little effort, taking it on board and, perhaps, trying it in low-risk situations before taking on the sabre-toothed tigers! Consider what you might have a right to say 'no' to that you have not exercised yet – staying late at work, refusing a promotion perhaps. (*Refer to the section on page 106*)

The right **to ask for what** *you want* is also based on the level of your self-esteem and may take some effort to put into action. It may also involve some serious consideration about exactly what it is that you do want. Examples at work might include training, help with a particular project, etc. A note of caution here: asking for what you want is not the same as getting it. This right involves not only you being able to ask but also the receiver having the right to refuse if it isn't what they want. The aim of communication here is that at least they will know what it is you want.

The right **to ask for information** links with the previous right. Often we are intimidated by 'experts' – accountants, lawyers, etc. and deny ourselves this right. Taking on this right can make a huge difference in the contributions you allow yourself to make in communications.

The right **to make mistakes and to be wrong** is one that often causes difficulty. It does not imply that we intend to make mistakes but rather when they occur (which our humanity ensures will surely occasionally happen) that we will learn from them quickly and move on rather than beating ourselves up for making them. Most of our learning comes out of mistakes, so we should welcome them as opportunities for development rather than dread them. Taking on this right allows you to own up to them as quickly as possible so that they may be resolved rather than trying to cover them up and possibly creating a much larger problem in the future for both you and your organisation. This is again a right that we often find easier to give others than to accept for ourselves.

The right **to choose not to assert ourselves** is a saving grace in a list of very positive statements. It means that we do not always have to be positive, dynamic and assertive. Perhaps in a meeting you will wish to decide not to make a strong contribution, not because you feel that you can't but because you make a choice that you will feel good about afterwards. This right gives you the freedom to choose rather than have no choice at all. This is a right that some people genuinely find harder to give to others than to themselves.

The final one is perhaps the most important. The right **to consider our needs to be as important as the needs of others**. *As*, that is, not *more*. Often we find ourselves putting others' needs first and then find that we haven't the stamina or resources to complete what we have agreed to do because we allowed our needs to be subservient to those of others. Are you the one who always stays late, who helps everyone else out? What about your needs? Who helps you?

A STRUCTURE FOR EFFECTIVE COMMUNICATION

So, you bump into your manager in the corridor who asks you to meet in their office in 30 minutes to discuss the progress on your project (which you are aware is behind schedule). How can you remain assertive and create an effective communication?

- Take time to prepare
- Consider what your objective and your fall-back position are
- Plan your strategy
- State your purpose and reason in 'I' statements
- Encourage two-way communication
- Negotiate
- Agree action
- Clarify
- Check how you are both feeling

Take time to prepare. Asking for time if necessary is very assertive. It is much better to ask for time to gather your thoughts and papers, if required, than to try to fake it 'on the hoof'. Consider how you are feeling. Repeat to yourself, if necessary, any of the relevant personal rights. Think about what the reason is for the communication and set your objective – what do you want to achieve from the meeting? Is it going to resolve the problem?

Often people try to have conversations about the symptoms of what is wrong rather than attempting to solve the real issue. Like the sailors who were asked to re-arrange the deckchairs on the Titanic, it may make the situation look better superficially but the fundamental problem of the ship listing has not been resolved. At work this may include talking about how you feel they treat you rather than opening the conversation on how you really want the relationship to be or asking for additional help instead of clarifying the scope of the project. Your objective should contain something that resolves the real issue for you.

Then consider a **fall-back position** (what would be acceptable to you if you can't achieve your objective). Most failures at communication occur because no fall-back position has been identified. If you can't get what you want and have no other position, how can a genuine two-way communication of respect and equality take place?

Some examples of fall-back positions:

- You want a pay rise, but your boss can't or won't give you one. A fall-back position might be they know you want one or understand that you think you deserve one, you make a date to discuss it again in three months or negotiate something different like a bonus, additional holiday, etc.
- Your project is behind schedule; your objective might be to extend the time frame and a fall back position might be to get some additional help.

Plan your strategy. Consider what might be in it for them. Human beings are inclined to act when there is something in it for them to do so. Plan your strategy on how to motivate them to listen to you and act in the way you want them to. Where is the best place to have this communication? When? How are you going to present it? In an appraisal, for example, you may find it helpful to hold it in a neutral environment (a meeting room perhaps) rather than your office.

State your reason and purpose in 'I' statements. It is often useful to prepare your opening statement. The opening is crucial in any communication; if you can enrol them at the beginning of a conversation, you are half-way there, but if you lose them at the beginning it will be an uphill struggle. Keep the opening fairly concise; a hidden danger in preparing opening statements is that the receiver might get drowned in a sea of words! Summarise what your position is and tell them what you want to talk about, using 'I' statements.

Putting your point of view in the first person is by far the most powerful form of communication. Using 'you' tends to put the receiver on the defensive or confuses the issue (if you mean 'I' rather than 'you') while using the royal 'we' or any form of plural (without genuine reason – such as speaking on behalf of a team) actually weakens your case and might even imply that you have been discussing the individual behind their back. Try to say everything in 'I' statements and see what sort of reaction you get. Make a list of how often you say 'you' or 'we'.

Some common examples of using 'you' and 'we' include generalisations such as 'When you're sitting in a meeting, you tend to think about ... '. This is obviously an assumption because you can't possibly know what anyone else is thinking so it can only be assumed that you are talking about yourself. Therefore, why not put it into the 'I' statement. The more confusions you give the receiver to decode, the more likely it is that they will misunderstand the purpose of your message. 'We' is often used when the sender is feeling threatened or isolated because it implies a false sense of strength. Examples include: 'Why is this report late?' and 'Well, we aren't getting the right information' (meaning that you, personally, aren't unless you state clearly that the whole team is having difficulty).

Encourage two-way communication. Once you have told the receiver what you want from the conversation, encourage them to respond. Use empathy appropriately and listening skills (explored later in this chapter).

Negotiate. Once you have both stated what you want, move towards a negotiated successful conclusion. This is where your fall-back position is vitally important. You know what your bottom line of satisfaction is so that you now have some room to move. Using respect, empathy and congruency, see whether you can create an outcome that is satisfactory to you both. (*See the section on negotiation later in this chapter.*)

Agree on action. When you feel that you have achieved a satisfactory outcome, gain their agreement and move towards agreeing the actions that will result from it (you may have to negotiate again here). Unless actions are agreed, it is likely that neither of you will be satisfied with the outcome of the conversation.

Clarify that you have both made the same agreement! How many times have you left a meeting satisfied with the outcome only to discover afterwards that the other thought you had both agreed something completely different. Clarification is a vital aid to under-standing and can hardly ever be used too often. Examples include: 'I am right in thinking that what we have agreed is ...?' 'Can you confirm for me what you are going to do as a result of this meeting?' 'How are you going to proceed with this project now?'

Check how you are both feeling. It may depend on the culture of your organisation whether you feel this is possible but what is crucial in gaining commitment is how the other is feeling. If they are comfort-able and satisfied with the outcome, it is likely they will deliver on their agreements. If, however, they feel resentful, threatened or uncomfortable, it is unlikely that they will carry out their part of the agreement. 'How do you feel about this?', 'How easy is this going to be for you to deliver ...?' can be valuable aids to clarifying feelings.

An example of how to rehearse a difficult conversation

Ask a friend to help and set a specific time to meet.

'John, thank you for agreeing to help me. The situation is that I have a meeting with my boss, James, in the morning for an update on how my pro-ject is coming on and it is not going to be easy to explain. Would you be pre-pared to respond as he might while I run through how I am intending to play it?' (Explain more about James, how you think he might respond, his view of you, your view of him, if necessary).

'James, you have asked for an update on the ... project. I am sorry to have to tell you that it is behind schedule at the moment. I propose that I tell you what I have done about it so far and what I would like to ask for your help with. How would you feel about that?'

'What do you mean – it's behind schedule?'

'It is running slowly because of various problems at the moment but I believe we can make up the time. I have put two more people onto collat-ing the figures we have received and wondered if I could ask you to attend a meeting between me and Justine tomorrow to persuade Accounts to give us direct access to the original data rather than the published reports?'

'Are you sure you can make up the time? That's the important thing. OK, what time is this meeting? What do you want me to say?'

In feedback, your friend may also be able to give you some objective advice about alternative strategies. In the above scenario, it seems that James is more concerned about achieving the time deadline than what has gone wrong and an alternative strategy would be to lay out the time issue clearly at the beginning of the conversation.

If every conversation is an opportunity to help you realise your goals, ambitions and dreams:

Who could you communicate with more effectively?

_____

_____

_____

What might be the benefit for you to do so?

_____

_____

_____

How are you going to do it?

_____

_____

_____

_____

HOW TO NEGOTIATE EFFECTIVELY

As already identified, negotiation plays an important part in any effective communication, but it also exists on its own as a form of communication that can cause difficulties for the inexperienced. This more formal negotiation may be between supplier and customer, feuding factions in a dispute or the employer and employee and generally involves agreeing the terms for an agreement.

In the past, negotiation has sometimes been seen as a game in which one side has won and the other inevitably lost and this has caused problems because the loser rarely has a long-term commitment to stick to the agreement or build a long-term relationship of trust and loyalty. A more satisfactory concept of negotiation is that of a dance where each partner takes turns in initiating movement, a process that is enjoyable for them both and is the basis for building a deeper relationship. Aiming for a win:win outcome is the only way to guarantee that agreements are lasting and create good relationships necessary for ongoing successful business.

There is a series of steps in any effective formal negotiation:

- preparation
- invitation
- presentation
- bargaining
- close

Preparation: the time to set your objectives, to consider what their responses might be and to create a strategy.

Any negotiation should be based on both a long-term and a short-term objective. For example, in the short term a salesman will want to sell his products to a retailer, but also as a long-term objective he will want to build an ongoing relationship so that he has the basis of a ready-made outlet for future products and so save himself a great deal of time in the future.

Objectives in any negotiation are so crucial to the achievement of a successful outcome that it is worth considering three aspects:

- **your ideal outcome**
- **a realistic outcome**
- **the minimum level of an acceptable outcome for you**

These outcomes should include not only price but conditions as well. Often payment terms, delivery dates and additional benefits can be just as important as the price that is agreed on. As with the fall-back position in an effective communication, it is vitally impor-tant to clarify for yourself what your bottom line (the minimum level that would be acceptable to you) is. Too often this bottom line is unclear and this leaves the possibility that you might either leave the negotiation with an unacceptable outcome or not have enough room to negotiate freely.

The following checklist may help you in your preparation before any negotiation.

Negotiation between —————————————————————

My ideal long-term outcome—————————————————

My ideal terms —————————————————————————

My realistic terms ————————————————————————

My minimum acceptable terms————————————————

What variations might I accept? ————————————————

Their likely long-term outcome—————————————————

Their likely terms —————————————————————————

Their likely objections ————————————————————————

What variables might be acceptable to them? ————————————

My strategy ——————————————————————————————

Invitation to negotiate: refers to the moment between the sale and the negotiation and should not be rushed. Clarify that they are sold on you or your product before inviting them to negotiate on terms and conditions. This sale is going to be the basis for the agreement on which you negotiate and if they are not convinced by the product, you will be in a weakened position. After all, you do not want to make a deal based on price only, you want to sell them your product first and then negotiate an acceptable (to both of you) price for it and this price is going to reflect how badly they want it. Make sure the sale is complete, then proceed with the invitation to move the conversation on to its next stage. For example:

'Are these pens what you are looking for? I am delighted that we can help. Then perhaps we can move on to discussing terms?'

The more effectively you can handle this move, the more credibility you will gain and the better your position will be of being able to manage the negotiation.

Presentation: is the stage at which you open the negotiation by setting out your ideal terms and encourage them to respond openly. It is likely that your two opening positions will be some distance apart but do not be too concerned. By building on the agreement already secured, you can build your relationship and demonstrate that your intention is for a mutually acceptable outcome. Using all your responsive skills of empathy (*page 69*) and active listening (*page 93*), you may be able to judge where their acceptable area of agreement is likely to be (and whether yours matches it).

Bargaining: is the most easily recognisable stage in any negotiation. If you consider your opening position as being at one end of a see-saw and theirs at the other, the bargaining stage is slowly moving towards the mutually likely area of agreement towards the centre.

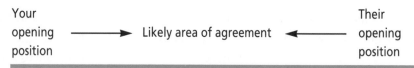

During this stage, it is vital to remember to display the core conditions of communication: equality, respect, empathy and congruence. Bargaining can be a threatening activity for both sides and the more you can inject the core conditions, the more likely it is that you can help keep it assertive and dynamic for both of you. Remember to give ground in return for movement from them, rather than making all the moves yourself. Find areas where you can offer something of value to your partner that costs you little to give. Remember to keep your eyes and ears open for signs of difficulties and resolve them as quickly as possible to keep the process going. Build on agreements all the time, reminding each other where necessary of the mutual interest in the 'sale'.

> *It is vital to remember to display the core conditions of communication: equality, respect, empathy and congruence.*

Closing: watch out for signs of agreement to close and move rapidly to clarify them. Any changes in body language will indicate a change in their thinking processes. Some examples are listed below.

THINKING/ANALYSING SIGNALS

Hands: hands-to-face movements, stroking chin, rubbing nose, taking glasses off, cleaning glasses

Head: tilted, often away to the side or above

Eyes: looking down or away, peering over glasses

Body: getting up, walking around, any exaggerated concentration (i.e. sharpening pencil, filling pipe, etc.)

AGREEMENT SIGNALS

Hands: relaxed, movement from face to chest, movement towards you

Face: smiling genuinely

Eyes: good relaxed eye contact

Body: relaxed, facing towards you, movement towards you

This stage is one of listening and responding in order to clarify and complete the process. Some examples of proven closing techniques are:

'Shall we draw up the contract now and sign it?'

'Sign the contract now and we can deliver on Monday.'

'Unless we can agree this' ... (threatening, use with discretion!)

'Both these approaches will solve your problem, which do you prefer?'

'If we can make this exception, can you get your side to agree?'

'OK, I think I've got all the information to draw up a contract.'

When the agreement has been clarified, check the standing of your relationship to ensure that a win:win agreement has been reached – if not, you may have to start all over again. Use open questions such as 'How do you feel about what we have agreed?' rather than 'Is this OK for you?' and summarise again how you would like the relationship to continue and encourage them to add to it.

'What opportunities for the future might there be?'

'Where do you think we might go from here?'

'How do you see this relationship developing?'

'How can we use this agreement to build ...?'

If you can achieve all this, you will have got an acceptable short-term agreement and built the opening to a successful long-term relationship.

Areas in which I want to develop my negotiating skills:

_____

_____

_____

_____

_____

_____

DEVELOPING GOOD LISTENING SKILLS AND PRACTICES

Do you feel that you are hearing enough from those around you?   *Yes/No*

Do you get enough ideas from those around you?   *Yes/No*

Are you getting all the information you need?   *Yes/No*

Do you understand how to receive information from those around you?   *Yes/No*

If you have answered 'no' to any of the questions above, it may be that you are not actively listening to what they have to offer you.

Given that good communication is fundamentally a two-way process and that so far this chapter has concentrated on how best to put across your message so that it is easier to understand, the time has come to consider the other half of communication. Active listening, the encouraging of the other party to continue and to develop their theme is very, very different from just allowing our ears to receive sounds and our brains to interpret them in whatever way it finds easiest. It could well be that the person with whom you are communicating has the answer to your problem, has a powerful contribution to make to your project or has some really good ideas that you haven't yet found for yourself.

How can you find out?

Active listening skills may be helpfully summarised as:

L   **look interested**

I   **inquire with questions**

S   **stay on target**

T   **test understanding**

E   **evaluate the message**

N   **neutralise your own feelings**

Look interested refers to the body language and posture of the listener. Giving your full attention to the speaker is perhaps the most important of the listening skills. It is generally much easier for someone to speak to you if you look at them, nodding appropriately and using body language to express interest in both the speaker and what is being said. Listening attentively is an enormous compliment to the speaker because it implies that you respect them and what they have to say. Because body language is an imprecise science, it is helpful to watch the speaker to see what they think of you and observe what they find appropriate and what is unhelpful. If they lean back and away from you, for example, you may be too enthusiastic for their comfort or invading their body space. A good listener will be watching the 'dance' to judge their own behaviour and its reactions. When in doubt, try to match your body language to theirs, follow what they do with their body and you will be well on the way to creating a good atmosphere for communication.

Inquire with questions. The use of questions is vital in encouraging others to speak and the type of question used can have a major impact. Unhelpful questions may be summarised as 'closed' – those to which it is possible to answer with either a single positive or negative word. This will not give you a full answer and therefore is of very little value to the process. For example, asking a subordinate to

> *Helpful questions include all 'open' forms.*

whom you have just delegated a difficult task 'Do you understand?' will be unlikely to gain anything other than a 'yes' . It takes a very brave individual to question their boss if they haven't understood and is likely to leave you with a false sense of security. Closed questions should be avoided wherever possible, as should rhetorical questions to which no answers are expected ('You like working with John? Yes, of course you do, I always have') and multiple questions when it is impossible to know which part you might be expected to answer.

Helpful questions include all 'open' forms – those to which it is impossible to simply answer 'yes' or 'no'. Open questions generally begin with 'How', 'What', 'When', Where' and occasionally 'Why' although this last can sound threatening and should be used with caution. Questions that develop the theme can be helpful. Such questions include 'What happened next?' 'Can you tell me more about how ..?' and 'And, then what happened?' A very effective form of question is one that uses the words of the speaker and 'reflects' them back.

For example:

> *'I was really upset when John was promoted above me'*
> *'You were really upset?'*
> *'Yes, I felt ...'*

Reflecting shows that you have been listening actively and by repeating a key word or phrase encourages the speaker to elaborate. A warning note, it is important to reflect their actual words rather than summarising or translating them. Continuing with the example above, if you had said 'You were angry?', they might well have responded with irritation 'No, I wasn't angry' and you would have lost the thread of communication.

Stay on target. This reminds us to keep focused on the topic. Think how often when you are listening to something important, you find your brain rushing off at a tangent. Also, keep the speaker on the subject; often if you are talking about a difficult subject, it is easy to be diverted onto safer areas and you will not resolve the situation.

Test understanding is reminding us again of the importance of clarification. If you are not completely sure that you understand what is meant, ask for clarification to check your understanding is correct. Use, for example 'Am I right in thinking that you are suggesting …?' Summarising and paraphrasing can also be helpful in this section.

Evaluate the message is about listening with your eyes as well as your ears. If the words they are saying are not ringing completely true to you, check it out. 'I hear that you say you are happy working in this team, but I observe that you are looking tense and I am wondering whether there is anything we can do to make you even happier?'

Neutralise own feelings is perhaps the hardest of all these aspects. If you are listening to someone and they say something to which you react, you will immediately stop being able to listen to them. For example, if you are discussing with a subordinate why their work is still unsatisfactory and they tell you that they do not find you easy to work for, if you react the opening for progress will be destroyed. To remain calm you need to remind yourself that when you are listening it is their time and your feelings are not relevant. Then, with practice, you can use empathy, respect and congruence to lead the conversation further, asking 'How could I help you better?'

When you are listening, it is their time – not yours.

Good practices in listening

When you are listening to someone, try to use it as an opportunity to find out more about them as a person and what they are committed to in their lives. Instead of just listening to what they are telling you, listen to the sort of words they use and how they describe things. Most of us, whether we are aware of it or not, send messages in our everyday communication about what our lives are about that are available to anyone listening for them. If you pick up these almost subliminal messages, you will be able to make a real contribution to other people's lives and find the key with which to communicate with them in the future.

Richard, in his thirties, a manager in a City financial institution was finding difficulty relating to his own manager and discussed with his coach how he might resolve the difficulty. He began to listen very carefully to his manager and realised that the words he was hearing had a great deal to do with control, discipline, delivery and responsibility. This gave him an insight into what his manager really wanted and he was able to phrase his objectives in words similar to those his manager had been using. The relationship was transformed and a sense of confidence that had been lacking in the past was immediately established.

Who might I benefit from by listening more actively?

_____

_____

_____

_____

_____

How will I do this?

_____

_____

_____

_____

_____

GIVING AND RECEIVING FEEDBACK CONSTRUCTIVELY

Does everyone around you know what they do best?	_Yes/No_
Do you know specifically what you contribute to them?	_Yes/No_
Do you receive criticism well?	_Yes/No_
Are you able to give criticism constructively?	_Yes/No_

Feedback is a wonderful way of finding out how you are being perceived, whether you are being effective and what you could be doing better. It is like a mirror held up so that you can assess yourself. Strangely enough, this is often not how it is seen, particularly in a work context.

Positive acknowledgements

Before discussing criticism, it is worth reminding ourselves that one positive acknowledgment can be worth a thousand criticisms. Given that most of us want to be liked and approved of, if someone tells you that they like the way you do something, you are likely to do it more. And the more you do things well, the less likely you are to do things poorly and they may never have to point them out to you.

Acknowledgements should always be very specific; just telling someone that they are great isn't very helpful, but if you can give specific evidence they will learn what it is you like and it will build their confidence and self-esteem. For example, 'Howard, thank you for that report. Because you got it in on time and included all the material on the merger in such detail, it really helped me in the meeting' rather than 'Howard, great report, thank you'.

How often honestly do you compliment your colleagues, subordinates and your own manager about how they behave? If people are making a major contribution to your life and achievements, how can they know and do even more unless you tell them?

Acknowledgements I could make to others

People who make a major contribution to my achievements	Their contribution to me	How I could tell them I appreciate it
_____	_____	_____
_____	_____	_____
_____	_____	_____
_____	_____	_____
_____	_____	_____

Constructive feedback

Consider your own attitude to criticism. It's probably negative. In our culture it is common to dread giving or receiving criticism. It is not seen as a helpful or constructive process. **Rename criticism for yourself and see it transform into something valuable.** You may find in the future that it becomes one of the most supportive aspects of your development and how you contribute to the development of others.

Susan, a manager in a service organisation says 'I used to become overwhelmed with a red mist of rage whenever I heard what I considered criticism. I have now transformed how I listen to it by changing the name I call it. Now whenever I feel this red mist overwhelming me, I stop for a moment and speak firmly to myself "Hang on, listen, this might just be some very helpful **feedback** that will give me a pointer as to how to develop and improve my effectiveness" – it has paid enormous dividends to me as I can often now allow other people to contribute to my development.'

GIVING CONSTRUCTIVE FEEDBACK

- be clear about what you want to say and why
- check out what the feedback says about you, the giver
- start with genuine positives
- link, if necessary, with 'and' rather than 'but'
- refer only to the behaviour, rather than the person
- be specific and descriptive
- be selective and communicate as soon as possible after the event
- only refer to situations or behaviour that can be changed
- own the feedback (use 'I' statements)
- help them to find alternatives

  Warning note:

- be aware that you could be opening up other issues that you may have to deal with

Be clear about what you want to say and why. Is it genuinely to contribute to their development and effectiveness? If you simply want to put them down and make them feel bad, don't expect to be able to do this constructively, it's impossible.

Check what the feedback says about you, the giver. We all have particular issues that we get upset about and often it is these that we criticise most in others. For example, some people have an issue about time and are incapable of being late for anything – this is their hang-up, if you like. It is important to them to recognise that being upset about others' attitude to time may say more about the individual it bothers than it does about other people. Check for yourself what you tend to criticise in others most and whether you are being unreasonable.

Start with genuine positives. Since many of us have difficulty hearing criticism without considering that we have failed at every aspect, it is important to open with a statement of genuine respect or acknowledgement. If you like having the individual in your department or are pleased with some aspects of their progress, tell them before you move onto what you still wish to see improved. Give them something to hang onto while you tell them what they may have difficulty in hearing. Genuine positive statements will help you build an atmosphere of respect or trust but only if these are *genuine*. Don't lie or tell them something superficial – they will instinctively know and the whole point will have failed. Sometimes it can take an effort to find something you can genuinely acknowledge – but it's well worth it.

Link, if necessary, with 'and' rather than 'but'. If you give a genuine compliment about the individual's work and then use the word 'but', it has the effect of wiping out completely all the nice things you have just said. If, however you link it with a phrase such as 'and there is one more aspect that I think would benefit you', it sounds very much more acceptable. Try it out for yourself. It is possible criticism could be transformed into constructive feedback for ever if only we could remove the word 'but' from our vocabularies.

Refer only to the behaviour rather than the person. If you want to achieve a change, you will be much more likely to do so if you keep talking to the individual as someone you respect and value who has some aspects of their behaviour that you would like to see changed. For example, 'James this budget is not up to your usual standard' rather than 'James you are hopeless, this budget is a disaster'. In Christianity, this is referred to as 'love the sinner and hate the sin' and in psychology as 'we are all wonderful people who occasionally behave badly'. If you imply that the person is no good, you will obviously not be treating them with respect and equality and therefore communication will break down (and it is likely that you will not achieve your aim).

Be specific and descriptive. Rather than refer to the individual always being late/sloppy/unprofessional (which is very unlikely to be true, if you are honest) refer only to one or two specific situations. Give them as much descriptive detail about exactly what it was that was unsatisfactory so that you can help them understand your view of the situation. 'This budget doesn't seem to include the allowance for maintenance that we discussed' rather than 'This budget is no good'. Don't allow them to divert you with excuses, stay on target – this particular behaviour or product is not acceptable.

Be selective and communicate as soon as possible after the event. Because our culture is so uneasy with criticism, it is common to save up complaints until the straw that breaks the camel's back lets loose a flood of up to a year's problems! This is unhelpful and unfair. Even when an individual is listening constructively to feedback, it is very hard to take on board more than two, or at the very most three, items so a flood is not going to achieve anything more than a breakdown in communication. I would also suggest that you impose a statute of limitations on criticism. After all if you receive criticism some time after the event, it is often almost impossible to remember clearly exactly what happened. It is always best to receive feedback as soon after the situation as possible, with one proviso: always ask whether it is a good time to debrief or give feedback after a mistake. Very often immediately following a mistake, the individual themselves is too upset to be able to listen to anything constructive. Ask them when would be a good time to discuss the situation if you want them to listen to you and change their behaviour as a result.

Only refer to behaviour or situations that can be changed. This may sound obvious but sometimes needs to be reinforced. Often when we are upset or irritated about a situation we complain in the form of a criticism that is hugely unfair. The individual has no control over whether they are tall, short, male, female, pregnant, retirement age, etc. It is perfectly natural to be upset or annoyed about some of these things but completely unacceptable to criticise them for it. 'If you hadn't been ill on Tuesday, none of this would have happened' is simply self-indulgence on your part, there is nothing the individual can do about it.

Own the feedback. Referring back to the structure for effective communication, it is important to speak in 'I' statements if you want to communicate. If you speak in terms of 'We', 'Everyone says', etc., it weakens your message and puts the receiver on the defensive. Also, if they ask you to be more specific about the issue, you may not be able to elaborate. Only refer to situations that concern you personally and about which you can be specific.

Help them to find alternative approaches. Don't take on the whole responsibility for changing their attitudes; ask them how they could do it differently in the future. The more you can encourage them to come up with solutions, the more likely it is that they will be committed. If you tell them exactly what it is that you want them to do, the less likely it is that change will occur. For example, 'Given what we have been talking about, how do you think you will go about this next month?' rather than 'What I want you to do is ...' The whole purpose of constructive feedback is, after all, to help develop the individual and their skills.

Finally, **be aware that you may be opening up other issues that you may have to deal with.** Genuine communication will sometimes open up issues that you may wish you had not initiated. Very often poor behaviour is a signal that an individual is not happy in their position or even with you as their manager. Part of your preparation should include how you will respond if they tell you things you would rather not have heard.

Who could I give feedback to more constructively?

_____

_____

_____

_____

_____

About what?

_____

_____

_____

_____

_____

How can I go about it?

_____

_____

_____

_____

_____

RECEIVING FEEDBACK POSITIVELY

- listen actively
- clarify exactly what is being said
- assess the feedback
- challenge any non-specifics
- admit the truth about the feedback
- don't give excuses
- thank the person for giving the feedback if it is constructive
- choose whether or not you are going to change your behaviour as a result

Listen carefully. Take whatever steps you need to minimise the red mist – tell yourself that you might hear something that will be useful to your growth, put your emotions on one side and listen as carefully as possible. Clarify exactly what is being said, make sure that you are hearing what they are trying tell you. Check with them what you have heard so that there are no misunderstandings and no false interpretations. 'Am I right in thinking that you are happy about the majority of this report but that the summary is too long?' rather than jump to the conclusion that it is all unsatisfactory.

Assess the feedback. Run through in your head what they have said against your view of the truth. Try to do this as honestly as you can. 'I know I put a lot of effect into this report but, honestly, might it be even better if I edited the summary a bit?'

Challenge any non-specifics. Ask for more specific details of any aspects that you are not sure about. 'You are always late/sloppy ...' is unhelpful while a more specific observation may have value for you. 'Are you saying the whole summary is too long or are there some sections that are too woolly?'

Admit to any truth about the feedback. If there is even a grain of truth in the feedback, own up immediately. Don't prevaricate – it wastes so much time and won't achieve anything. 'Yes, I can see that you might be right – what do you think I should do about it?'

Don't give excuses, they are irrelevant. Rarely does it matter why something happened, the point is that it did. The purpose of feedback is to ensure that it doesn't happen again rather than justify why or how it occurred. Keep your mouth shut.

Thank the person for giving the feedback if it is done well. If the feedback is valuable to you and your development, it deserves your thanks and since so much criticism is poorly given, it helps transform an organisation if you compliment an individual who genuinely attempts to give it constructively. 'That's great, I can see that these changes will make it more effective, thank you for your help.'

Choose whether or not you are going to change your behaviour as a result of the feedback. Don't lie about your intentions; it will only lead to another session in the future where they may be even more irritated if you have misled them. It is your choice as to how you are going to behave in the future and you will need to assess the consequences. Ask for their help if you feel it might be difficult for you to change.

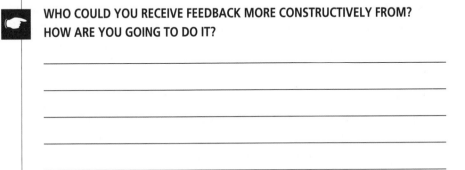

WHO COULD YOU RECEIVE FEEDBACK MORE CONSTRUCTIVELY FROM?
HOW ARE YOU GOING TO DO IT?

_____

_____

_____

_____

_____

SAYING 'NO'

Can you say 'no' at work without feeling guilty?	*Yes/No*
Do you find yourself doing things others have refused?	*Yes/No*
Have you ever wished you could have said 'no'?	*Yes/No*
Are you a 'yes' person who regrets it later?	*Yes/No*

In our culture, there is such a strong impulse to be liked and approved of that we tend to say 'yes' to every request and then, because we are human, regret it later. The danger in agreeing to do things that you don't want to is that you probably won't do them particularly well because your heart is not in it. Giving yourself the right to refuse at least the requests you don't want to fulfil will save you all the time wasted regretting it, the emotional upset of blaming yourself and the likelihood of doing the task unsatisfactorily.

Check again the personal right to say 'no' and consider what genuinely you have the right to say 'no' to at work (*see page 80*). At work, there are both requests (to which you have every right to refuse) and instructions (which you will have to suffer the consequences for if you refuse) and it is important to clarify the difference. You might be able to ask 'What will happen if I refuse?' or 'I don't particularly want to do this. Can we talk more about it?'.

It is so unusual for people in our culture to decline requests and instructions, that even when you summon up your courage and say 'no', the receiver simply does not hear it and continues unabated. There are some helpful guidelines to saying 'no' so that you are heard and that the receiver is left feeling comfortable:

- decide whether or not you really want to say 'no' and why
- ask for time, if necessary
- choose a key phrase that sums up your position
- keep repeating your core phrase until they hear it
- don't allow yourself to be side-tracked
- use empathy for their problem and offer alternative solutions
- don't take on their problem

Decide whether or not you really want to say 'no' and why. If you really don't want to do something and you agree to against all your instincts, the chances are that you won't enjoy doing it and probably won't even do it well. Doing something you don't want to might even damage your relationship a lot more than you fear saying 'no' might. Consider why you want to refuse and be very clear about it.

Ask for time to make your decision rather than be rushed into a decision that you will regret later. It is better to listen to their request carefully and agree to get back to them shortly with a decision that you feel comfortable with. Don't allow yourself to be rushed or manipulated into anything.

When you've made your decision to say 'no' (if that is what you really want to do), **work it into a simple phrase** that is genuinely the truth for you. If you simply don't want to do something, then say so. Excuses and using the word 'can't' are liable to be challenged by the sender of the request. In order to remain congruent in your communication, it is vital that you only attempt to send a completely genuine message.

Don't allow yourself to be side-tracked. Keep the conversation on target, avoid red herrings and additional reasons why they think you should fulfil their demands. Keep repeating your core phrase like a broken record until it is clear that they have heard you.

Use empathy for their problem and offer alternative solutions. One of the reasons senders of requests find it so hard to hear a refusal is that it implies that we do not hear the seriousness of the situation or care sufficiently about them. Using empathy for the sender will make it clear that you do care about them and the seriousness (to them) of their problem. If you also volunteer to help them think of alternative solutions, you will be adding your support even if you don't want to solve their problem for them.

Don't take on their problem. Remember that it is their problem – it isn't yours. Offer to help them discover alternative solutions but don't take their problem away and offer to solve it for them. If you do, you will have a millstone around your neck for many years to come as they hand all their problems over to you to solve!

Repeat your core phrase as often as you need to.

An example:

'James, good news, I have decided to recommend you for the position of sales manager for the eastern region.'

'The eastern sales manager? I didn't know it was vacant? When would it mean taking over? (exploring and thinking)

'Oh, about a month, plenty of time to wrap up here and get organised.'

'I really appreciate you thinking of me when you know how committed I am to taking on more responsibility (empathy) but I don't want to leave Head Office at the moment while we are the middle of the reorganisation.' (core phrase)

'Oh, don't worry about that, the eastern job will give you plenty of valuable experience and a good rise in salary.'

'I really appreciate your support (repeating empathy) but I don't want to leave the reorganisation programme right now. (core phrase)

(hearing him) 'But you said you wanted promotion.'

'Yes, I do and I really appreciate your support. (repeat empathy) In six months' time I would be thrilled to take on something like this but I really don't want to leave the reorganisation programme right now.' (repeat core phrase)

'Well, I must say, I am really disappointed.' *(he's really heard now)*

'I am sorry if this causes you any embarrassment. I really appreciate your support. (repeat empathy) I feel that I have a real contribution to make to the reorganisation programme and while we are half-way through it, I feel that I would be leaving something really important unfinished.' (moving the conversation on)

'Well, yes, that's true and you would be hard to replace but I thought you would like this opportunity and hadn't thought of anyone else.'

'And in six months' time, this move would be perfect. Would it help if we sat down and thought about other possible candidates?' (offering to help)

'Hmm, you might be right about the reorganisation programme, I hadn't thought it through clearly. It would be difficult for me to complete it on time without you. But let's talk about who else ...'

Situations where I might want to say no:

_____

_____

_____

_____

_____

Reasons for saying no:

_____

_____

_____

_____

_____

How can I go about refusing assertively?

_____

_____

_____

_____

_____

Further reading

Developing Assertiveness (A. Townend) (1993) Routledge

Putting Assertiveness to Work (S. Morris and G. Willcocks) (1995) Pitman Publishing

Getting to Yes (R. Fisher and W. Ury) (1987) Arrow

You Just Don't Understand (D. Tannen) (1991) Virago

Managing with the power of NLP (D. Molden) (1996) Pitman Publishing

A Woman in Your Own Right (A. Dickson) (1982) Quartet

TAKING ADVANTAGE OF WORK CONDITIONS

Confidence may be seen as a process in which you first *behave* it, then develop into *believing* it and finally *being* it

Do you know what people think of you within your organisation?   *Yes/No*

Are you ever taken less seriously than you think you deserve?   *Yes/No*

Are you sometimes ignored in meetings?   *Yes/No*

Have you been overlooked in promotion short lists?   *Yes/No*

Do you wish you could feel more confident sometimes?   *Yes/No*

The next step is to consider the environment within which you operate because however much you refine your communication skills, your message will be affected by how you are perceived and what the culture of your organisation is. Before any journey, the experienced traveller needs to consider all the prevailing weather and travelling conditions in order to be both well prepared to meet any eventuality and to consider whether there is a route that is better suited to their personal circumstances. It is exactly the same on your journey towards achieving your potential.

This chapter will:
- review what 'culture' is in an organisation
- show you how to identify the playmakers in your organisation
- illustrate how important your 'image' is
- provide some ideas how to manage it
- discuss how you can behave more confidently
- discuss the role of influence
- explain how you can create a powerful network
- discuss mentoring
- help you develop your own manager

IDENTIFYING YOUR ORGANISATION'S CULTURE

The culture of an organisation has been described by Tom Peters, the US management guru, as 'the way we do things around here'. There are huge differences to be considered in the culture of different businesses. The way an advertising agency operates will be very different from the way in which a manufacturing plant operates. The Civil Service will be very different from the head office of a multinational commercial organisation. And within each industry, the individual organisations will have unique cultures. As these are the travelling conditions through which you are passing, it is valuable to recognise them before considering how to adapt best to them.

How can you begin to identify what the culture is in your particular organisation? Fill in the following questions after careful consideration.

YOUR ORGANISATION'S CULTURE

Consider the management structure. Is it like a pyramid with rigid channels of communication from the top downwards? Or is it like a matrix, more flexible with communication moving freely across departments, upwards and downwards?

_____

_____

_____

_____

_____

_____

What do the physical features of the organisation imply? What do you see as you walk around and what does it say? What are the building, furnishings and facilities like? What do people wear to come to work – casual/trendy/ formal suits and ties and does dress vary greatly between senior and junior members of staff?

_____

_____

_____

_____

_____

What does the organisation's written communications imply? Press releases, annual reports, sales brochures, etc. all have a particular focus; what are your organisation's?

_____

_____

_____

_____

_____

How does your organisation treat outsiders? Customers, clients, shareholders, stockholders, visitors, etc.?

_____

_____

_____

_____

_____

Who are the heroes and heroines of the organisation? Who are the people about whom stories are commonly told? What sort of stories seem to sum up what the organisation is really about?

_____

_____

_____

_____

_____

Who are the decision makers? Who are the people who make things happen? Who are the fast-trackers? What sort of people are they?

_____

_____

_____

_____

_____

(Source: _Corporate Cultures_ (Dealt and Kennedy) Addison Wesley)

The answers to these questions will give you some idea of the culture within your organisation. It does not matter whether you approve of it or not, changing any culture is a slow evolutionary process so you have two choices – move on to a culture that suits you better or adjust your communication and image to that within which you are operating. Deciding to ignore it is a guaranteed path to struggle and misunderstandings.

Organisations and celebrities employ specialists to manage their public relations because they understand implicitly that everything they say and do adds to their 'image' in the mind of their consumers. They know how important it is to manage this image to gain a reputation that will enable them to flourish.

It is the same for an individual within an organisation. You might think it doesn't matter and is somehow rather 'tacky' – you may even believe you don't have an 'image' and anyway if you do, that it is who you are and people are just going to have to understand and accept you for who you are. But you need to understand that your image determines how your messages are decoded and how seriously you are taken.

> A senior female manager who wishes to remain anonymous tells a story of how when in her thirties, she finally had her hippy-length blond hair cut and styled, she received a phone call from the chief executive. 'A lot of nice things are being said about you at board level'. 'Great' she said, 'can you be more specific?' 'They really like your hair' he said. She was stunned.

After all, you accepted when you went for your interview that the picture you put across was particularly important and you probably spent some time considering what to wear, what to say and how to present them with a perception of you that was the one you wanted. Sadly you may now have let it slip a little. It's a bit like courtship and marriage – how often do people make a real effort while they are trying to attract what they want and then let themselves 'go' when they've achieved it.

Firstly, of course you have an image – everyone does. Anyone could come into your organisation tomorrow, ask a few people whether they know you and what people say about you. You would be amazed, they could give you a potted version of your image within a matter of hours.

So you definitely have an image within your organisation – the next question is 'Is it one that you feel represents you in the way you would like to be seen?'

Discovering your image

Checking what your image really is isn't quite as easy as it sounds because people often have difficulty giving feedback on what may be uncomfortable truths – particularly if they like you. Sometimes it is easier to find out what nicknames you have behind your back and what stories are told about you. Your manager may be able to tell you what the senior management team say and think about you – if you give him/her some warning and explain why you want to know.

If you are concerned that the senior management team are not recognising your potential, it may well be because they do not perceive you as the person you believe you are. Often adjusting your image in an organisation involves trying just a little more consciously to demonstrate the behaviour you want them to recognise.

Image is made up of:

- visibility
- stories told about you
- known successes or failures

Visibility refers to the way in which you stand out among your colleagues. There is nothing worse for career advancement than being invisible, but some forms of visibility are more beneficial than others. Physical characteristics such as age, height, gender and race will make anyone who does not fit the standards of the majority of their colleagues immediately highly visible and therefore anything they do is immediately noticed. If you are in the minority in any of these physical characteristics, make it work for you. Where female members of a management team are more rare, these women can regard their visibility as either a positive or a negative aspect – and many choose the positive. This may result in complaints from their male colleagues that the women seem to have far more influence than they did.

The second aspect to visibility is how you present yourself visually. Having already established (*see page 70*) that more than half the message you transmit is done visually, it is important to behave in the manner in which you wish to be seen.

Posture. Whatever height and body shape you are, stand tall, straight and smile appropriately. This immediately demonstrates confidence, self-esteem and a readiness for action. Slouching implies the opposite and should be avoided at all costs.

> If you really don't think any of this matters, consider how John Major is suffering in the opinion polls and ask yourself whether his reputation as the 'Grey Man' is at least partly to blame. Does he really look like a dynamic leader, ready to face whatever difficulties lie in the future? Did Michael Foot's visual image affect his chances of becoming Prime Minister? Certainly the polls and commentators indicate so.

Dress and grooming. If you want to be seen as having greater potential and being available for promotion it is worth considering dressing and grooming yourself as if you were going for an interview – one step up on the job you are presently doing.

In each organisation and industry there will be a culture of appropriate dress that it is unwise to flout. If trouser suits for women, facial hair for men, etc., are deemed to be unsuitable and you want career advancement, it is foolish to rebel. There are some simple and obvious guidelines:

- Always have clean, tidy hair and hands.
- Make sure your clothes and shoes are clean and neat.
- Keep your style appropriately up to date (nothing makes you less likely to be promoted than being stuck in a 1960/70/80s time warp).
- Add colour to your working wardrobe (a scarlet tie or scarf can add considerably to your visibility).
- Avoid wearing grey or beige from head to foot (you will blend into the background).
- Keep your accessories simple.
- Keep your business outfits looking professional.
- Invest in one really good suit or jacket to lift your confidence on difficult days.

A note: really good suits, jackets and shoes may be bought cheaply in the twice-yearly sales or at designer discount houses. You may indeed find that the perfect designer jacket, if you shop wisely, will cost less than a chain store panic buy and prove to be much much better value.

Voice. As indicated by the research on page 70, 37% of your message is transmitted through the tone of voice you use. It is widely accepted that babies respond better to high pitched sing-song voices and adults to lower tones. Since you want to be taken seriously by adults it is worth considering how your voice is modulated. Margaret Thatcher is known to have worked to lower her voice by two tones between becoming party leader and Prime Minister and it was reported in 1995 that John Major worked to lower his voice before the Conservative Party Conference. It is a point worth serious consideration. Research shows that a lower voice is seen as having more authority and, since when we are nervous our voices tend to rise, a high pitched voice sounds lacking in confidence. Often simple breathing techniques will provide the lower confident tones that are required (*details can be found in Stage 10*)

Stories told about you are a little more difficult to influence but you need to make sure that you know what they are. Sometimes you can encourage how often a story is repeated if you elaborate on it, giving more detail – but only do this if it shows you in a good light. If the story that makes you wince as your most embarrassing moment is regularly discussed it is best to treat it lightly – a light smile might even add to your reputation as being unstuffy and genuinely human.

Correcting a negative image. It is not easy but always remember as the world of celebrities knows, any publicity is better than no publicity at all. If neither the senior management or junior staff comment on you at all, you really are in trouble. If you feel that you have an image within your organisation that you dislike, don't try to confront it and deny it – often this only reinforces it. 'Methinks they do protest too much' as Shakespeare commented. The only effective response is to demonstrate the opposite of what you are accused of.

For example, someone thought of as panicking needs to demonstrate that they remain calm in a crisis, declaring 'I am fine, what I think we should do is plan how to respond' rather than 'I am NOT panicking'. When the negative image is referred to in the future, it may be worth challenging it by saying, assertively (*see page 104*), 'I am not aware of any panic. Can you tell me specifically why you think I panic?'. You might gain some useful feedback.

Known successes or failures are perhaps the most obvious ways of influencing your image. In a culture that has difficulties in celebrating success, it can require some effort to take this on board. Consider creating a culture around you of success which would include celebrating and broadcasting others' success as well as your own. Large charts in your department of your successes will motivate your own staff as well as sending a message to outsiders. Remember that the success of your department will rub off on you as well and might even create an environment where you are seen to 'grow' stars and be a highly sought after manager within the organisation. You will benefit in hundred ways as well as likely gaining promotion. But always acknowledge other people's successes genuinely and avoid the mistake of the First World War general who nominated his batman for the Victoria Cross by declaring, 'the chap was incredibly brave – he followed me everywhere'.

Blow your own trumpet

Your role in your organisation almost certainly involves delivering on objectives, so when you do deliver, make sure the right people know. Some ideas worth considering are:

- Copy reports to senior management as well as your boss.
- Invite senior management to any success celebrations.
- Keep a file copy of your successes in written form for future reference (i.e. interviews).
- Always offer solutions when you have to report problems.
- Offer to help other departments with their problems.
- Volunteer for projects in meetings with senior management.

My current image:

_____

_____

_____

_____

How I want to project myself

_____

_____

_____

_____

Action to be taken:

_____

_____

_____

_____

DEVELOPING CONFIDENCE

In preparing to write this book, a wide variety of managers from different organisations and industries were asked what advice they would like to give to new managers. They said 'Realise that everyone has doubts, trust yourself and have a go. As a manager you have to lead and sometimes take a leap of faith.' Nelson Mandela in his autobiography states that 'There are times when a leader *must* move forward ahead of his flock, confident he is leading his people the right way'.

In the 'manager's jacket syndrome', when the bigger job is offered, the individual goes out and buys a jacket, thinking somehow that the world will look different and that he will understand everything he has to do. And of course it doesn't work like that. The individual puts on the jacket and still feels exactly as he did before. What is important to understand is that nearly everyone feels like that at some point in their career and that isn't the issue. No one, however confident they appear, feels totally confident all the time.

KEYS TO BEHAVING WITH CONFIDENCE:
- being aware of your qualities and strengths
- being aware of the contribution you feel you have to offer
- believing that the job needs to be done
- being prepared to take the gamble and to do your best
- drawing on all your training and experience

Confidence may be seen as a process in which you first **behave** it, then develop into **believing** it and finally **being** it. Any new task or process requires a degree of consciously adopting new forms of behaviour which when they become comfortable lead to increasing confidence.

When you are asked to take on a new task that is particularly challenging or demanding, assess it by doing the following exercise:

ASSESSMENT OF NEW TASK

Is this task important to either me or my organisation? Why?

_____

_____

_____

_____

_____

Do I feel I have anything to offer this task? What?

_____

_____

_____

_____

_____

What are the qualities and skills required for this task? (List them)

_____

_____

_____

_____

_____

What qualities and skills do I have that match the above?

_____

_____

_____

_____

_____

Who could I ask to help me with the areas I feel I do not yet fulfil?

_____

_____

_____

_____

_____

Once you have identified that you think the task is important and that you have something to contribute to it and others want you to do it, you have a choice. Will you take it on or not? When you have chosen to accept it and gathered support for the areas you are concerned about, you need to proceed confidently, drawing on your strengths and the strengths of those around you. **It will certainly help to continually remind yourself of what you believe you can contribute rather than focusing on your concerns.**

CONSTRUCTIVE POWER AND INFLUENCE

There are so many negative connotations to the concept of power and influence that you perhaps first need to recognise that everything you say and do has an influence – it is up to you whether the influence is positive or negative. A complainer sends a negative influence into the organisation, an offerer of solutions a positive influence – which do you want to be?

It may be that you cannot recognise that you have any power to influence the organisation within which you operate. Power lies in several different sources; to identify yours, fill in the following questionnaire:

FORMAL AUTHORITY

Do you have a formal right to make genuine decisions? *Yes/No*

Do you need to give approval before others take action? *Yes/No*

Do you supervise anyone else's work? *Yes/No*

Do your decisions affect the long-term organisation's work? *Yes/No*

Does your manager typically support your decisions? *Yes/No*

Do you have support from others to your *right* to do the above? *Yes/No*

POWER OF EXPERTISE

Does it take at least a year to learn to do your job adequately? *Yes/No*

Do you need a qualification to do your job? *Yes/No*

Do you have the highest qualification in your field? *Yes/No*

Are you the only person who can do your job? *Yes/No*

If you left, would they have difficulty in replacing your function? *Yes/No*

Is your expertise related to a major aspect of the
organisation's work? *Yes/No*

Do people frequently consult you and follow your advice? *Yes/No*

Do senior managers show that they value your contribution? *Yes/No*

RESOURCE POWER

Can you give or withhold access to the following resources at work:

- Money *Yes/No*

- Information (non-trivial) *Yes/No*

- Promotion   *Yes/No*

- Training   *Yes/No*

- Senior managers and other powerful people   *Yes/No*

- Computers, administrative facilities, etc.   *Yes/No*

- 'Perks'   *Yes/No*

Are you the only source to other people of these resources?   *Yes/No*

Are others aware of your power in this area (eg past refusal)?   *Yes/No*

INTERPERSONAL POWER

Are you on good terms with people in other departments?   *Yes/No*

Are you on good terms with people at other levels?   *Yes/No*

Have you built contacts with the organisation's powerful people?   *Yes/No*

Do people confide in you?   *Yes/No*

Do you usually speak at meetings?   *Yes/No*

Are you an active listener?   *Yes/No*

Do other people take your views seriously?   *Yes/No*

Do you avoid passive or aggressive behaviour at work?   *Yes/No*

Can you hold the attention of a group or larger audience?   *Yes/No*

(Source: *Career Life Planning for Women Managers* (Ryan and Fritchie) Manpower Services Commission)

PROFILE OF POLITICAL RESOURCES – SUMMARY

Score one point for each Yes answer:

High   5 +

Medium   3

Low   1

Authority   Expertise   Resource   Interpersonal

It is likely that you will have identified at least some element of power based in each of the power sources. This is your current political resource profile.

You may wish to take action to alter this profile and the following two questions can help you decide what to do:

- Do any people who get to the top of your organisation have any characteristics in common?

- Are there any future trends which might demand different characteristics for success in the future?

The profile I wish to develop is:

- Authority

- Resource

- Expertise

- Interpersonal

My action plan for achieving this is:

_____

_____

_____

_____

_____

_____

_____

_____

_____

_____

_____

_____

_____

Having discovered what a potentially powerful person you are, how are you going to use it?

- Do you tend to keep information to yourself?
- Do your team have enough information and authority to do their tasks effectively?
- Do you share your power?
- Who is your power role model – and why?

Most people have a love/hate relationship with power and influence. Some love it and use it to control and manipulate others because they believe that it is a finite resource, like money, and that if you give it away, you will be left with none. Others are frightened by it and see only its negative effects.

This book suggests an alternative view: that power is an *infinite* resource (like love) and that the more you share it with others, the more you will receive and that power can be a wonderfully positive influence in both the workplace and the world. For example, the more you encourage the spread of valuable information, the more will become available to you. The more you delegate authority, the more responsible your people will become and you will also have gained their support and trust.

If you have had a previously uncomfortable relationship with power and influence, it is likely that you have been at the receiving end of some manipulative uses of it and that it is your negative experiences that are colouring your view. Now that you are aware of how much power and influence you have, use it responsibly and with integrity and you could become a powerful force for good in your organisation. Power gives you the ability to enable things to happen.

How I intend to use my power and influence in the future:

_____

_____

_____

_____

_____

_____

_____

_____

_____

_____

_____

_____

_____

_____

_____

_____

_____

_____

_____

_____

_____

_____

_____

_____

NETWORKING

'I don't know – but I know someone who does'

One of the most effective ways of developing your power is to develop your networking skills. Networking is the formal recognition of all the people in your life who give you access to information, expertise, resources and personal introductions. It has been said that you can reach anyone on the planet within five phone calls – so long as you start with the right person from your network. So it is enormously beneficial to maintain a strong network, continually adding to it.

Begin by considering your present network. List all the people in your immediate circle with a note as to what they are a resource to you for.

For example:

Jane – Finance – information and explanations

John – Sales – information, feedback on products

James – Marketing – access to Marketing Director

June – my department – history of organisation

Also consider your personal friends outside work who may also have valuable links to competitors, potential customers as well as valuable expertise and information.

Each person on the planet has at least six friends and if each of them have another six, then within just a few enquiries you will have access to an enormous number of people. Whatever it is that you want to find out, it is likely that someone you can contact will have the information for you.

Draw a visual representation of your power network as it currently exists and consider any areas you would like to develop.

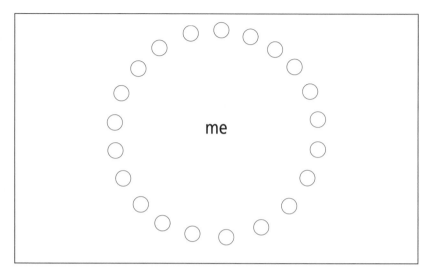

me

How can you develop it? Consider everyone you meet as a possible source of information/access. Keep visiting cards and make a note on the back of what you talked about and what they are interested in. For example:

John worked in Russia for two years and has contacts with brokers as well as his clients.

If you discover areas that are currently missing from your network, actively search out possible inclusions. At work you could deliberately build better relationships with the department responsible for the area you know little about and outside work, ask your friends whether they have contacts in, say, advertising and marketing.

Develop your relationships with your network. Hold regular meetings, social or work-related. Make sure that you keep in touch with the people you expect to be most helpful to you and try and identify what you can do for them so that a genuine two-way relationship is nurtured and developed. A network is such an important resource that it is well worth spending the time to keep it dynamic and alive. If you do this, it will be there and available for you whenever you need it.

A powerful network can provide a real advantage in your career as you will have access to information that is not readily available.

Examples from the sources for this book include:

- information about working conditions in similar organisations
- advance information about potential customers
- advance information about potential vacancies
- briefings on specialised subjects from experts
- introductions to important contacts

Clarify your boundaries of confidentiality. There is nothing guaranteed to destroy your relationship quicker than industrial espionage! If you hear something on your network that may be of value to your organisation, consider carefully how you are going to use it. You will need to protect your source, as a journalist does, if you want to continue the relationship.

> *Grown and developed well, your network of friends and contacts can become your own personal research department.*

If you have a source in the competitive organisation, you may need to clarify the boundaries between each other as well as telling your own employer what you will or will not discuss.

Grown and developed well, your network of friends and contacts can become your own personal research department, so take the advice of the network involved in preparing this book and plan to develop your own.

ACTION PLAN

How I am going to develop my network:

_____

_____

_____

_____

_____

_____

_____

_____

_____

_____

_____

_____

_____

_____

_____

_____

_____

_____

_____

_____

_____

_____

_____

_____

_____

_____

_____

FINDING A MENTOR

A mentor is a valuable support to any one wanting to develop their potential and achieve success. Your mentor may be older than you and successful in their own right but it is essential that they are committed to your success and have your best interests at heart. Mentors are generally *not* your line manager, often not even working in your organisation, they do not tell you what to do or have a specific agenda – they help you achieve what you want to. Because they are not your line manager, they are not focused on the short-term achievement of objectives but on the long-term strategy and goals. They are objective, supportive, encouraging and a champion for you.

Mentoring has always been around. In the past, older, wiser persons identified young people with potential and adopted them as their 'protégées', but these days, it is just as common for the young individual to seek out a mentor for themselves.

How can you go about it? First, consider carefully exactly what you want from a mentor and then identify individuals who you think would fit the bill.

Managers from my network have for example:

- approached speakers after a conference
- written to famous individuals
- identified individuals from newspaper articles
- asked their own networks for introductions
- approached the authors of books
- approached friends of the family

When you have identified a potential mentor, be aware of the likely reactions to an approach. Nearly all the experiences of my network

have indicated that the potential mentor was very flattered to be considered as such and many of them made an appointment to meet to
discuss the possibility. However, since mentoring can be a time-consuming process, it is possible that they may feel that they cannot take
on such a commitment. It may however be possible to arrange a short-
term mentoring agreement to help you develop a particular area.

HOW TO BENEFIT FULLY FROM YOUR MENTOR:

- develop a trusting relationship
- be prepared to take constructive feedback on board
- be prepared to share problems openly
- be prepared to listen to an objective view

QUESTIONNAIRE

Do I want to find a mentor?   *Yes/No*

What sort of person will they be? (List of strengths and qualities)

_____

_____

_____

_____

_____

_____

Possible people to approach

_____

_____

_____

_____

_____

_____

Examples of successful mentoring:

> Jennifer d'Arbo, Chairman of Moyses Stevens Investments. 'I loved that man more than anyone else in the world; he invented me. He was a great entrepreneur in his own right. He was the kindest, most generous giver. I met him when I was about 21. When I went into business he gave me my trade references. He had to make them up as we went along because I didn't have any. Whenever I needed advice, or whenever I was going to do something dotty, like buying a bankrupt department store, Lionel would say, "Oh wonderful, darling, wonderful, what a good idea. Come over and talk to me about it". Then he would have a whole list of names of people to give me for advice. He was a star.'

> James became Chair of a family-owned company while he was still in his thirties following the sudden death of his father. Because he had only recently begun to understudy his father's role, he found taking on the Chair a real challenge. Over the following few years, he relied on the advice and support of a retired colleague of his father's with whom he felt comfortable to discuss any matters that were concerning him. 'I don't know how I would have managed to get through my learning process without the comfort of knowing that there was someone who was on my side and supplied me with such sensible advice and support', he says.

DEVELOPING YOUR MANAGER

If you want to be managed well so that you can achieve all your objectives and develop yourself, then you have no option but to develop your own boss. However good your manager is, there is no way that he/she can instinctively know how you can most effectively be managed unless you tell them.

Taking responsibility for your own development as well as making your image within the organisation as effective as possible will almost certainly involve you in enrolling your own boss in the process. What will be the benefits for your boss? You will need to 'sell' them on the idea so some serious consideration will need to be given to this aspect, as there may also be disadvantages from their point of view: possibly increased time and attention as well as the concern that you might be aiming to take their job.

These benefits might include:

- **more effective achievement of objectives (credit to boss)**
- **you taking on more responsibility**
- **you taking on more tasks**
- **better relationship leading to fewer misunderstandings**
- **more time for boss to do what he/she wants to do**

How and when can you begin this upwards development process? In an ideal situation there will already be opportunities to communicate your needs, these will include:

- **appraisal session**
- **when you are being delegated a task**
- **when you are debriefing a task**

If you do not have such opportunities available to you, you may have to ask for a specific meeting to discuss how you can be most effective. Aspects you will need to consider and prepare for are:

- What motivates you?

- What are your long-term goals?

- How much constructive feedback do you want?

- How much positive praise do you need?

- What training do you want?

- How do you learn best (experiment, teaching, mixture of both)?

- How much supervision do you like?

The process needs to be balanced continually between what it is you want and what it is they want. The first step is to clarify exactly what it is they want which may include you asking them to be more specific about the task (or your role) that has to be done with measurable criteria for success. Too often tasks are set without either side agreeing what will constitute its successful achievement and if you don't understand what is required of you, you will be unlikely to achieve it. When you are clear about exactly what is required of you, you need to express what it is you need to be able to do the job which might include any of the items listed above.

Now that you have reached the position in the structure for effective communication where both sides have stated their position, you are in a position to negotiate. Your line from here onwards should be 'I will be able to deliver what it is you want more effectively if you will ...' so that the benefit for them is made clear. As in any effective communication, you may not get agreement for everything you want so you need to have established a fall-back position.

Another aspect that you may be able to influence is that of clarifying the boundaries to be managed in each position. Sometimes if your manager has been recently promoted, they may find it difficult to let go of feeling that they can do your job better than you can rather than concentrating on the boundaries of their new position. For example, if you have been asked to write a report, you can coach them to help you frame it so that it satisfies the final audience. 'What do you think I ought to bear in mind with regard to what the Finance/Marketing/Production directors will be looking for?' In this way, you will encourage your manager to be focusing upwards while you do the job you have been asked to do.

If it seems your boss is looking over your shoulder and making suggestions all the time, you may want to acknowledge their input and recognise their concerns by arranging a firm date for a progress review:

'That's a valuable suggestion. Can you leave it with me to work through and then perhaps we could meet tomorrow afternoon and I'll show you a full draft?'

If, on the other hand, you are not getting the support you want, you may want to consider asking for a meeting:

'I think it's going well and there are several areas where I would appreciate your experience, could we meet this afternoon to go through it?'

Key words to remember in conversations to manage your manager are: **'helpful'**, **'valuable'** and **'experience'**.

Action plan for developing my boss:

- benefits for boss

- what do I want out of it?

- what am I going to tell them about my long term goals?

- when is the best time to have this conversation?

Further reading

Reinventing Influence (Mary Bragg) Pitman Publishing

Status (Philippa Davies) Piatkus Books

The Gods of Management (Charles Handy) Pan

Corporate Cultures (Dealt and Kennedy) Addison Wesley

Career Life Planning for Women Managers (Ryan and Fritchie) Manpower Services Commission

Getting the Best Out of Yourself and Others (B. Rodgers/I. Levey) Fontana

PUTTING CREATIVITY
TO WORK

Tackling a problem from an unexpected
direction can be truly advantageous

Do you sometimes feel that life is running you?   Yes/No

Are you more likely to react to events than to initiate them?   Yes/No

If things aren't going your way, do you want to give up?   Yes/No

Do you ever wish you could be more dynamic?   Yes/No

Do you find it difficult to think of creative options?   Yes/No

The way you react to events, whether in your personal life or in your working life, depends a great deal on how well developed your creative thinking skills are.

You will have to manage situations where the world is not working out the way you wanted it to and one of the hallmarks of your success is how well you respond pro-actively to the difficulties that emerge. **How you think affects what you think about and the quality of the solutions that emerge.**

This chapter will explore:

- what strategic thinking really is
- how to plan a strategy
- how to assess the opportunities and threats that emerge
- how to develop your creativity
- how to brainstorm successfully
- the role of creative visualisation

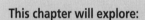

WHAT IS STRATEGY?

'The obvious way forward will lead to fighting, the surprising approach will lead to victory.'

Strategy or the art of how to achieve your goal was originally based on military tactics and has been in existence longer than perhaps most would think. *The Art of Strategy* from which the quote above is taken was written by Sun Tzu more than 2,500 years ago. An effective strategy might be summed up as having:

- a clear long-term goal
- creative tactics by which to achieve it

This might be summarised as 'working smarter, not harder' which may explain its popularity in business jargon today. As the world market-place becomes more and more competitive, strategic planning becomes more and more important. Strategic planning is an art that is valuable to any business and its development will pay dividends for you personally as well as organisationally.

As an example, it is worth considering the current grocery market and exploring the strategies of the major players. Some years ago supermarkets and grocery stores were all based on the local high street and attracted passing trade based on price and image. Tesco began closing some of its small stores and embarked on a campaign to spread its appeal to a more up-market customer. Currently we can see that Tesco, Sainsbury and Asda tend to concentrate on large, clean, bright out-of-town stores with plenty of parking and a wide range of products at reasonable prices. Safeway have tended to retain their high street stores and offer the convenience of easy-access shopping. Marks and Spencer have found a market with working people offering high quality convenience and ready prepared food in the high street at prices considerably higher than other supermarkets. Local independent grocers offer easy-access shopping and tend to rely on convenience and long opening hours. Recently there has been a rise in large new supermarket chains offering cheap, no-frills shopping. There is enormous variety in the route to success in any market and changes can be seen almost monthly in strategy. Consider when you are next shopping for groceries what your store's strategy might be and how successful it is.

But how does an organisation develop a strategy? One way is by beginning with a strengths/weaknesses/opportunities/threats (SWOT) analysis:

Strengths and weaknesses analysis. Once this has been identified, you have some choices about whether to work purely from your strengths or whether to spend some time developing your weaknesses so that they are reduced. In the above example, it might be said that Tesco by moving up-market in its appeal resolved one of its weaknesses and that Marks and Spencer concentrated on its reputation for quality rather than focusing on price.

Opportunities and threats. This involves drawing some conclusions about what is going to happen in the future (both in society and in what your competitors might do), identifying trends and matching them with your strengths and weaknesses. In the above example, it might be that Marks and Spencer correctly identified a trend of working people wanting quality ready-prepared food to serve at home and that Tesco, Sainsbury and Asda identified a trend for people to do one major 'shop' a week with easy access to parking at a reasonable price.

What is the relevance of strategy to a programme of self-development? In any organisation it is a vital business skill and any development of your understanding and knowledge of it will pay you dividends, but it also has a direct relevance to your future. You have already begun the process. In Stage 1 you identified your own strengths and weaknesses. Stage 2 (*page 35*) concentrated on discovering where you want to get to and this chapter will focus on how to get there and use your thinking processes to help you.

This book is not suggesting that you should consider your manager, colleagues and other likely candidates for the position you want as 'the enemy' but rather that you create a strategy that enables you to be seen as the obvious candidate for the position you want. It is worth considering that if you do get the job you want in the long term, how do you want the people around you to behave? It is likely that if you have 'stabbed them in the back' and behaved as if they were your enemies, that they will not be supportive of you. An effective strategy might involve positioning yourself in a favourable light while building support from those around you so that you are in a position to deliver your objectives effectively when you get the promotion.

How to assess opportunities and threats. For an organisation, it is vital to continually assess the national and international trends in social behaviour, in your particular industry as well as assessing what your competitors are likely to do.

Royal Dutch Shell has a whole department responsible for scenario planning where they assess both the likelihood of trends and how they could respond to any opportunities and threats to the supply or sale of oil and petrol products.

IBM has been identified as having misjudged the popularity of personal computers which led to a downturn in its profitability.

Many of the defence industries failed to plan for the resulting decrease in demand following the fall of the Berlin Wall and the reduced perceived threat from the Eastern Bloc.

It is well worth keeping an eye (reading newspapers, trade journals as well as listening out for clues) on trends for yourself and for your own career. These might include:

- is your industry likely to expand or retract over the next ten years?
- are some countries better placed to benefit than others?
- what are the trends with regard to qualifications and skills?
- what qualities are likely to be valued in the future?
- who are the likely contenders for senior positions?

If your industry is likely to contract over the next ten years, you may wish now to consider transferring to another sector which is more likely to expand. The earlier you spot the signs and respond, the more likely that you will emerge ahead of the game. Many industries have boom times in particular parts of the world at specific times and their employees may have to adapt rapidly as conditions change.

Tom, a manager in an oil company, had already spent two years working in Head Office when he realised that as the reserves in the North Sea were depleting, senior positions in the UK office were likely to be reduced and that opportunities for promotion limited. He volunteered to be considered for relocation and now is based in Thailand in a good position to benefit from the expansion of the South East Asian oil market.

The trends with regard to qualifications and skills may include MBAs, financial and accountancy training, languages as well as experience. You will be the one to decide what would be the best things for you to do but the earlier you can identify the trends the better placed you will be to benefit from the insight. Currently anyone working for an international company would do well to consider learning at least one language to fluent conversational level and plan to spend at least one year based abroad.

Establishing what qualities are likely to be valued in the future leaders of your organisation is rather more complicated. For the past 20 years, commentators and gurus have expressed the view that a more 'caring,sharing' style of leadership will be required but we have yet to see widespread signs of it being implemented! The British Institute of Management's *Management Development to the Millenium* report (July 1994/5) identified from a survey of its members that the key skills required for the year 2001 would be:

- **strategic thinking**
- **responding to and managing change**
- **orientation to total quality/customer satisfaction**
- **financial management**
- **facilitating others to contribute**
- **understanding role of information and IT**
- **verbal communication**
- **organisational sensitivity**
- **risk assessment in decision making**

Consider your own industry, identify possible trends and consider developing your skills in any areas from the above list, as well as any others, that you consider will be most valuable in the future.

Identifying the key people for the future can be helpful in planning your strategy but a word of warning, if you identify who you think will be the high-flyer and hitch your wagon to this rising star, you may be left out in the cold if something goes wrong for them.

A manager running a department with the full support of the chairman and chief executive, concentrated on the junior members of staff so that they felt involved and motivated while he rather ignored managers at a similar level and above who became resentful of his department's success and freedom. After the company went public, the chairman and chief executive were ousted and this particular manager found himself in a position where he decided to resign as a sudden realisation dawned on him that the people he had been ignoring for so long were preparing to take their revenge.

The lesson to be drawn from this example might be that you need the support of as many people, in as many different roles across the organisation, as possible to help you achieve your potential, so treat them all with respect.

Be nice to others on your way up, because you will need their support when you have got there.

CREATING YOUR STRATEGY FOR SUCCESS

Personal strengths:

_____

_____

_____

_____

_____

Personal weaknesses:

_____

_____

_____

_____

_____

Trends for your organisation and area of work:

_____

_____

_____

_____

_____

What will be the requirements for success in the future:

_____

_____

_____

_____

_____

Opportunities for you in the future:

_____

_____

_____

_____

_____

Possible threats to you in the future:

_____

_____

_____

_____

_____

What can you do to maximise the opportunities?

_____

_____

_____

_____

_____

What can you do to minimise the threats?

_____

_____

_____

_____

_____

DEVELOPING CREATIVITY

This section is not necessarily about thinking of pretty woodland scenes, painting a picture or writing a piece of music. Creative thinking involves doing things differently, in a way it hasn't been done before, doing the unexpected – which, if you remember was one of the elements of strategic thinking Sun Tzu identified. Tackling a problem from an unexpected direction can be truly advantageous.

An unexpected drop in price of your goods may gain you new customers while your competitors struggle to come to terms with your action and consider how to respond. Every customer wants to receive more than they expect, so the element of surprise, something that exceeds the customer's expectations, is what every organisation ought to be looking for in their strategic planning.

How does this relate to a personal development plan? In two ways, first, the more you can use creativity to develop your own strategy for success, the more likely you are to be able to foresee both the likely and unexpected trends. Second, the more able you are to blend creativity with your logical planning and evaluation skills, the more likely you are to be able to provide that extra something that makes you the ideal candidate for promotion.

EXERCISE

Draw yourself nine dots at equal distance from each other as illustrated and draw four straight lines without taking your pencil off the page so that each dot has a line passing through it. (If you already know this exercise, try doing it with three straight lines only – again without lifting your pencil off the paper.)

```
O   O   O

O   O   O

O   O   O
```

Although this is an exercise that is well known and has been around for many years, it still illustrates the creative process particularly well. You may have glanced at it and thought 'That shouldn't be too difficult', lifted your pencil and immediately begun. After a few attempts you probably stopped, confused and even frustrated and began to try thinking logically and carefully about it. Your frustration is probably based in the assumptions that you are using to think about the exercise, that the nine dots form a box within which you are supposed to be drawing your lines. Let the assumptions go – there is no limit to the area of space within which you may draw your lines. Begin again. When you have completed the exercise or reached complete despair, check your attempts with the figures on *page 168*.

EXERCISE

Imagine a cake which you are asked to divide into eight equal portions using only three slices of your knife.

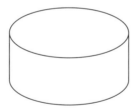

If you are having difficulties, you will probably find that you have again made an assumption: either that you may not move the cake around or that the cake you are envisioning is not three-dimensional. Try again. When you have completed the exercise or reached complete despair, check your attempts with the figures on *page 168*.

The creative process: consider what processes you went through as you completed the exercises above. It is likely that they match the figure below:

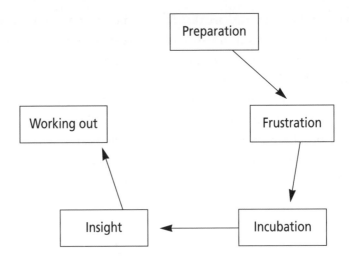

(Source: *The Creative Manager* (R. Evans and P. Russell) (1989) Unwin Hyman)

- *Preparation* is concerned with analysing the task, gathering data, looking for patterns, trying out ideas, questioning assumptions.
- *Frustration* occurs when we are unable to resolve the issue, feel bored, irritated or despondent and doubt our own ability.
- *Incubation* is a time when we give up trying, put the issue on hold and hand it over to the unconscious mind.
- *Insight* is the inspiration, the 'Aha', the moment we normally associate with creativity.
- *Working out* involves testing the insights and putting them into practice.

It is important to see creativity as a process rather than simply the moment of insight as both the frustration and incubation stages are just as important and without them the insight rarely occurs.

How can you use creativity to help you? By understanding that it will give you solutions that are elegant and unexpected.

Use your creative thinking process to help you solve any problems that emerge during both the planning and implementing stages of any projects that you set up.

- allow yourself time to prepare as fully as possible so that you are clear what the problem is you are working on solving

- allow the frustration that emerges as part of the process, welcoming it rather than allowing yourself to get angry and give up

- allow the time and space necessary for incubation. Once the problem is in your head, move away from it, make a cup of coffee, take a walk, sleep on it even, but allow your unconscious mind time to solve it. (How often have you battled for the right word while writing a report and as soon as you get up to make a cup of coffee, it immediately appears in your mind?)

- enjoy the insight, the 'Aha', and learn for yourself what helps your unconscious mind to produce it

- work it out into the form of a solution as soon as possible and test it out against the original problem

One of the most helpful uses of creativity is to create different options for yourself. Having choice is hugely freeing and allows space for creativity to occur, while having no choice

Allow the frustration that emerges as part of the process, welcoming it rather than allowing yourself to get angry and give up.

leaves you feeling restricted and is likely to lead to a situation where you can feel threatened (and you saw the results of that in Stage 3 when we investigated aggressive and passive behaviour).

Having prepared all the information for your strategic planning on *page 147*, begin to create at least six scenarios of what might happen, both expected and unexpected and how you would react to each of them. Life has an interesting habit of producing the most unlikely events. It rarely unfolds in a logical pattern; creativity and flexibility are the key factors necessary to enable you to cope with it. The reason for creating six is to be able to provide yourself with enough options to think and plan through.

- Best scenario:
- Second best scenario:
- Most likely:
- Least likely:
- Second most disastrous:
- Most disastrous:

Thinking through strategies for dealing with the worst possible outcome that you could possibly imagine gives you the confidence of knowing that whatever comes up, you have thought it through and can overcome it.

Richard Branson is reported as focusing in every new project planning meeting on the 'most disastrous outcome' on the basis that if he and Virgin can survive that, then the project is usually worth progressing with.

The same process is now available to you whenever a challenging situation comes up, take some time out and consider all the possible outcomes. When we are faced with a difficult situation, we tend to be so completely overcome by it that we can only see one possible outcome, usually the worst possible, and we are left in what is called 'survival' where we have no options, no freedom and no room to be pro-active. If you can come up with six different outcomes, you will be able to find alternative ways of managing them and suddenly you have some choice, some room to manoeuvre. When you have worked through the different possible outcomes, identify your preferred outcome and consider whether there is now anything you can do to make it more likely.

Sonia, the Chair of a charity, found herself in the uncomfortable position of being asked to face the trustees on a motion of no confidence. Rather than giving in to panic, she prepared a number of different scenarios which were:

- **Best outcome:** calling their bluff and winning the confidence vote by refusing to debate the issue: a classic stand-off

- **Second best outcome:** debating the issue, apologising for mistakes made by the board, presenting the options and implications, giving the trustees the full picture and getting a mandate to govern

- **Most likely:** arguing case and the motion fails to carry, carrying on without a mandate, no real authority or confidence

- **Least likely:** mover of no-confidence motion withdraws it

- **Second least likely:** organisation unites behind new chair and new composition of board

- **Second worst outcome:** losing vote, board continues for six months until new one can be elected, no mandate or authority

- **Worst outcome:** losing vote, board being fired and new one elected immediately, losing all continuity. New board likely to fail because issue not really resolved

As soon as she had realised that she could and would survive (she would still be alive, with a happy family and could always find another job, even if it wasn't as well paid and satisfying) even the worst outcome, the threat to her personal future receded and she was able to work creatively again and focus on the welfare of the organisation, the continuity and reinforcement of its institutions and re-establishing trust.

After considering all the options and their implications for herself and the organisation, she identified the second best outcome as being the most realistic and more likely to be attainable and this became her preferred option as she began working on a strategy for the meeting.

By the time she got to the meeting, she was fully confident she would survive any outcome. She opened by acknowledging that the board had made some mistakes and set out the options and implications that faced them. She even offered to step down if the trustees could appoint a new board who could unite the organisation. The vote of no confidence failed.

How can you use scenarios to your advantage?

BRAINSTORMING

Brainstorming is the most well known and probably the most effective creative thinking process but it isn't always used to its full potential. The first requirements of brainstorming are a large sheet of plain paper and an open mind. Brainstorming can be effective either with a group of people or on your own, but a genuine open-mindedness is crucial.

Set up the session thoughtfully. Arrange a large enough room with a table for everyone to sit around where they can all see and hear each other easily.

Tell them that you are looking for at least 100 ideas as quickly as possible and that silly-sounding ideas are welcomed as these may well inspire the perfect answer. Ask for no comments or reactions to each idea but just a flow of ideas from all around the table.

Begin by reading out the problem and asking for a few minutes' thinking time for people to be clear about the problem and to begin jotting down ideas. If you are working with a group, ask people to shout out ideas as they think of them and appoint a 'scribe' to write them all down. If you are on your own, small 'post-it' notes are a good way of jotting down ideas and then moving on to a clean piece of paper for the next.

The purpose of brainstorming is to create as many ideas as possible (aim for 100 within ten minutes) without any personal or group censorship. Don't worry at all if some of the ideas are silly or stupid; surprisingly often a really silly idea will spark something else that is just perfect and if that silly idea hadn't been expressed, nothing would have happened.

Once you have captured 100 ideas you can begin to assess them. Gather all the similar ideas together and, if appropriate, unite them into one single idea. Certainly creating categories and linking similar ideas can be very helpful. Then begin to discuss each idea or category.

Some teams have set themselves guidelines to remove as many assumptions as possible and to allow creativity to flow. The principles listed below are those laid down by the Sony team responsible for the Data Discman:

1. Believe everything can be half the size you initially thought of

2. Decide the size the product should be, even before considering what it should consist of

3. Set a clear, simple target

4. Agree the target and motivate yourself for success before considering the detailed substance of the project or product

5. 'Difficult' means possible, the term 'impossible' should be excluded from the discussion

6. Before explaining or attempting to explain the idea, make the product

7. Brainstorm in your hotel, do not end your discussion or return to work before your discussions are ended

8. The most promising of ideas must be kept secret from your boss; you must make the product before telling him or her

9. If you want help, ask the busiest people; they are the ones who will have the best ideas

Although some of these principles are radical, they illustrate how this particular team removed many of the assumptions that might have restricted their thinking. One of the most interesting aspects is how they focus on a successful outcome rather than focusing on whether it is possible. This confidence leads to an atmosphere where creativity is encouraged.

How can you use brainstorming more effectively?

_____

_____

_____

_____

_____

CREATIVE VISUALISATION

One of the most powerful inhibitors to doing something for the first time is the fear of failure. When you have done something successfully several times it becomes easier and you are more able to concentrate on improving your performance rather than simply surviving the situation. Creative visualisation (or mental rehearsal) is a proven way of doing something successfully in your mind so that your brain believes that it has achieved it successfully at least once before.

The Reader's Digest some years ago published the results of a fascinating experiment. High school students of similar basketball ability were divided into three groups and each given a different practice schedule.The first group practised free throws on a basketball court for one hour each day; the second group did no practice at all and the third group practised free throws in the their minds only for one hour each day. The results were that the first group improved their average by 2 per cent, the second group's averages deteriorated by 2 per cent while the third group improved their average by 3½ per cent.

We can deduce from the results of this experiment that real practice has some measurable value especially against no practice at all but what might lead to mental rehearsal being more successful? It has been suggested that because of the nature of reality, failure and mistakes occur in practice which lead the brain still to be concerned about the outcome of each shot and we know that when we are nervous, we rarely achieve our potential. The advantage of mental rehearsal is that it is possible to create a perfect outcome each time. You can even adapt the outcome if it is not going according to plan, for example, if your basketball shot in your mind is going too high or low, you can mentally adjust the trajectory until it is perfect.

Rehearsing mentally can be used in any situation and is particularly useful when you are very nervous and the situation is particularly important: exams, driving tests, appearing on stage or making an important presentation are all examples of situations where thousands of users have benefited from its use.

> *The advantage of mental rehearsal is that it is possible to create a perfect outcome each time.*

Mental rehearsal will never negate the need for preparation but will help you avoid making a mess of a situation where you have prepared fully but your nervousness lets you down. If you have a major presentation to make, for example, when you have completed your preparation, consider what it is that most concerns you and see if you can 're-frame' it in your mind to allow the possibility of success.

'Too many people, I can't connect with them'
Maybe you could focus on one at the beginning and smile at them so that you feel connected and then smile around the group.

'They are all waiting for me to make a mess of it'
Is that how you feel listening to a presentation? Maybe at least some of them are really interested in what you have to say.

When you have re-framed the negative thoughts and fears, mentally rehearse it as if it is a major triumph. Because you want your brain to believe that you have already done it wonderfully well at least once, it helps to move the time frame to a period after the challenge, so imagine that it is now the evening of the day in question and review how well it went. Ask yourself the following questions based on the premise that it had been a brilliant success:

- What did you wear and why?
- How were you feeling?
- What did you do immediately before the meeting to relax?
- How did you open your presentation?
- What was their reaction?
- How were you feeling?
- What were the main points you got across?
- What helped you?
- How did you complete your presentation with a flourish?
- What was their reaction?
- What did people say to you afterwards?
- How did you feel?

Elaine, an office manager in her thirties, was due to take her driving test (part of her personal development plan) for the third time and was becoming more and more nervous. At lunchtime her mentor sat her down in a private office and explained the process. 'It is Friday morning and we are going to have a conversation about the previous day on which I want you to understand that you have passed your driving test. I want you to concentrate on this and answer the following questions.'

' I am so thrilled that you passed your test. Congratulations. How was it all? What time did you wake up?'

'I woke at about seven.'

'How were you feeling when you woke up?'

'I felt surprisingly calm.'

'What did you wear?'

'I decided that I wanted to look smart and yet be comfortable so I wore my blue shirt and matching skirt with flat navy shoes.'

'What did you have for breakfast?'

'I had some cereal and a cup of tea, I didn't want to eat too much'.

'What time did you leave for the test?'

'My instructor came to pick me up at ten and we had a final lesson before my test at twelve.'

'How was the lesson?'

'It was fine. It felt like a practice rather than trying to learn any more.'

'So you got to the centre by twelve – how were you feeling?'

'Fine. We didn't have to wait too long until I was called.'

'What was the examiner like?'

'He was great. He looked rather like my instructor and I felt quite comfortable with him. He wasn't scary at all ...'

This continued right through the entire process including the drive home and the congratulations from friends and family. At the end she promised to review it again before she went to sleep and guess what – she passed!

The more you can concentrate on the situation having been achieved with great success and the more you can see and feel yourself being successful, the more likely it is that you will be able to replicate this when the time comes. Our brains find it difficult to allow us to do something new or difficult without flooding us with tension and fear. Mental rehearsal or creatively visualising ourselves being successful is a great builder of confidence and relaxes the tension that often caused past failures.

Mental rehearsal is a form of programming yourself into believing that not only are you able to do something but also are able to do it well. If, for example, you simply cannot see yourself doing a particular task, you will be most unlikely to be able to achieve it. You need to be able to believe that you can do it and do it well to allow that to happen. Self-belief is crucial to success and mental rehearsal is a proven way of providing that self-belief.

Areas where mental rehearsal would be of value to me:

Possible answers to exercises on *pages 154 and 155*:

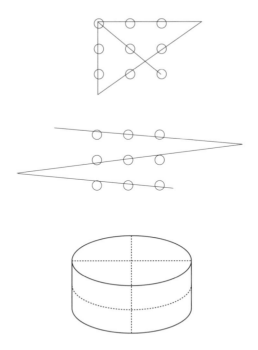

Further reading

The Creative Manager (R. Evans and P. Russell) (1989) Unwin Hyman

A Whack on the Side of the Head (R. Von Oech) (1990) Thorsons

Creative Visualisation (S. Gawain) (1978) New World Library

The Mind of the Strategist (K. Ohmae) (1986) Penguin

The Essence of Management Creativity (T. Proctor) (1995) Prentice Hall

Imagination Engineering (P. Birch & B. Clegg) (1996) Pitman Publishing

The Art of War (Sun Tzu translated S. Grifith) (1971) Oxford Paperbacks

UNDERSTANDING THE ART OF PRESENTATION

It generally takes me three weeks to prepare a good impromptu speech

(Mark Twain)

Do you dread making presentations?	*Yes/No*
Do other people make better presentations than you?	*Yes/No*
Do you dread writing reports?	*Yes/No*
Are other peoples' reports more effective than yours?	*Yes/No*
Do you think reports and presentations are a waste of time?	*Yes/No*
Do you put off preparing presentations until the very last minute?	*Yes/No*

However effective you are at selling your ideas in a one-to-one situation, it is certain that you will be expected to make either verbal or written presentations of your ideas in order to influence groups of people and the skills required to achieve this goal are vital to your future success. You may have been on a course and 'know' all the techniques but **the success of your future presentations will depend on how much you take responsibility for the development of the skills and practise each and every presentation.**

This chapter will:

- explain how to manage your emotions before making a verbal presentation
- remind you how to structure your presentation
- help you decide what information to include
- remind you how to plan your presentation
- help you develop your own practice regime
- cover proposals and reports

MANAGING YOUR NERVOUSNESS

In a recent survey in the USA, more people expressed 'having to speak in public' as being more terrifying than anything else –

171

including their own death. This extraordinary result draws attention to the fact that very often not knowing how to manage the emotions that are present is as important as not knowing how to construct the presentation.

There are probably very few people who would be the first to volunteer to make a presentation – for many it is not a favoured activity. Most people will suffer from some nervousness before making any sort of presentation or having to speak in public – and the more nervous you are, the less likely you are to do yourself justice. Some nervousness, however, is helpful because it focuses the mind on the task in hand and encourages you to take it seriously and follow the steps necessary to reduce the emotion to the level where it inspires you to give your best.

- **Prepare, prepare and then prepare again. Remember that failing to prepare is generally preparing to fail! Follow the guidelines given later in this chapter for gathering the appropriate material, visual aids as well as creating a structure with appropriate memory cards for you to follow.**
- **Practise actually speaking the material until you are comfortable and confident about it, especially the opening (*see the section later in this chapter*).**
- **Mentally rehearse the material and visualise yourself being successful (*see Stage 5*).**
- **Relax and practise the breathing exercises immediately before you begin (*see Stage 10*).**

Managing stage fright

Some slight nervousness before making a presentation can be helpful to spur you to do your very best but real stage fright has the ability to render a sufferer completely silent and immobile. People who do not suffer from any form of stage fright can have no understanding of just how debilitating it can be and their encouragement and attempts to motivation can have the opposite effect. Some people suffer from stage fright to a limited extent, that is that on the occasions when they are required to make work presentations or even dramatic performances they feel fine but in certain other situations can be terrified.

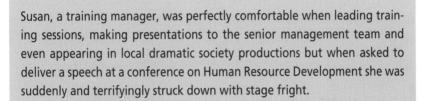

Susan, a training manager, was perfectly comfortable when leading training sessions, making presentations to the senior management team and even appearing in local dramatic society productions but when asked to deliver a speech at a conference on Human Resource Development she was suddenly and terrifyingly struck down with stage fright.

So what causes this uncomfortable condition? Many many different things which may include:

- large groups where the speaker feels that they cannot connect with such a large number of individuals
- the fear of being judged by superiors
- the fear of standing up in front of one's peers
- the fear that no one will be interested in the subject
- the fear that others are more expert on the subject
- the fear of failure
- the fear of making a fool of yourself
- being so self-conscious that you cannot communicate

How can you manage the fear? Unfortunately there is no way of removing fear completely, but there are processes you can work through to make it less debilitating.

The first step is to decide whether you are going to make the presentation or not! Often you will have some options that you can consider. In many cases these will include:

- Issuing a paper and taking a question session only.

- Delegating the presentation to another member of your team.

- Holding a workshop session rather than a presentation – asking questions, stimulating discussion and reaching a decision by consensus.

- Declining the invitation (if appropriate).

However, you may need to consider the following long-term benefits:

- If you believe in your subject and have a particular view, you will probably be able to present it better than anyone else. Your view may not be accepted unless you do the presentation.

- A good verbal presentation is much more likely to influence a decision than a written report.

- If making presentations is important in your role and your future success, the more practise you can get the better.

When you have established whether or not you are actually going to make the presentation, try and identify what it is that is causing you such difficulty. Imagine yourself taking up your position to make a presentation, become aware of your feelings and make a note of all the concerns you have. When you have identified all the causes of your problem, try and find a way to transform them. For example:

Sea of faces: if you are presenting to a large group of people and feel unable to connect with them, consider how people you envy as presenters manage the situation. It may be that they smile at the whole room to encourage a friendly response, it may be that they focus on one individual to begin with and then spread their attention around the group after they have created a connection with one person. Find a way that works for you to build connections before you begin your presentation.

Can't breathe, won't be able to make a sound: when you reach the podium, gather your thoughts, take a sip of water and take an abdominal breath to release the tension (*see page 265*). Find a simple sentence to begin your presentation with so that you can practise it and be comfortable with your opening comments. Once you have begun successfully, the rest is much more likely to go well.

They won't be interested in what I have to say: consider how you feel when you are listening to a presentation. It is likely that the audience wants to be interested in what the speaker has to say, they don't want to waste their time so will be expecting you to have something to offer them – a new opinion, a different way of approaching a problem, etc.

They are much cleverer than I am, they know more about it than I do: if they are genuinely clever then they will have chosen to listen to what you have to say. Trust them – they obviously believe that you have something to offer them.

Making a fool of yourself: the audience is most unlikely to want you to make a fool of yourself, they are there because they want to hear what you have to say. You will only make a fool of yourself if you do not prepare fully. Think carefully about what you consider making a fool of yourself would involve, prepare your presentation carefully and practise until you have reduced the risks to the very minimum.

Being judged: This is one of the commonest fears among people making presentations as part of their working life. The important thing to remember is that the audience is much more interested in what you have to say rather than how you as an individual behave. Prepare your material carefully, plan how you can deliver it in the way most likely to allow people to understand it and practise it until you are comfortable with the material. In this way it is possible to **shift your consciousness away from yourself and onto the material** and this will allow to you communicate it, rather than just speaking it.

PREPARING A VERBAL PRESENTATION

Before any verbal presentation, it is well worth creating a structure to help you remember everything.

Structure for preparing a presentation:

1. Planning

2. Preparation

3. Practice

4. Presentation

Planning

During the planning process you should consider:

- How long your presentation should be
- Who your audience will be and how to appeal to them
- How to choose what material to use

The length of your presentation may be determined by your organisation and its culture. Certainly if your audience are expecting a ten-minute presentation and you run on for 20 minutes, you are likely to lose their attention! When you are making a presentation, the time always seems to go much more slowly than you imagine. Talking, even for one minute, against a stop watch is surprisingly hard to do even about something that you know a lot about. So before you move onto the preparation stage, make sure you know how long your time slot is and whether it includes time for questions.

Your audience should be the prime motivation for what angle your presentation will take, so find out as much about them in advance as possible. You are almost certainly going to be attempting to convince them of the benefits of your idea, product or service, so it is important to be as clear as possible about what they might want. For example, senior management may want to hear of possible savings while the salesforce may want to hear how easy it is going to be for them to sell.

To make a really effective presentation, it is obviously important to include all the relevant information. In the planning stage, it is well worth taking time to do some additional research. You may well consider that you know everything there is to know about your particular idea, product or service but do you know what the options are, what competitors are planning, whether there is a genuine demand for it in the market-place or whether it has been considered before? The more rounded and well-thought-out your arguments are, the more likely they are to be accepted and even if you don't use all the material in your final presentation, the better prepared you will be for any difficult questions that might come up. It makes your preparation much easier if you have too much relevant information rather than trying to pad out too little.

When you are clear about your time slot, who you are going to be presenting to and have collected a wealth of information, you are ready to move onto the next stage.

Preparation

'It generally takes me three weeks to prepare a good impromptu speech'
(Mark Twain)

Preparation is the key to success in presentation skills. It takes time and effort. Get started early rather than leaving it until the last possible moment. The more preparation you have done, the more confident you will feel about the actual delivery.

Preparation is the process of working out:

- a structure for your presentation
- choosing your material
- considering what visual aids, if any, to use
- writing your presentation out and then preparing memory aids
- planning how to present most effectively
- planning how to deal with questions

A structure for your presentation: this is vitally important and should consist of a beginning, a middle and an end or an introduction, a presentation of the argument and a conclusion. This can be summarised in the old chestnut which is still highly relevant today:

- Tell them what you are going to tell them.
- Tell them.
- Tell them what you have told them.

The **opening** of any presentation is the perfect opportunity to engage the audience in wanting to listen to you and your arguments. It should include introducing yourself if they don't all know you, building credibility and an ice-breaker or attention-grabber which might include:

- a true but surprising statistic
- creating rapport
- a summary of the problem you intend to solve
- a brief summary of your approach

Always remember that this is your opportunity to get the audience to give you their full attention, so never run yourself down, even humorously. This is the moment to sell yourself as an expert, as someone whom it will be worth listening to. Never tell them you are scared or feeling insecure about standing up in front of them, they will immediately stop listening to you. Now is the time to 'fake' confidence, if you don't feel it. If they believe you are confident about what you are going to talk about, they will be able to feel confident about listening – and vice versa. And as soon as they begin to listen, you will become more confident anyway.

A word of warning about telling jokes – a good joke appropriate to the topic (and the audience) at the beginning of a presentation can work wonderfully well, but a poor joke or one that misfires will start you off on a losing streak and will mean that you have to work terribly hard to regain their trust and confidence. If you want to tell a joke, practise it with a group of people prepared to give you genuine feedback and judge its reception carefully. Start collecting fascinating statistics immediately

> *Now is the time to 'fake' confidence, if you don't feel it.*

so that you have a choice available to you for each presentation you have to make. You can find them in research about your industry, in yearly trends published in newspapers and, if you have a good network, from your own sales and finance departments. Collect any that refer to your particular industry or department and to issues that might affect it in the future, you will find them of enormous value.

Examples for customer care presentations include:

- *It costs five times as much to develop a new client as it does to keep a present one.*
- *98% of unhappy customers don't complain and never return to the supplier who failed to satisfy them.*

Other types of opening, each presenting a range of opportunities for different lead-ins include:

- **A question:** rhetorical or otherwise, preferably something that people are likely to respond to positively. 'Would you welcome a better way to ...?'

- **A quotation** which might be humorous or to make a point, might relate to the situation, or draw on a common memory. 'At the last AGM, the MD said ...'

- **A dramatic statement:** a story with a startling end, perhaps. Talking about direct mail advertising, the speaker asked the group to count, out loud, from 1-10. Between 2 and 3, he banged his fist on the table and shouted 'And that is how long our direct mail has to catch people's attention – 2½ seconds!'

- **A curious opening:** simply a statement sufficiently odd for people to wait to find out what it is all about. 'Consider the aardvark, and how it shares a characteristic of some of our managers ...' (thick skinned!)

- **A checklist:** perhaps a good start when placing a shopping list in mind early on is important 'There are 10 key stages to the process, first ...'

Creating rapport is your opportunity, at the very beginning, to create an appropriate group feeling. You may want to set a pattern of saying 'we' rather than 'you', as in 'what we need to ..' rather than 'what you need to ...' to create a comfortable atmosphere, you may want to add, discreetly, a compliment or two ('as experienced managers, you will understand ...'); mention some common interest; mention some point to verify your competence in the area under discussion ('as an engineer myself ...'), being careful not to boast overtly and, above all, be enthusiastic. It is said that the one good aspect of life that is infectious is enthusiasm. Use it.

The **main body**, or middle, of the presentation should contain the exposition of your argument. It will take up the major part of your presentation and builds on the attention you gained in your opening. It should flow in a logical manner and contain the options, your preferred solutions, any costs and any benefits so that it can be easily understood.

The **end**, or **conclusion**, of the presentation should clearly imply that you are about to finish speaking. It should wrap up the arguments and summarise your conclusion so that there are no misunderstandings. You should indicate what action you require – perhaps a vote or an agreement – before you thank the audience for their attention and take your seat again. Always try to end on a high note. The group expect it, if only subconsciously. It is an opportunity to build on past success during the session or, occasionally, to help make amends for anything that has been less than successful. You may want to consider some of the following ideas:

- **Matching your opening gambit at the end.** 'I began by asking you a question, now let us finish with another ...'
- **An immediate gain.** 'Put this new system into place and you will be saving time and money immediately'
- **A story or quotation linked to the subject that encourages a positive outcome.**

Visual aids: remember the figures in Stage 3 that 55% of the information that people absorb is presented visually. Some form of visual aid can, therefore, be extremely valuable.

Visual aids include:
- yourself
- the product itself
- whiteboards/flip charts
- overhead projectors
- videos

You are the most effective visual aid. The way you look and your body language will communicate a large part of your message. If you want your audience to take away with them the message that this is an exciting idea, you will only achieve this if you communicate it with enthusiasm. If you want them to understand the seriousness of your message, you will need to communicate it with credibility. Any message is communicated through congruity (*see page 69*) and you can adjust your demeanour through your practice sessions (see later in this chapter). Always stand up so that the audience can see you; it is much much easier to listen carefully to a message if you can see the speaker. Even in a small group, sitting at your place around a table and delivering your presentation may have an acceptable outcome, but how much more effective it will be if you stand up, walk to the side table where you have laid out your visual aids and deliver it from there. The group won't be able to take their eyes off you and therefore are much more likely to give their full attention to what you have to say.

Products: consider for a moment how difficult it is to describe a packet of breakfast cereal and how easy it is to hold one up so that everyone can see it. If you are talking about a product, take it with you and show everyone what it is you are talking about. If you have an art department, take a mock-up, even consider creating a mock-up yourself in order to communicate it better.

Whiteboard and flip charts are invaluable to presentations to small numbers of people. If you are using statistics or figures, always write them up so that people can remember them. Most of us have real difficulty in holding a list of numbers in our heads; if you want the audience to remember them, put them in a visual form. Also write up the key point of your presentation so that people are more likely to remember it and take it away with them. If your writing is not neat, write it up in advance and turn the pages of the flip chart as you go along. Visual aids should always be neat and easy to read.

Overhead projectors (OHP) are a very useful tool for presentations to larger numbers of people but are often over-used. Points to remember:

- Don't do your whole presentation on the OHP, use it as a visual aid only.
- Speak to the audience, not to the screen.
- Point at the slide carefully with a pencil, not at the screen.
- Make sure that you have all your slides in the right order and that you are comfortable working the OHP.
- Don't put too much material on each slide.

Only print as much on a slide as you would on a T shirt. Printing large chunks of text on a slide is intimidating to an audience and they will be unlikely to remember it.

Videos: can be very useful in an all-day presentation in order to provide variety and case studies but should be treated with reservation by presenters. They are often used to fill time and to avoid making a real presentation at all! If your chairperson has made a video to communicate with the staff across the country and you have been asked to show it and speak about it, fine. Show the video, but always remember that the real presentation doesn't start until you begin to speak to the audience in person.

Choosing your material is the next important stage. After your research, it is likely that you have potentially far too much material and you now have your time slot into which you have to fit it. How do you prioritise what to say and what to exclude? The criteria for choosing your material needs to be: what exactly are you trying to say and what are the arguments to support your case?

Another useful watchword to remember is **KISS – Keep It Simple, Speaker**. Simplicity allows the audience to understand and remember what it is you want to communicate.

An effective presentation will always be clear about its purpose, the 'what it is you really want to say'. Write out a critical path analysis of your objective, for example:

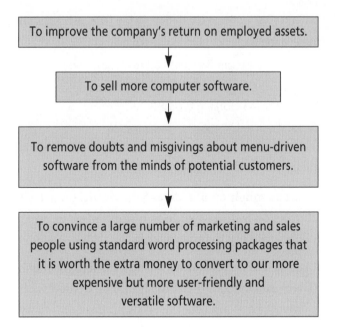

You may want to include what all the options are, the pros and cons of each and a clear and precise argument for your conclusion.

Use:

- short words
- short sentences
- short paragraphs or sections
- as little jargon as possible
- signposts of your intentions
- descriptions that paint pictures
- group topics and points together in small sections

Writing it out and preparing memory aids. This is often the area that lets a potential presenter down. When you have planned what you want to say and sorted through all your information, write out a draft of your speech, read it out loud in front of a mirror and time yourself. When you have created a presentation that runs to approximately the correct time frame, check that you have everything in the right, most logical, order. This is the moment to take the opportunity to do a scissors-and-paste job on a table top (or on your PC). Cut up each section or paragraph and lay them out in a different order to see if you can improve the flow or argument.

When you are completely happy with it, stick them onto a long piece of sellotape and re-type the whole thing in 'spoken' English. Too often because presentations are planned, they are delivered as if they were prepared as a dissertation. A proven way of helping to avoid this is to type them up in a 'poem' form that allows you to build in pauses, breath spaces and phrases.

'Good morning. (SMILE)
To those of you who don't know me,
I am James Taylor
and I am responsible for managing the
company's pension scheme.
I am based in Luton (in the finance department)
and am visiting each of our sites around the country
to explain how we intend to
improve and expand
the existing pension arrangements.' (PAUSE)

'Now some of you may think pensions are boring ...'.

You can adjust where you want your lines to begin and end, you can add any comments in brackets to remind you to smile, breathe, pause, use a visual aid, etc. But the huge advantage of this method, is that you can personalise the presentation and ensure that it reflects how you want to be able to deliver it.

When you have finished typing it, print it out and deliver it again, preferably into a tape recorder. The advantage of this is that you can hear how it comes across. Are you speaking too fast? Is it clear? Is it interesting? Are you speaking with enthusiasm? Does it still run to the right length? Does it truly reflect how you want you presentation to be? Make any adjustments until you are happy with it. Use this draft to practise with until you are confident with all the material you are intending to use.

When you are confident, transfer paragraph or section headings from your typewritten copy to numbered cue cards and create a list of bullet points.

So the above example might become:

---

1. Good morning

2. Me and Pension scheme

3. Boring?

The advantage of cue cards is that you will not be able to 'read' your prepared speech to the audience (reading generally encourages people to deliver the material much too fast and to avoid looking at the audience and inhibits using genuine inflection and enthusiasm) and yet you will be supported from losing your flow by a list of consecutive bullet points. It is helpful to make sure that your numbered cue cards are bound with a piece of string so that you can turn and read them easily but not destroy the order if you unfortunately drop them. When you have prepared your cue cards, file your typed speech and practise from the cards only.

Consider how you are going to deliver it most effectively. As already indicated, relevant strategies include:

- **Standing up where ever possible.**
- **Creating a position where everyone can see you.**
- **Preparing in advance appropriate visual aids.**

Make yourself as comfortable as possible so that you can deliver it with personal confidence:

- Take an abdominal breath before you begin.
- Wear clothes that are comfortable but smart (this is not the moment to wear the new shoes that squeak etc).
- Relax your body as much as possible.
- Stand straight and relaxed, avoid fidgeting.
- Practise using appropriate gestures that release tension in your body and add interest to what you are saying.
- Establish comfortable eye contact with as many of the audience as possible (begin with those immediately ahead of you and then look to each side).
- Make sure you have a glass of water to sip, if required.
- Empty your pockets of jangly items.

Make sure that you are comfortable with the area where you are to make your presentation. If it is going to take place within your building, make sure that you visit the room the evening before to check that everything you will need is in place and that it is in good working order. Your checklist might include:

- paper on the flip chart
- cleaner for the white board
- sufficient pens
- spare bulb for OHP
- chairs for the meeting
- space for you to make your presentation
- appropriate lighting/fresh air/silence
- how to divert phone calls

The more you make yourself comfortable with the environment within which you are going to make your presentation, the less likely it is that you will be thrown by any unexpected events.

If you are making your presentation in an external venue, where possible arrange to visit it the previous evening or very early in the morning to check it out and arrange to have any missing items delivered well in advance of your timeslot.

Managing audience participation and questions: one of the best ways of keeping an audience's attention is to encourage them to participate. The question is: how do you want to manage questions? You can encourage questions all the way through, which may work well with a small group but may throw you off your stride. You may invite questions at the end of each section which provides the audience with an opportunity to challenge or clarify any misunderstandings as well as allowing you to complete each section before moving onto the next. In a large group, you may wish to make your presentation uninterrupted and ask for questions at the end. Whenever you decide is an appropriate time for questions, remember to ask for them and allow enough time.

If you are asked a question to which you do not know the answer, be honest. Never attempt to fudge the issue, you will lose any credibility that you may have spent such an effort creating.

Practice makes perfect

In researching this book, one of the most commonly quoted pieces of advice was to practise presentation skills as often as possible. Many managers quoted their role models, who appeared to be completely confident and at ease with making presentations, as practising, not only in private but also with their staff and asking for constructive feedback. It seems uniformly that presentation skills are not natural or effortless even for those who make it appear so. Good presentation skills lie in the commitment to practise. Politicians and television presenters learn how to use autocues, make speeches and offer the off-the-cuff sound bite –

what makes you think that it will be easier for you than it is for them?

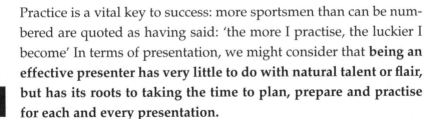

Practice takes many forms:

- opportunities in leisure time should be seized as a low-risk way of increasing confidence
- practising in private in front of a mirror is a good way of learning material and assessing timings
- practice with friends and family can be very useful and often even more difficult than the real thing – if you can manage that, the event will seem comparatively easy
- practising with your colleagues – a mutual session where you each hear the other and offer good feedback
- mental rehearsal can help you develop your confidence before an important presentation (*see page 163*)

Practice is a vital key to success: more sportsmen than can be numbered are quoted as having said: 'the more I practise, the luckier I become' In terms of presentation, we might consider that **being an effective presenter has very little to do with natural talent or flair, but has its roots to taking the time to plan, prepare and practise for each and every presentation.**

You may never reach the stage where you enjoy making presentations, but it is an achievable goal that you will be making presentations that other people will enjoy listening to if you follow the golden structure:

- plan
- prepare
- practise
- present.

ACTION PLAN:

What are you going to do to improve the effectiveness of your future presentations?

_____

_____

_____

_____

_____

_____

_____

_____

_____

Do you need to find opportunities to make more presentations? What might they be? Who might be able to help you?

_____

_____

_____

_____

_____

_____

_____

_____

_____

_____

PREPARING WRITTEN PRESENTATIONS

At some stage in your career it will be part of your job to write either a proposal or a report so you need to know how to do it most effectively. The two forms of written presentations require very similar skills and may be summarised as follows;

A report:

- contains information about what has happened in the past
- seeks primarily to inform the reader
- records objective facts

A proposal:

- examines what might happen in the future
- seeks primarily to persuade the reader to make a particular decision
- expresses opinions, which are supported by objective facts

Similarly to preparing verbal presentations, it is helpful to consider a structure:

- planning
- preparation
- producing the written presentation

Planning: this is the stage to consider:

- **what is the the objective of the document?**
- **what form should it take?**

The objective is vital. You need to consider who is going it read it. What is their level of knowledge of the subject? What will they use it for? What aspects will they want it to cover? What aspects are not important? If you have been asked to write it by your manager, check exactly what they are expecting you to produce – it is going to take you some time so make sure that you give them what they are expecting.

What form should it take? How long should it be? Will it be helpful to include graphs or tables of figures? Are you going to bind it in some way? What form of presentation will be helpful? If it is for external use, is there a preferred way of presentation?

Preparation:
- **research**
- **choosing your material**
- **creating a structure**
- **writing it up**
- **checking and review**

Research: as in any presentation, it is important to gather all the material and research the subject so that all the necessary aspects are fully covered.

Choosing your material: the best way of choosing your material is to check it back against the objective that you identified in the planning stage. This will give you the agreed criteria against which to identify what is important and what may be left out.

Creating a structure: this is just as important in a written proposal or report. It makes it easy to read and understand if the arguments follow a logical pattern.

Plan :
- an opening where you tell them what you are going to cover
- a middle section where you follow through the arguments
- an end or a summary of what you are suggesting

If it is a lengthy document, more than six pages, you may want to consider putting your introduction and summary on separate pages. If it is even longer (some government reports run to several volumes), it is worth considering adding an index and an executive summary at the front. Remember that your readers may be busy people and you need to tempt them to read your masterpiece. A good summary should convince them that you have done a valuable piece of work and let them see the conclusions. If they still have questions, the index will allow them to find the section easily that contains your evidence.

Make it easy to read and attractive to look at. Don't fill up each inch of the paper with blocks of printing – allow plenty of white space, wide margins, consider double-spacing and include bullet points of the points you are covering and consider visual aids, such as simple tables and graphs. Remember that although your report is in a visual form, the more attractive it is to look at, the more people will be inclined to read it. Similarly, biggest is not necessarily best – a heavy, academic-looking report is likely to promote despair among its recipients. Keep it simple where possible.

Write it up and allow yourself plenty of time for revisions. Don't fall into the trap of thinking that because you have done all the research and planning you can put it off until the very last minute. Most writers find that they need at least a night's sleep before being able to assess what they wrote the previous day, even before handing it to an outsider for feedback.

Write it against notes of your structure so that you can follow the well thought out flow of your arguments and points for and against. Unless you are very experienced, it is difficult to just sit down and write anything more than a paragraph without some notes.

Use simple English, avoiding jargon where possible. Match your approach to your audience but try not to fall into the trap of using 'report' language.

> Taking into consideration all the possible factors, there is clearly a dilemma here between the two opposing potential situations, that of existence and that of non-existence, leading to an ultimate and possibly irreversible decision.
>
> *or*
>
> To be or not to be; that is the question.

Checking and review: make sure that the spellings are correct and that figures are accurate. This form of copy-checking takes time and an objective eye may be of help. Most typists find it very difficult to check their own work; particularly when it looks neat and clean it is easy for spelling mistakes to creep through to the final version.

Check the flow of the document. How easy is it to read? How attractive does it look?

Ask a colleague or your manager to read it and give you feedback. Allow enough time for them to do this and for you to make any revisions necessary. Bind it, send it out and keep at least one copy for yourself. A good report or proposal should be saved in your personal file for future reference.

ACTION PLAN
How are you going to improve your reports and proposals?

_____

_____

_____

_____

_____

Further reading

How to Write Proposals and Reports that Get Results (R. Jay) 1994 Pitman Publishing

Making Successful Presentations (P. Forsyth) Sheldon Press

Effective Presentation – how to be a top class presenter (T. Jay and R. Jay) Pitman Publishing

Improving Your Presentation Skills (M. Stevens) Kogan Page

MAKING MEETINGS WORK
FOR YOU

Make the purpose of any meeting dynamic
and positive

Do you spend a large amount of your day in meetings?   *Yes/No*

Do you think meetings are a waste of time?   *Yes/No*

Do you find yourself in meetings that have no relevance to you? *Yes/No*

Do you always know the purpose of the meetings you attend?   *Yes/No*

Do you find yourself sometimes making no contribution to them? *Yes/No*

Do your meetings often start late and overrun?   *Yes/No*

A large proportion of a manager's time is likely to be spent in meetings and many managers report that meetings are the least effective use of their time. This chapter will focus on how to manage meetings effectively, and in the chapter on time management (*page 275*) we will also look at some ways of reducing the time wasted in meetings.

This chapter will cover:

- whether a meeting is necessary
- what the purpose of the meeting is
- why agendas are crucial to a successful meeting
- creating a structure for the meeting
- who should attend and when
- to chair or not to chair
- creating time boundaries to ensure efficiency
- how to create minutes or action notes
- continual improvement

WHAT IS A MEETING?

Ideally a meeting is a gathering of interested parties responsible for:

- making a decision
- moving a situation forwards
- exchanging ideas
- receiving information
- debating alternative approaches

so that they may collectively make a good decision.

Too often it is a gathering of people:

- without a clear focus
- who are not quite sure why they are there
- who listen to what is said without any real interest
- who have no decision to make

Is a meeting necessary?

Is there a decision to be made or a way forward to be agreed? Does the decision or the action need to be made by the group of individuals involved? Will a better decision or action be agreed if there is a debate by the individuals involved? If not, it may be worth considering saving everyone a great deal of time by issuing a memo or speaking to them individually. Too often, meetings are called to announce a senior manager's decision and a great deal of time is spent without a useful outcome if the participants do not understand that they have been called together to hear the information rather than discuss it and make a collective decision.

Face-to-face communication between a group of individuals can have many benefits:

- build understanding of differing points of view
- build genuine support between departments
- understanding of differing requirements
- create better team relationships

It might be said that *when a meeting is good, it is very very good and when it is poor, it is dreadful*, so perhaps the first learning point in this chapter is to suggest that you **have fewer meetings and make them more effective**.

If you are responsible for calling meetings, make sure that you consider carefully whether they are necessary and encourage everyone who attends to take them seriously, prepare in advance if necessary and make their full contribution.

If you are asked to attend meetings that you consider unnecessary, speak to the person who has requested your presence and clarify with them why they think it is important, and necessary, that you attend.

The purpose of the meeting

Unless you are clear why you are calling, or attending the meeting, it is unlikely to be effective. You might find it enlightening, at the next meeting you call, to begin by asking each of the attendees what they think the purpose of the meeting is – you might get some very different answers!

Too often we hear 'Let's have a meeting on Tuesday to talk about ...'. If the only purpose of a meeting is to talk about an issue, there is an implication that no decision or commitment is to be made. If the purpose of a meeting isn't positive or dynamic, how can the attendees be expected to treat it with the seriousness you think it deserves. **Make the purpose of any meeting dynamic and positive.**

'I want to call a meeting on Tuesday to review progress on the … situation and agree the way forward' is much more likely to be successful than the suggestion that you will all talk about it. Even an ongoing team meeting can be opened with the purpose of reviewing the previous week's/month's activities and agreeing the way forward.

AGENDAS

Meetings can often be transformed from talking-shops that waste a great deal of time to valuable discussion forums and decision-making processes if there is an agenda. If you can issue, in advance, a list of the items that need to be addressed, you will focus the minds of those attending, encourage them to prepare in advance and arrive with all the necessary materials. Ask the attendees what they think should be included in the agenda. In the case of the regular meeting, this can be done at the end of the previous one.

Creating an agenda can also help you clarify whether the meeting is necessary or not. Some organisations reserve time at the end of the week to discuss any urgent matters that might have come up and if no agenda items have been reported by lunchtime on the particular day, the meeting is cancelled.

When preparing an agenda, be realistic about how much can be achieved. Too many items will have a demotivating effect as either only a small proportion of them will be dealt with properly or the entire list will have to be rushed.

STRUCTURE

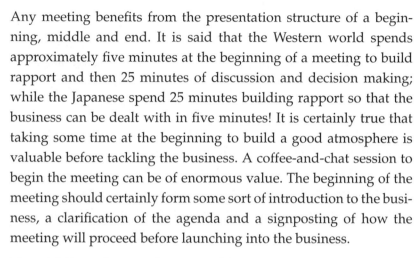

Any meeting benefits from the presentation structure of a beginning, middle and end. It is said that the Western world spends approximately five minutes at the beginning of a meeting to build rapport and then 25 minutes of discussion and decision making; while the Japanese spend 25 minutes building rapport so that the business can be dealt with in five minutes! It is certainly true that taking some time at the beginning to build a good atmosphere is valuable before tackling the business. A coffee-and-chat session to begin the meeting can be of enormous value. The beginning of the meeting should certainly form some sort of introduction to the business, a clarification of the agenda and a signposting of how the meeting will proceed before launching into the business.

The middle, or the main business of the meeting, is also worth some consideration as to structure. It is worth planning at least one easy item to begin with so that an atmosphere of co-operation and achievement can be developed. It is also worth planning to take the first item at least fairly slowly giving everyone a chance to speak before attempting to build more dynamic energy into the process.

Creating an agenda can help you prepare for the meeting by planning how to manage the items most effectively. Consider carefully which order to put items in to encourage good decision making.

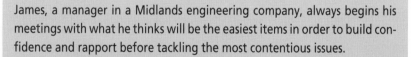

James, a manager in a Midlands engineering company, always begins his meetings with what he thinks will be the easiest items in order to build confidence and rapport before tackling the most contentious issues.

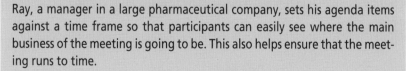

Ray, a manager in a large pharmaceutical company, sets his agenda items against a time frame so that participants can easily see where the main business of the meeting is going to be. This also helps ensure that the meeting runs to time.

If the business is more complex than had been imagined, the group should take the time to decide how to proceed. It may be necessary to postpone some items until the next meeting or simply to speed up and limit the amount of time each person speaks – but the meeting itself should decide. If items are rushed through and decisions made without full agreement, their chances of success in implementation are low! The purpose of a decision-making meeting is to gain commitment from all parties to any decisions reached, so any decision made without commitment is worthless.

If the meeting is due to last more than two hours, plan how to take appropriate breaks. An effective meeting needs everyone to be giving their full attention and this will be lost if people are longing for another cup of coffee, a breath of air, etc. Taking a five-minute break can dramatically improve concentration and energy.

The end of the meeting is important to round off and complete everything.

It should consist of:

- an indication that the end is in sight
- a request for any other business
- a summary of actions required
- setting a date (and agenda) for the next meeting if required
- a review of the meeting (*see section on process page 211*)

WHO SHOULD ATTEND AND WHEN?

Identifying who should attend a meeting is generally straight-forward: the people central to making the decision or carrying it out. But there are some general guidelines:

- Keep the numbers low, wherever possible. Too many people make it difficult for everyone to have their say and to make a decision. Resist the temptation to include people who *might* be useful, it is a waste of their time and will probably interfere with the process.

- If some participants are only involved with some sections of the agenda, consider including them for these only. This is the advantage of a timed agenda and will save time and increase motivation.

- Sometimes deciding who to exclude can be a more contentious issue. Often attendance at a meeting is a status symbol and exclusion can cause distress. Be aware of the consequences but try to limit to attendance to those whose presence is necessary.

- Disruptive individuals – conflict at meetings should be avoided where possible but balance the advantages with the disadvantages carefully and warn the chair of any likely conflict so that it can be managed.

- The group may want to include an individual who chooses not to attend. Consider carefully that if they do not want to attend, how much value will they actually bring if they are forced to attend? Sometimes you can bring pressure on them but it may not prove to be helpful. Try inviting them for a short time period and explain why you want them there.

CHAIRING MEETINGS

A meeting will only be effective if everyone involved in it takes some responsibility for making it so, but, even so, there are likely to be some issues that individuals will be so involved in that the meeting is likely to run away with itself unless there is one person nominated to take control of the process. Some groups of people do manage to run their meetings effectively without anyone taking the role of chair but more commonly it doesn't lead to a successful outcome.

Simon, a solicitor, regularly attends 'chambers' meetings of the partners who believe that they should operate as a co-operative. He complains that 'we even have to vote on whether the meeting is going to make a decision or not'.

The chair needn't be the most senior person in the group. It is worth considering whether to rotate the role of chair so that each person involved takes a turn, gathers experience and becomes involved in the responsibility of creating effective meetings. The chair has the responsibility of facilitating the process rather than forcing the meeting to make decisions and should:

- encourage everyone to speak, using open questions
- encourage co-operation and good listening practices
- take everyone's point of view seriously
- encourage movement towards agreement
- encourage agreed actions and clarify so that they are clearly understood
- keep to agreed time boundaries
- continually work to improve the process and results
- be aware of the dynamics of the group
- manage the agenda

When a group of people are gathered together for any purpose, they tend to take on roles and behaviours which may be very dissimilar to their normal patterns. Some that you may recognise and some pointers as to how to handle them are:

Quarrelsome: do not get into arguments with this one. Ask for comment from other strong members of the group to maintain balance. Stop them from monopolising by bringing in other members of the group. Emphasise the need for constructive comments.

Positive: a great help in any discussion. Let their contributions add up. Use them frequently and make sure you have them on your side wherever possible.

Know-all: pass their views back to the group for comment. Show recognition for their enthusiasm but emphasise the value of other contributions.

Talkative: keep them on the subject for discussion, emphasise the need for relevance. Interrupt tactfully but ensure the group feels that you are not being vindictive. Try and limit their speaking time without antagonising them or losing the value of their contributions.

Shy: involve them, ask questions that they will feel confident to answer to increase confidence. Show encouragement where possible and protect them from attack by other members.

Uncooperative: show how the discussion personally affects them. Play on their ambitions and recognise their knowledge/experience and their value for the group. Emphasise the need for constructive comments.

Uninterested: ask them for contributions in areas of their interest/detailed knowledge. Encourage their efforts, show how decisions will affect them personally.

Highbrow: protect them from attack. Keep them involved but emphasise the need for practical solutions. Keep pressing them to talk in terms of what must actually be *done*.

Questioner: tries to trap the group leader. Pass their questions back to the group. Do not allow yourself to show any antagonism towards them.

Group dynamics

It is important to be aware of where the group is, at any time, during the decision-making process. A good way of visualising this is:

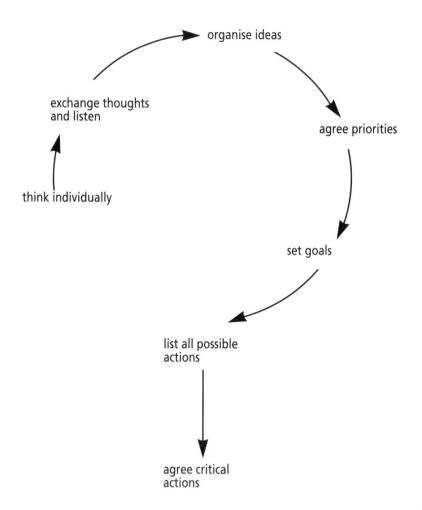

It is important to allow time for the group to complete each stage before pressing them to move to the next one.

CREATING TIME BOUNDARIES

One of the biggest complaints about meetings in organisations is that they very rarely start or finish on time. Ineffective, time-wasting meetings mean that the individuals involved don't take them seriously. A guarantee that they will start and finish on schedule is likely to encourage the prompt arrival of attendees. If you have a persistent latecomer, you may want to consider having a private conversation with them about any difficulties, help resolve them and make a request for prompt arrival in future.

One of the ways to build concentration on the matter in hand is to suggest time-scales for discussion. Individuals who talk too much may be helped by limiting any input to, say, two minutes per person. Individuals who find it hard to put across their point of view may be helped by the chair asking for a sentence from each individual around the table about their view before the full blown discussion begins – sometimes this has the additional benefit of discovering that the group are in complete agreement without having to listen to a lengthy presentation by the proposer.

The length of meetings may depend on the culture of the organisation but it is generally agreed that a well-chaired one-hour meeting will achieve a great deal more than a loosely run three-hour session. The more people are encouraged to focus on the issues at hand, the more likely they are to reach effective results. Aim to have fewer, better meetings.

MINUTES OR ACTION NOTES

It is important to produce some form of paper log at the end of a meeting, if only to record who has agreed to take any action, so that it may be followed up and reviewed. If actions are not noted, it is quite likely that no one in the group will take responsibility for putting them into practice and therefore the meeting was a waste of time because nothing happened as a result of it.

On the other hand perhaps too many meetings demand the presence of a note taker to produce a full, typed list of minutes that may not be issued until just before the next meeting, which allows very little time for a member of the group to be reminded that they agreed to take a specific action. There are some legal requirements for full sets of minutes but not nearly as many as you would think. Ask yourself whether minutes are truly important and whether they justify the attendance of a note taker or whether some brief action notes taken by the chair or a nominated 'scribe' will be sufficient. These notes may even be added to the agenda paper and photocopied immediately after the meeting.

AGENDA

Production Meeting 4pm 10th June
TD, JB, NF, VS, TB, CT, SC.
I. monthly production figures

ACTION
JB to talk to Accounts to
speed paperwork (report)

2. customer feedback

TD to meet SKD Ltd 12th
June (report)

Whatever form is chosen, issue each individual with a copy as soon as possible, preferably within 24 hours to remind them of agreed actions.

CONTINUALLY IMPROVING YOUR MEETINGS

Meetings may usefully be seen as having two parts:

- the content (the subject matter or task on which the group is working) and
- the process (the way in which the group is working)

The **process** is what is happening between and to group members while they are working, i.e. morale, feelings, atmosphere, influences, participation, leadership, conflict, co-operation, etc.

For a meeting to be effective, it is important to encourage openness, honesty and asking for support where necessary. Too many progress review meetings are ineffective because the participants only tell of their successes and hide their difficulties because they are afraid of criticism or appearing to have failed in some way. A meeting should be seen as an open forum where reports are genuine rather than tailored to allow an individual to look good (or bad).

Helpful process behaviours are:

- **initiating** – proposing tasks and goals, defining group problems, suggesting procedures, etc.
- **seeking information** – asking for facts, ideas and suggestions
- **giving information** – giving ideas, suggestions, relevant information, etc.
- **clarifying** – sorting out what has been said or suggested, clearing up any confusion

- **summarising** – pulling it all together, restating suggestions, offering conclusions, etc.

- **harmonising** – reducing tensions, reconciling differences, taking other points of view seriously

- **gate keeping** – helping keep channels of communication open, encouraging participation, making sure ideas are heard and discussed

- **encouraging** – being friendly, warm, responsible to others, accepting other contributions graciously

- **developing ideas** – listening and supporting them

- **giving feedback** – positively, showing respect for others' contributions

The more you can use these behaviours, the more likely you are to encourage them in others and your meetings will become more and more effective. As a chair, you should acknowledge these behaviours and encourage them in the group.

Unhelpful process behaviours are:

- **counterdependency** – opposing or resisting any authority in the group, on principle

- **dominating** – asserting personal dominance, disregarding others, wanting your own way at all costs

- **withdrawing** – non-participation because you feel uncomfortable (bored, alienated, etc.)

- **pairing up:** finding an ally or allies against the rest

These behaviours should be avoided at all cost.

One way of improving the group's process in meetings is to arrange for a feedback session at the end. Some useful questions to consider are:

- How are our plans for co-operating going?
- What is helping or hindering our efforts?
- What progress have we made with our task and what helped this?
- Are there any delays and what is the cause?
- What have individuals done that has helped and why?
- What principles are emerging that can be applied more widely?
- When we resume our task, how can we co-operate better?

Each individual attending a meeting must take some responsibility for its success. Too often people complain about meetings and yet

Do not let yourself be a complainer, do something about it.

do nothing to improve them. Do not let yourself be a complainer, do something about it. If you are part of the meeting, you are part of its results.

A simple process check at the end of a meeting might include verbal answers to the following questions:

- What did I enjoy about this meeting?
- What was valuable about this meeting?
- How could this meeting have been improved?

What can you do to improve the meetings you attend?

_____

_____

_____

_____

_____

Further reading

How To Be A Great Communicator: the complete guide to mastering internal communication (D. M. Martin) Pitman Publishing

How to Win at Meetings (G. Janner) (1990) Gower

Putting it Across (A. Heylin) (1991) Michael Joseph

IMPLEMENTATION – PUTTING IDEAS INTO ACTION

All writers and athletes talk about the 'block' or the 'pain barrier' as something that simply has to be gone through and it is just as relevant in business and personal development

Do you find yourself saying you'll do things that you don't?   *Yes/No*

Do you find yourself delaying putting ideas into action?   *Yes/No*

Do you follow your boss's deadlines but not set yourself any?   *Yes/No*

Do you want other people to do it all for you?   *Yes/No*

Putting ideas into action is the most crucial part of any self-development programme. It is likely, during your career, that you will work for a number of different employers, in a number of different industries. It is unlikely that any one organisation is going to provide a development or career plan for the whole of your working life. Your future success is your responsibility rather than anyone else's. You need to plan success for yourself rather than rely on your organisation to do it for you. Implementing ideas and putting them into action are part of your route to success.

This chapter will cover:
- why implementation is so often a problem
- creating a structure to support you
- preparation
- planning
- project management
- goal setting
- prioritising
- decision making
- problem solving

THE DIFFICULTY IN IMPLEMENTATION

Some people expect books like this to **make** them do the things that they knew they ought to be doing. An anonymous source speaks for many:

> *'I've been on courses, I know what I ought to be doing but somehow when I get back to work, it all gets forgotten. Can you help me actually get it together and carry out out some of the things I have managed to avoid?'*

The answer, of course, is 'No'. No book can make you do anything, only you can do that, but the rest of this chapter is designed to help make it easier for you to put your plans into action.

In order to resolve this difficulty, let's have a look at some of the reasons why you might not put into action what you say you are going to:

- Should never have agreed to do it in the first place.
- No commitment – you feel that you should but don't really think it that important.
- Because no one has set a time frame for you, it simply falls off the bottom of the list.
- Your personal development takes second place to others' demands.

Should never have agreed to do it in the first place: too often people offer to do things because it seems the right, the nice, the socially acceptable thing to do because everyone wants to be liked and approved of. Re-read the section on saying 'no' (*page 106*) and consider whether you really want to be the sort of person who doesn't follow through on their word. How did you feel when someone else agreed to do something and then let you down? Angry and upset? How do you feel about the person who hasn't delivered? You think they are unreliable, untrustworthy and obviously don't respect you? Is that the sort of person you want to be? What does your behaviour say about you?

It is generally much more acceptable to say 'no' at the beginning rather than let them down later on. **Only agree to do things that you are committed to delivering.**

Lack of commitment: how often do you say that you are going to be on time for meetings, keep your in-tray under control, not leave things to the last minute and then forget about it? Knowing what you would probably benefit from and actually doing it are very, very different things! Don't fall into the trap of saying that you will change your behaviour unless you are really committed to making the effort that it will take. Human beings rarely change their behaviour until the consequences of not doing so become too ruinous. Unless your boss gives you grief about being late or you are genuinely suffering from leaving things until the last minute is it likely that your commitment will be high enough to make the change. If your behaviour works for you, you probably won't change it. In order to be successful in your life, it is important to build on successes. Failing to make changes that might be helpful to you is demotivating. Keep your word to yourself as well as others. Don't set yourself up to fail by believing that you *ought* to do something that you have no commitment to complete.

Balance up the advantages and disadvantages of making a change before deciding to do it.

Not having a set time frame: when your boss asks you to do something by Wednesday, you probably do it without too much difficulty but when you decide, for yourself, to take on something it is much more likely to fall off your list of priorities. You are probably programmed to react to urgency rather than importance (*see page 275*) and to put much more of your effort into the task (the what it is you do) rather than the process (the how you do it). Consider carefully how the task might benefit from changes to the process and balance the advantages. Then prioritise it in line with all the other things you have to do. Always set yourself time frames to any projects you take on; unless you have some deadlines you will be unlikely to complete them (or in busy times even begin them).

Set your own time frames.

Your personal development comes last: putting yourself and your own development behind others' needs is unlikely to lead you to success. Taking responsibility for your career and its success means that you need to be putting a high priority on your personal development. It is highly likely that the more you develop yourself, your skills and qualities, the more your organisation will benefit, so the two aspects are not mutually exclusive. Making changes to the way you do things in order to improve their effectiveness does take time, but it is a small injection of time in the short term in order to gain time and improve results in the long term. If your boss doesn't understand that even after you have explained why you want to make some changes, you might need to consider if you are working for the right organisation for you.

Prioritise on the basis of longer term results.

What difficulties have you identified that held you back in the past and what can you do about resolving them?

_____

_____

_____

_____

_____

_____

_____

_____

CREATING A STRUCTURE FOR IMPLEMENTATION

A structure for implementation includes creating an order for preparing and managing the implementation of your project and is similar to scaffolding; it holds everything together until the project is complete when it can be removed without everything collapsing.

The structure we will consider is:

- vision
- commitment
- goal setting
- preparation
- planning
- project management
- delivery

Vision: unless you are clear about where you are going and what it will be like when you have reached your goal, the chances of it being achieved are greatly reduced. A clear vision about exactly how the conditions of the final goal will be, will give you your objective. This objective should be SMART:

- Simple, specific
- Measurable
- Achievable
- Realistic
- Timed

Unless an objective is SMART, it will encourage you to set goals that you will fail to achieve and therefore reduce your confidence to manage and achieve future goals and projects.

Preparation: this is your thinking time. A time to check:

- **What is the objective of the project?**
- **Are you committed to it?**
- **Is it smart?**
- **What are its benefits to you and your organisation?**
- **The possibility of creating a visual representation from the idea and talking about it.**

The more you can clarify your objective, your commitment to it and its benefits, both to yourself and your organisation, the more likely it is that you will be prepared to make the effort necessary to achieve it.

Visual representations: one of the pieces of advice that came up regularly in researching this book was that the people who managed to put their projects into action often created a visual display that inspired them to keep going. A visual display is anything that becomes a representation of the final goal or an inspiration to make progress. The advantage of creating a visual representation of your project is that it transforms it from an idea in your head into a positive form that exists in the world.

Mary, a manager in the television industry, attended a course on Time Management and discovered that by making only small changes she could save up to two hours per day. This impressed her so much that she wrote out 'I can save two hours a day by keeping my in-tray under control' and pinned it to her wall to motivate her. After only a few weeks, she was attending to her in-tray daily and saving even more time than she had estimated.

John, a manager in an engineering company in the Midlands, who has to regularly write reports finds that by first finding a new plastic file, labelling it with the title of the project and leaving it on his desk, its very presence reminds him continually of what it is he needs to do and he gets started without too much difficulty.

Others create a visual timetable of their project during the planning stage and pin that to their wall to create a visual check of how their project is progressing.

As well as a visual representation, it is also important to talk about your ideas and goals. In fact, anything you can do to get it out of your head and out into the world will enable you to be more likely to achieve it. As we said in Stage 3, communication is the key to turning ideas into reality. The more you talk about it, the more real it will become, the more you will find yourself fleshing out your plans and the people to whom you talk will remind you of what you said that you wanted to achieve.

Create visual representations and talk about your projects.

Planning: this is the time to work out what you need to do to achieve your goal. It might include:

- research/investigation
- draft/weigh up options/balance/tender documents/preliminary decisions
- share/delegate
- deliver/completion
- create time scales for each section

A point to bear in mind when planning your time scales is always to build in a contingency for emergencies and unexpected occurrences.

Every financial budget will contain a contingency – use the same guidelines for planning your time scales.

So if you have to write a report within two weeks, your planning might include:

Week One:	Day 1:	ring up network to do research, arrange necessary meetings
	Day 2–4:	read appropriate material, meetings, etc.
	Day 5:	assess material, plan report
Week Two:	Day 1:	draft report
	Day 2:	read and ask others to read
	Day 3:	review and redraft if necessary
	Day 4:	consider how to present and final review
	Day 5:	deliver

A personal development project has many similarities except that it is likely that there is no set time scale. **Create your own time scale.**

Angela, a manager in a manufacturing company in the north east of England, discovered to her horror that she would be expected to make a presentation at the annual sales conference in six months' time. She had been on courses about presentation skills but did not feel that she was very good at it and certainly didn't look forward to the sales conference. While watching her favourite film star collect an Oscar on television, she thought 'that is how I want to be able to feel – confident, happy, looking good and relaxed'. The next morning she cut out a picture of the occasion from her newspaper, pinned it on her wall and created a plan.

October:	annual sales conference
September:	make at least two presentations outside work to build confidence
August:	plan material for sales conference
July:	take all opportunities to speak at meetings, off-the-cuff and prepared
June:	prepare practice presentations and work with coach
May:	research opportunities for practice (women's groups, local church/politics/campaigning groups, etc., national careers courses, specialist organisations, etc.)
April:	read handouts from presentation courses and find a good book
	find a coach or friend to help practise

The sales conference went well and she was congratulated on her presentation. She knows that personal development has no completion date and that there are still some areas she can improve on, but she has achieved her goal of doing herself justice at the sales conference and has improved her profile within her organisation.

What aspects of setting objectives, visual representations, preparation and planning can you use for your benefit in the future?

_____

_____

_____

_____

_____

_____

_____

_____

_____

_____

_____

DEALING WITH DIFFICULTIES

As Murphy's Law so succinctly puts it 'Whatever can possibly go wrong – will' so it is important to have a strategy for dealing with any difficulties that may arise.

Strategies for handling difficulties:

- don't panic

- recheck your commitment

- keep to your schedule

- talk to someone to revive your motivation

Don't panic. Things will rarely go exactly to plan and if you have planned your project sensibly and built in a contingency for unexpected occurrences, it is likely that you will be able to respond to the problem if you don't panic. More time is lost on projects through panic than any other cause. Accept Murphy's Law (even unwillingly!) and prepare to handle the difficulty.

Rechecking your commitment: often when something unexpected happens to knock your plans off course, a desire to give up the whole project appears. Whenever this happens, it is important to return to your original objective and consider carefully whether you are still committed to it. It is possible that you may discover that you were only committed to the project if it was going to be fairly easy to achieve. If this is the case, consider dropping the project for the time being and re-assessing it at a future date. There is no point battling on with something that you have lost your commitment to. On the other hand, very few things worth having come easily and you should consider carefully what you might lose by dropping the project. Often if you can handle the anger and upset that appear with the unexpected occurrence, you will find after a very short time that you are ready to move on to handling it by taking remedial action.

!

Very few things worth having come easily.

Keeping to your schedule: everyone has times in their projects where the very thought of taking action is enough to produce a negative response. Self-discipline has little to do, in the opinion of the sources for this book, with the real world – it is a concept that is easier to identify and discuss in hindsight than in the moment. So what do you do when the thought of taking action on your project makes you to want to volunteer for the Foreign Legion? Some serious self-talk and bribery. Ask yourself how you will feel if, having got this far, you give it up now and waste all that effort? Is this the sort of person you want to be? (Don't even think about your past experiences and the sort of person you *suspect* you really are – this is about who you want to be.) This is an opportunity to break all sorts of habits from the past when you might have given up. If you are still committed to a successful outcome for the project, bribe yourself. Now is not the time to take a break from the project, you have to dig in and take some action for a limited time before allowing yourself a treat.

'I am going to make that phone call before I have a cup of coffee'
'I am going to write three pages and then do something else'

All writers and athletes talk about the 'block' or the 'pain barrier' as something that simply has to be gone through and it is just as relevant in business and personal development. A writer will simply write though a block, even if it isn't of a very high standard and an athlete learns to 'dig in' and continue until the barrier is past. So take a deep breath and simply carry on and remember it is from overcoming difficulties like this that success is achieved.

'How can you eat in elephant? In bite-sized chunks': remember to build in plenty of stages in your time schedule so that it becomes more achievable, have measurements to check your progress against and consider setting yourself daily targets. There is nothing more encouraging than getting yourself ahead of schedule. At the end of each stage, give yourself a treat for achieving it on time. Part of your self-talk might include reminding yourself that you only have to do this stage at the moment so that you are not intimidated by the size of your project.

Talk to someone: one of the most effective ways of reviving your motivation to achieve your project is to find someone to talk to about it. Avoid the temptation to talk about why you are finding it so difficult which will only depress you more and is likely to convince you that it is impossible. Find someone you can talk to about why you decided to take on the project in the first place – the more you remind yourself of your original decision and commitment the more likely you are to re-invigorate yourself. You might want to consider asking the person you are talking with to coach you (*see page 49*).

What are you now going to put into action that will help you deal with difficulties on your projects in the future?

_____

_____

_____

_____

_____

_____

_____

_____

_____

_____

_____

_____

_____

DECISION MAKING

In researching this book, a common concern was a dislike of making a decision and on investigation this seemed to be based on the fear of making the wrong decision resulting in:

- no decision at all, leaving people and resources standing around not knowing what to do
- a decision by committee, whereby at least people know what to do but it has involved so many compromises that the final result is rarely satisfactory
- making a decision and then sticking to it in the face of evidence that it isn't working

The first learning point is that **there is no perfect decision**. Some may prove to have been better than others in the light of experience, but each decision can only be judged on the information and the circumstances existing at the time. In hindsight every decision is likely to look suspect but can be justified by the person who made it (think about any decision you have made in the past).

So what can you do? The second learning point is that **most short term decisions are better than no decision at all**. At least people will know what they should do, time will not be wasted and will give you time to balance all the information available. Worrying overly about making the perfect decision will leave everyone in a state of chaos instead of beginning to respond to the situation.

The third learning point is that **any decision should be flexible and reviewed regularly**. The world keeps changing and a decision that looked good yesterday may well need reviewing in the light of new information and circumstances.

The fourth learning point is that **advantages and disadvantages should be weighed up before a decision is made**. It is worth taking a little time to consider what your criteria are for the advantages and disadvantages. Are they personal to you? Long or short term? For the benefit of the whole organisation and its stakeholders or just your department? None of these is *necessarily* right or wrong but it is interesting to note how you reach your decisions and whether you are comfortable with them in the long term.

The fifth learning point is that **any decision has consequences which should be considered**. A decision has the effect of ripples on a pond which should be assessed carefully. Often deciding to do 'the right thing' will have such dramatic consequences that the decision should be considered very carefully. Making redundancies, taking a high-risk gamble, disciplining a friend were all examples quoted by the sources for this book. This does not mean that you should walk away from a difficult decision but that you must consider how you will manage the consequences because if you don't, what seemed like a 'good' decision might look like a potential disaster when the consequences become apparent.

How do you make your decisions? Are there any changes that you would benefit from and, if so, what are they?

_____

_____

_____

_____

_____

_____

_____

_____

PROBLEM SOLVING

The first important thing to remember is that if you have a problem, you need to take responsibility for it. Blaming someone or something else for your problem doesn't work. If your boss is stopping you doing something, who has the problem? You do – the manager probably doesn't even know there is a problem, because it isn't his/hers. You need to be able to take action to solve it.

There are three different sorts of problems and it is important to be able to distinguish between them:

- simple ones

- complex ones where the current issue is only a symptom of the whole

- unsolvable ones

Simple problems are easy to solve. Difficulties arise when you try to treat all problems as simple problems.

Complex problems are the most common. Very often the issue that arises is only part of the whole and therefore when you solve that one, another one will immediately appear to replace it. You need to treat problems 'holistically', that is as part of a whole. In a work situation, your problem may appear to be that a subordinate has not delivered what you wanted. The issue might be that they:

- didn't understand what you wanted

- don't have enough time to do it properly

- are unhappy in their job

- don't believe in your project

- don't like you

231

If you treat it as a simple problem and repeat what you want, if they don't like you, it is quite likely that you will not receive what you want.

Unsolvable problems: there are very few genuinely unsolvable problems – certainly not nearly as many as people think. If you treat all problems as if they might be complex rather than simple, far more will become solvable. Most 'unsolvable' problems do have a solution but not perhaps in the circumstances you presently find yourself.

Solving a problem: there is a well-proven structure to problem solving:

- clarify what exactly the problem is
- identify possible causes
- choose likely cause and investigate
- try it
- check it
- repeat cycle if necessary

How do you solve problems? Are there any changes you would benefit from and, if so, what are they?

_____

_____

_____

_____

_____

UNDERSTANDING FINANCE

Finance is like the rules and the scoring
system for the game of business

Is finance a bit of a mystery? *Yes/No*

Do you wish you understood it more? *Yes/No*

Do you know the difference between a balance sheet
and a profit and loss account? *Yes/No*

Do you hope you can avoid the topic altogether? *Yes/No*

If you are in the lower or middle ranks of the management hierachy, you can possibly get away with being a little vague about finance, but there is no such thing as a top class manager who doesn't need to understand it. It doesn't mean that you have to be a maths whiz – far from it! The basic principles of finance are stunningly simple and there are many business decisions that must be made using 'rule of thumb' financial techniques that can be done in your head.

This chapter will help you understand:

- payback
- the importance of cash
- gearing
- profit and loss
- revaluation and depreciation
- capital and assets
- the balance sheet

PAYBACK

Payback is a simple way of assessing whether or not it is worth investing in a project. There are many more complicated ways of doing the same thing, but the beauty of payback is that it is quick to calculate, everyone can understand it and it works! Some of the biggest, most successful companies in the world prefer to use payback for their investment decisions.

Suppose you are a marketing manager in a small company. You have an idea that you think will increase sales – it involves spending £100,000 on a special promotion. You write up the idea on one side of paper and take it to a management meeting.

The managing director listens to your description of the benefits of the investment – you reckon that the promotion will increase sales at a rate of £5,000 extra profit per month.

'So, what's the payback?' asks the MD.

(Everyone does the sum in their heads: 100,000 investment divided by 5,000 monthly profit = 20 months before you get the investment back.)

'The payback is 20 months' you answer brightly.

Of course, all the rest of your assumptions have to be right for the payback figure to be right – if the promotion doesn't bring in any extra profit then the estimated payback figure will be wrong. But let's assume that you know what you are doing and that your fellow managers do too.

'Well,' says the M.D. 'That sounds promising. Jill has an investment proposal too.'

Jill is in charge of overseas sales. She wants to spend £200,000 on opening a showroom in Dubai. She reckons that the company will make £5,000 a month in extra profit.

'The payback is 40 months' says Jill. (200,000 investment divided by 5,000 extra monthly profit = 40 months before you get your investment back.)

Now the discussion can get started; let's assume the company can't, or doesn't want to, invest in both projects at the same time. The fact that your scheme has a shorter payback will be a significant factor in deciding which project to go with first.

Summary:
- payback is simply the time it takes to get back the money you invested
- the shorter the payback, the better
- in practice, a payback of less than 3 years is considered attractive

ACTION PLAN

Every time you contemplate a project, do the simple payback sum in your head. Ask:

- how much are we investing?
- how much will profits increase monthly?

Divide the investment by the profit increase and you get the number of months it will take to get the investment back.

CASH FLOW

The main reason why businesses go bust is that they run out of cash. This is particularly true of small and medium-sized concerns, where the owners and managers do not have the clout, political connections and access to sophisticated financial markets which so often saves large companies quoted on the stock market from ruin.

You could say that a company running out of cash is like a person who dies when their heart stops beating. As an explanation of the cause of death, it can be unsatisfactory – there may be deeper reasons for the death of a person or business. Nevertheless, if your heart stops, or your company runs out of cash, that's the end of story in most cases.

Why do businesses run out of cash? You might think that companies only run out of cash if their sales dry up or they make huge losses, but this isn't true. Many other factors can impede the flow of cash into your company. Consider the following scenario:

THE CASH FLOW CRISIS

You are a senior manager in a small company turning over £1m a year. Suddenly you get a massive order from a reliable foreign government – it's worth £2million, it will take nine months to fulfil and the company will make £750,000 profit. Fantastic. It is going to be a big job but you're sure the bank will come up with any extra cash you need – after all, the customer is a reliable government.

You do your sums carefully and you work out how much extra you need to borrow to fulfil the order. You distinguish between the kinds of bills you can delay paying if you have to, such as:

- suppliers' invoices
- heating and lighting costs
- rent and rates

and the kind of bills that you really must pay on the nose, in particular:

- wages and salaries

The trouble is, an expansion in the amount of work a company does tends to increase its 'people costs' considerably, in particular their wages and salaries, and it is very,very hard to delay paying your people – they don't like any delays at all and it could be against the law. Thus you are increasing your risks, you are borrowing more money to finance a huge expansion in the work your company does, and you are taking on more people – by definition, expensive people (all people are expensive) who are not going to wait for their money if you have made a mistake in your sums.

This puts you out on a limb. If you are cautious, you might get the customer to make staged payments so that you get some of the money as you go along which will help reduce your borrowing requirements. But even with staged payments, the chances are that there will be a period where you are risking borrowed money in the hope that your customer will pay.

Now think of some of the things that could go wrong:

- your customer could insist on a delayed delivery – and thus,
- delayed payment
- your customer might simply pay late
- your supplies might arrive late
- an economic crisis might force interest rates up
- your costs might go up due to factors beyond your control

When you take on a big job, any hiccup of this kind can cause you to run out of cash. That is why it is very important to watch your cash flow, which is simply the pattern of cash coming in and going out of your bank account, very closely to make sure that you are not getting into trouble.

Positive cash flow

The previous scenario was a 'negative cash flow' situation. It is called negative because you are spending money before you can get it back. Most businesses work this way. There is another way – the 'positive cash flow' method, which is harder to arrange, but has distinct advantages.

Suppose you are in a business that sells direct to the public. When you sell your product, the customer pays in cash, on delivery. If you can arrange for lengthy credit terms from your suppliers, you can get yourself a positive cash flow:

- the supplier delivers to you but gives you plenty of time to pay
- you deliver to the customer and get paid in cash
- so you get the money in the bank before you have to pay it out

Businesses with a positive cash flow can expand without using borrowed money, which can be a tremendous competitive advantage. There is a danger, though, if your sales suddenly start to drop off, you could end up with a pile of unsaleable goods that you can't pay for.

Either way, you always have to watch your cash flow like a hawk. Remember profits are vital, but without good cash flow control your business will grind to a halt.

ACTION PLAN

Look at the various businesses your company operates and think about their cash flows. Which ones are positive and which negative? Ask yourself if there is anything that could be done to improve the cash flows: if you don't know the answers, ask colleagues who do. Perhaps there are suppliers who could be persuaded to give better credit terms, or potential customers who will pay cash-on-delivery (COD). Get into the habit of assessing all business ventures in terms of their cash flow.

GEARING

Gearing means the ratio between the money that a business has borrowed and the capital that it owns itself. (In the USA, gearing is called 'leverage'.) Supposing your business has cash and assets worth £100,000 and borrowings of £10,000, your assets to borrowings ratio is 10:1 and you are low-geared. If your business is in the reverse situation with assets of £10,000 and borrowings of £100,000, you are high-geared.

The level of gearing is very important in a business:

- High gearing gives you high risk – your profits can be enormous, but so can your losses
- Low gearing gives you low risk – you haven't borrowed much money, so your profits are simply linked to the capital in your business

Perhaps the easiest way of understanding the implications of gearing is to think of the property market, where gearing is very important.

Scenario A: suppose you buy a £100,000 house for cash. If the property market goes up by 10%, you can sell it for a £10,000 sound profit. (Ignore inflation and buying/selling costs for the sake of simplicity.)If the property market goes down by 10%, and you sell the house, you lose £10,000.

Scenario B: not everyone who buys a £100,000 house has all the cash and, if they do, they might think it was better to borrow part of the purchase price. Let's say you buy the house for £50,000 in cash and take out a £50,000 mortgage. If the property increases in value by 10%, you still sell it for £10,000 more than you paid but that's now a £10,000 profit on an investment of £50,000, which is a return of 20% – double that of Example A. Likewise, if you lose £10,000 when you sell, you lose 20% of your capital.

Scenario C: the property market is cyclical and during periods when there are rapid increases in value, more people increase their borrowings in the hope of increasing their profits. Suppose you buy a house of £100,000 but take out a £100,000 mortgage to pay for it. If you sell it for a £10,000 profit, that £10,000 is all yours, even though you didn't put any capital into the property. If you lose £10,000, you will end up owing the lender that sum, but you don't have a house any more because you have sold it.

What's a healthy level of gearing? This is an unanswerable question, it all depends on what business you are in, whether or not your judgement of the future proves to be right and whether you can get out of your debts if things go wrong. Business owners who aren't in a hurry to get rich – perhaps because they are rich enough already – tend to favour low gearing because it is less risky. Businesses in a rush to grow tend to favour high gearing.

PROFIT AND LOSS

The profit and loss account is one of the standard documents that every business must produce each year. It tells you how much profit, or loss, the business has made during the preceding 12 months.

Here is a simplified profit and loss statement:

The XYZ Manufacturing Co. Ltd			
Sales			1,000,000
Less:			
Materials	200,000		
Labour	400,000		
Overhead	200,000	(800,000)	
Trading profit			200,000
Investment income		10,000	
Net profit			210,000

The left-hand column shows categories of expenditure and the right-hand column shows the income, where figures in brackets are minus numbers, so, in our example, the (800,000) is simply the total expenditure, which must be subtracted from your total sales income to give you your trading profit.

Profit and loss statements often have many more categories of expenses than the three in the example, but the principle remains the same. The trouble with profit and loss statements is that they don't tell you very much about the business – except for its size and roughly how it spends its money. Some of the important things that a profit and loss statement doesn't tell you are:

- it doesn't tell you how much capital is invested in the business. Without knowing this, the profit figure isn't very informative.

Suppose, for instance, that the XYZ Manufacturing Company in the above example had £100m invested in plant, buildings and stock; its £1m annual sales and £210,000 profit would be a very poor return on its capital. Conversely, if it had only £100,000 invested in the business, the profit would represent a good return.

- it doesn't show which costs relate to which sales. Suppose you sell two products, one of which is massively profitable and another which sucks up all your money and produces a loss. You cannot detect this from the profit and loss account because it only shows the overall costs

- it doesn't tell you if you need to replace equipment or invest money to keep the business going

- it doesn't tell you if you have got any cash available

There is one other matter that profit and loss statements do show, though – changes in the value of investments and fixed assets, which are things like buildings and machinery. Suppose, for instance, that your company owns an office building which has recently shot up in value. The increase in value would be indicated on the profit and loss sheet. Suppose that your company has a machine which has lost value during the past year because it has been used so much – the loss in value is also indicated. Thus, the XYZ Company's profit and loss statement might actually look like this:

The XYZ Manufacturing Co. Ltd		
Sales		1,000,000
Less:		
Materials	200,000	
Labour	400,000	
Overhead	200,000	
Depreciation of fixed assets	50,000	(850,000)
Trading profit		150,000
Investment income	10,000	
Net profit		160,000
Revaluation of property	100,000	
Total gains		260,000

This kind of revaluation is important, but it is not an exact science, since you never know for certain what something is worth until you actually sell it.

REVALUATION AND DEPRECIATION

Let's look at these changes in valuation more closely. First, we'll take the decrease in the value of the machinery, which, in the profit and loss statement above, is given as £50,000. This decrease is called depreciation: it is the same principle as the depreciation in the value of your car. Let's say you buy a three-year-old car for £4,000. If you look after it properly and don't have any bad accidents, you can be reasonably confident of selling it in the future. The chances are, though, that you won't get as much for it as you paid because the buyer will want a 'discount' of a few hundred pounds off, based on its age – the longer you keep the car, the bigger the discount will be. This is depreciation, and you must try to account for it by knocking off a bit of the asset's value each year, even though you haven't sold it. There are two problems with depreciation.

The first problem is that the day will come when your machine has to be scrapped and you will need to buy a new one. If you have under-estimated the depreciation rate, you may still think that the machine is worth something. In addition, the cost of replacing the machine may have increased dramatically. For this reason, it is important to assess the reality behind the depreciation figures each year.

The second problem is that sometimes companies depreciate their fixed assets too quickly, and end up with, say, machines that are still productive but are valued at zero in the books. This has the effect of making the return on the capital in the business look better than it really is. When you finally have to replace the machines, the return on your capital will drop suddenly.

Revaluation works the same way, but in the opposite direction. Most things that you buy have a limited life and become worth less over time. Some things, in particular land and buildings, tend to increase in value over time. If you don't keep your valuation of such assets realistic and up to date, you don't know what is really happening to your business. A good example of the danger of doing this was the 'asset stripping' craze of the 1960s and 70s. At that time there were many stodgy old businesses with very valuable buildings which they forgot to revalue. The asset strippers came along and bought control of these businesses (usually through the stock market) for a fraction of their real worth and then sold off the property for a fortune. They didn't care about the businesses themselves and often let them go bust. People are more aware now, but even so, if you don't know what your business is really worth, you could end up selling it for a song.

CAPITAL AND ASSETS

In business, capital refers to the money that is used in the business to generate profits. Suppose you decide to set up a small company on your own. You might put in some of your savings, borrow money from a bank and get good credit terms from your suppliers. These are all types of capital:

- Money you borrow is called 'loan capital'.
- Money you put into the company in return for shares is called 'share capital'.
- Goods you receive on credit which you haven't paid for represent more money; they form part of 'working capital' (which is a slightly strange concept to which we will return shortly).

'Assets' are things the business owns. These include cash, buildings, leases, equipment, stock, the value of a brand name and so on – in short, assets are anything the company owns which is worth money, including money itself. There are two main types:

- **fixed assets** which are the things you are keeping to run the business, including buildings, cars, machinery, furniture, telephones and so on

- **current assets** which are mainly things that you own and intend to sell, such as materials, stock and work in progress. It also includes the money people owe you and depending on your accounting policy, the cash in your bank account, the cash which you have received but haven't banked yet and cash you have drawn out to make purchases

Working capital is your current assets plus your current liabilities. Current liabilities are mainly debts that you owe to suppliers and the tax man, plus interest you owe to banks and any short-term money you have borrowed (in practice, this usually means a bank overdraft).

Why do you add current assets and debts together and call them working capital? It's simple – it's all money that you are using in the business at the moment:

- The current assets are things you are going to sell, hopefully at a profit
- Current liabilities are debts you owe but haven't paid yet so you are enjoying the benefit of their value.

Working capital is very important in a business because it is the money that is circulating through it each day. It isn't the same as cash, because parts of it are tied up in things, such as stock; you could call it 'theoretical' money which is moving through the system. At different times, your business will have different amounts of working capital in it. **As the business grows, you will have to watch it as carefully as you watch your cash flow.**

Suppose demand for your products or services goes up. You can sell as many of your widgets, or whatever your company supplies, as you can produce. So you start producing more and more, pay everyone overtime and maybe take on more temporary staff. You are going to need more money. Why? Because you will be using more raw materials, more electricity, more paper and more of all the things that go into producing your product. How are you going to pay for them? The main ways are:

- The owners of the business can put more money in.
- You can borrow from a bank.
- You can ask for more credit from your suppliers.

Whichever way, or combination of ways, you use, it all increases your working capital.

Suppose that after a while your customers start asking you for credit. You could refuse, but you decide that it is worth agreeing to their demands. Once again, you need more working capital because the money they owe you will arrive more slowly, but you will still have to pay your debts. You could decide to slow things down a bit; for instance, you could stop making so much of your product. The trouble with this is that you could lose customers.

The amount of working capital in the business is changing all the time. To work out how much you have at a given time, you have to take a snapshot of the business by freezing everything for a moment. Then add up all your current assets and liabilities. For example:

The XYZ Manufacturing Co. Ltd – Working capital

CURRENT ASSETS

Materials	50,000
Work in progress (*this consists of materials you are making into your product but haven't finished yet, plus an estimate of how much you have spent on them in terms of wages and a proportion of bills such as rent and heating*)	150,000
Finished stock	70,000
Cash in hand	10,000
Cash in the bank	40,000
Trade debtors (*this is the money customers currently owe you*)	50,000
TOTAL	370,000

CURRENT LIABILITIES

Trade creditors (*this is money you currently owe to suppliers*)	170,000
Other liabilities (*this includes things like dividends to shareholders, VAT and tax debts*)	80,000
TOTAL	250,000

Your working capital is thus the two totals added together:
370,000 plus 250,000 = 620,000

You also need to know your 'net' working capital, which is the difference between the current assets and current liabilities. So your net working capital is 370,000 minus 250,000 = 120,000

Now you can unfreeze the business and get going again. If you take another snapshot a day later, or even a few hours later, you will probably get different figures because you will have bought more things, made, delivered and sold more things.

The main thing to remember is that working capital is a measurement of the money flowing through the day-to-day processes of your business.

THE BALANCE SHEET

The balance sheet is a document which, like the profit and loss account, must be produced by any business at least once a year. It incorporates many of the elements which we have discussed in this chapter. The balance sheet tells you about the present condition of your company – like a working capital statement, it is a snapshot of your business at a particular moment in time. It gives you the answers to the following questions:

- **Where is the money that we put into the business?**
- **How safe is that money?**
- **How much cash do we have?**
- **How much cash can we get quickly?**

The balance sheet has two columns. The left-hand column shows you what you have done with the money. The basic categories are:

- **Fixed assets** – these are the things that you have bought to keep running the business, such as buildings, machinery and furniture.
- **Current assets** – these are the things you are working on in order to sell.
- **Investments** – these could be shares and bonds that you have bought.

The right-hand column shows you where the money has come from. The basic categories are:

- **Share capital** – money the owners have put in in return for shares in the company.
- **Loan capital** – money the company has borrowed for a fixed term, normally several years at least.
- **Reserves** – money that the business has generated from profits but hasn't paid out.

The two columns have to 'balance'; that is, they have to add up to the same amount. That is why it is called a balance sheet.

The XYZ Manufacturing Co. Ltd

BALANCE SHEET

Fixed assets	1,000,000	Share capital	600,000
Current assets	400,000	Loan capital	900,000
Investments	200,000	Reserves	100,000
	1,600,000		1,600,000

What does this example tell you about XYZ Ltd's gearing?

_____

_____

_____

_____

_____

_____

How much cash do you think it could get hold of quickly?

_____

_____

_____

_____

_____

_____

SUMMARY

You don't have to be an accountant to understand the basic principles of finance, but you will need an accountant to guide you through the detail. All sorts of laws and regulations affect the way accounts are prepared, and the bigger the company is, the more complicated its accounts will be. A good accountant is happy to explain things – that is what he or she is there for – so don't be afraid to ask.

Remember there are three basic documents for a business that tell you about three different things and taken together tell you a great deal about the health of your business.

- The profit and loss tells you about the past.
- The balance sheet tells you about the present.
- The cash flow forecast tells you about the future.

One other point – accountancy is an art as well as a science. For example, you may think your machinery is worth £100,000 and has five years of working life left in it, but someone else may think differently. Two accountants may take two different views. Ultimately, it is down to judgement and experience. Business is the art of the possible, not an exact method of predicting and controlling the future. As you develop your own business skills, you will become more and more able to assess the state of the company as it really is rather than how you would like it to be.

ACTION PLAN

Get hold of your company's published accounts and go through them carefully. Try to understand the implications of each item and how they fit together. Discuss them with your colleagues, and accountants. Do this and your financial understanding will grow in leaps and bounds.

Further reading

Budgeting for Non-financial Managers (I. Maitland) Pitman Publishing

Handbook of Finance for Non-financial Managers (P. McKoen and L. Gough) Pitman Publishing

UNDERSTANDING AND MANAGING THE PRESSURES

Men are disturbed not by events but by the view they take of them

(Epictetus)

Do you ever find yourself too tired to enjoy life? *Yes/No*

Do you find that you can't complete your work each week? *Yes/No*

Are you expected to achieve more than you consider reasonable? *Yes/No*

Do you find yourself saying that it will be easier next month/year? *Yes/No*

Do you have more than five days' sick leave per year? *Yes/No*

Do you sometimes have difficulty sleeping? *Yes/No*

If you answer 'yes' to several of these questions, then it is likely that you are suffering from some degree of pressure. As more organisations become 'leaner' in the search for competitive advantage, individuals are becoming more concerned for their job security, they are working harder and for longer hours and a toll is being taken on their health and well-being.

It is your life and your health that may be at risk so it is vital that you learn how to recognise and manage the pressures if you want to work effectively and enjoy life.

This chapter will focus on:

- what 'stress' really is and why you react badly to some things and not others
- how to recognise your personal warning signs
- how to relieve the pressures and build resistance for the future
- understanding what causes additional vulnerability
- creating an action plan to keep yourself fit for work and play
- how to manage your time more effectively

DEFINING STRESS

Stress is something that we all talk about and our newspapers are full of. Only recently Professor Cary Cooper of Manchester University published a report estimating that Britain loses 30 million working days per year through stress at a total cost to the economy of £2 billion. We know that stress has a major impact on both ourselves and the economic well-being of our industries – but what exactly is it?

It is generally much easier to understand what causes us stress rather than to define what it is. It is likely that you will be able to fill in the following list without too much difficulty.

Some of the things that have caused me stress recently:

_____

_____

_____

_____

_____

Now look through your list and see how many of the items relate to things that haven't been as you thought they should have been. For example: train delays, traffic jams, arguments with your partner or boss, being in a negative-equity situation with your home, feeling insecure in your employment, etc. Generally most of the situations people find stressful contain at least an element of 'this is not how it is supposed to be' and that causes the reactions that we commonly refer to as stress.

Back in the first century AD Epictetus wrote 'Men are disturbed not by events but by the view they take of them', which explains why what one of us might find stressful, another might find simply challenging or stimulating. So we might agree with the definition that Peter Russell currently offers us that 'Stress is your unwanted reactions to a situation you perceive as a potential threat to your physical or psychological well being'. Stress may be caused by a situation, but the situation itself isn't inherently stressful.

Is there a formula to resolving all the stressful situations in our lives so that we can live calmly and control our surroundings? No, unfortunately there isn't. However, we

Stress may be caused by a situation, but the situation itself isn't inherently stressful.

may well be able to reframe some of the situations we currently find stressful; once we are in a traffic jam, for example, we are not able to do anything about dissolving it but we can enjoy the chance it gives us to listen to the car stereo, think and relax. Life, being as unpredictable as it is, will always throw us some unexpected situations and we need to learn how to manage them better.

UNDERSTANDING VULNERABILITY TO STRESS

The seriousness of the effects of the stress we suffer from is linked to our vulnerability to stress. The effects are often cumulative: the more stressful situations we have to encounter, the more likely we are to suffer distress from them. This also explains why it is nearly always the straw that breaks the camel's back – one small event that we would expect to be able to take in our stride causes us to react in a quite unexpectedly dramatic fashion. Major life events create so much change in our lives that they reduce our resistance to stress and it is worth regularly taking stock of just how many you have experienced over the past 12 months.

The following questionnaire, based on the work of psychiatrists Holmes and Rahe at the University of Washington, lists scores for the life events that may cause an additional vulnerability to suffering the effects of stress.

Tick any of the events that you have faced over the past 12 months:

Life event	Points
☐ Death of partner	100
☐ Divorce	73
☐ Separation from partner	65
☐ Jail term	63
☐ Death of close family member	63
☐ Serious personal injury or illness	53
☐ Marriage	50
☐ Been fired from work	47
☐ Reconciliation with partner	45
☐ Retirement	45
☐ Change in health of family member	44
☐ Pregnancy	40
☐ Sexual difficulties	39
☐ Gaining new family member	39
☐ Business reorganisation	39
☐ Change in financial state	38
☐ Death of a close friend	37
☐ Change to different line of work	36
☐ Change in number of arguments with partner	35
☐ Mortgage of three times annual income or above	31
☐ Foreclosure of mortgage or loan	30
☐ Change in responsibilities at work	29
☐ Son or daughter leaving home	29
☐ Trouble with partner's family	29

☐	Outstanding personal achievement	28
☐	Partner starts or stops working	26
☐	Change in living conditions	25
☐	Revision of personal habits	24
☐	Trouble with boss	23
☐	Change in working hours or conditions	20
☐	Change of home	20
☐	Change in recreation activities	19
☐	Change in church activities	19
☐	Change in social activities	18
☐	Mortgage or loan less than annual salary	17
☐	Change in sleeping habits	16
☐	Change in number of family get-togethers	15
☐	Change in eating habits	15
☐	Holidays	13
☐	Christmas	12
☐	Minor violation of the law	11

TOTAL: _____

Before you assess your score, it is worth remembering that a questionnaire such as this can only provide a crude indicator of the cumulative effect of major changes in your life. A high score does not necessarily mean that you will be suffering from the effects of stress. It indicates only that you are at a higher risk and should therefore take as much care of yourself as you can.

If your total for the past year is under 150, you probably won't have any adverse reactions. A score of 150–199 indicates mild concern with a 37 per cent chance that you'll feel the impact of stress with physical symptoms. From 200-299 you qualify as having a 51 per cent chance of experiencing a change in your health. A score of over 300 could threaten your well-being unless you take particular care to look after yourself.

It is interesting to note that holidays and Christmas, both times when you are expected by your employers to relax, appear in the list of life events that are likely to trigger stress. There are probably two causes for this. First, people generally have very high expectations of holidays and Christmas which may not be fulfilled, particularly when they involve being in close contact with other family members for long periods of time. Second, when you are at work you tend to keep going and then if you are run-down, as soon as you stop illness erupts as a way of allowing the body and mind finally to be able to recuperate. This does not mean that you should avoid taking holidays but that it is helpful to manage your expectations more effectively and if you do fall ill, take note of how run-down you have become and plan how to manage yourself better in the future.

John, a manager in his late twenties, in the past 12 months had got married, moved house, got a mortgage that was three times his annual salary, was expecting their first baby and had been promoted so that his responsibilities had increased. All these events involved changes in his domestic arrangements, social and family life and, at what he had expected to be the happiest time of his life, he couldn't understand why he was so tired. After doing this questionnaire, he began to look after himself better and to relax whenever possible and is now beginning to enjoy himself more.

How your lifestyle can affect resistance to stress

The following items are factors which affect your general resistance to stress.

Score one point for each 'yes' answer:

1. I eat at least one balanced meal a day.

2. I get 7 or 8 hours sleep at least four nights a week.

3. I give and receive affection regularly.

4. I have at least one blood relative I can rely on within 50 miles.

5. I exercise to the point of perspiration at least twice a week.

6. I smoke at the most 5 cigarettes per day.

7. I take fewer alcoholic drinks a day than the government guidelines (3 units for men, 2 for women).

8. I have an adequate income to meet my basic expenses.

9. I get strength from my religious beliefs/philosophy of life.

10. I regularly attend club or social activities.

11. I have a network of friends and acquaintances.

12. I have one or more friend to confide in about personal matters.

13. I am in good health (including eyesight, teeth and hearing).

14. I can speak openly about my feelings when worried or angry.

15. I have regular conversations with the people I live with about domestic problems, chores, money and daily living issues.

16. I do something for fun at least once a week.

17. I am able to organise my time effectively.

18. I drink less than three cups of coffee (or tea or cola) a day

19. I take quiet time for myself during each day.

20. I am the appropriate weight for my height.

TOTAL: _____

A score of less than 12 positive answers indicates some vulnerability to stress, you are seriously vulnerable if your score is under 8 and you are extremely vulnerable if it is under 4.

Recognising your own personal warning signs of distress

Part of becoming aware of how you are being affected by the pressures in your life involves taking a regular 'stress warning signs inventory'. Early warning signs exist in four different areas: physical, mental, emotional and behavioural.

Go through the following list and tick the ones that you tend to notice when you are under pressure:

PHYSICAL SIGNS

☐ headaches ☐ clenched fists/jaw etc

☐ indigestion ☐ fainting

☐ palpitations ☐ frequent infections

☐ nausea ☐ rapid weight change

☐ vague aches and pains ☐ constipation or diarrhoea

☐ tiredness ☐ skin irritations

☐ allergies

MENTAL SIGNS

☐ indecision ☐ muddled thinking

☐ failing memory ☐ making mistakes

☐ loss of concentration ☐ less intuitive

☐ tunnel vision ☐ less sensitive

☐ bad dreams/nightmares ☐ hasty decisions

☐ worrying ☐ short-term thinking

EMOTIONAL SIGNS

☐ irritability

☐ more suspicious

☐ gloomy, depressed

☐ more fussy

☐ feeling tense

☐ drained, no enthusiasm

☐ under attack, paranoia

☐ cynical, inappropriate humour

☐ nervousness, anxiety

☐ feeling of pointlessness

☐ loss of confidence

☐ loss of satisfaction in life

☐ demotivated

☐ reduced self-esteem

☐ job dissatisfaction

BEHAVIOURAL SIGNS

☐ feeling unsociable

☐ restlessness

☐ loss of appetite/over-eating

☐ change in sexual needs

☐ disturbed sleep or insomnia

☐ drinking and smoking more

☐ taking work home more

☐ too busy to relax

☐ not looking after yourself

☐ lying

☐ anti-social behaviour

☐ low productivity

☐ accident-prone

☐ bad driving

☐ increased problems at home

☐ desire to take time off, run away

☐ loss of perspective

Take your most commonly recognisable early warning signs and transfer them to the space on the next page so that you can use them in the future as a trigger to take remedial action.

My most common early warning signs of distress:

_____

_____

_____

_____

_____

_____

_____

_____

GAINING RELIEF FROM THE PRESSURES

Some simple guidelines for relieving the pressures of your busy daily life and building resistance to stress in the future is vital in creating a structure to protect yourself from lasting physical and mental damage from stress.

- Relaxation
- Exercise
- Laughter
- Insight
- Engaging in relationships
- Fuel

Relaxation: in this case does not necessarily include lying on the sofa with a glass of whisky watching the television. Formal relaxation techniques are a good way to clear the mind and relax the body sufficiently after a hard day and prepare you for a good night's sleep so that you are ready to face the next day refreshed and renewed. Yoga and meditation classes are available all over the country and have been found to be very effective. Formal relaxation exercises are now available on audio tape which may be used on headphones on train journeys for those who commute on public transport, but for obvious reasons are not appropriate for use in a car.

Whatever technique you decide to use, it is worth considering how you manage the transition from work into social life. Make some time either on your journey home or when you first arrive to switch off from work and become again the parent, lover, friend that you need to be which may be very different from your working role. Take a walk, watch nature for a few moments, inspect your garden, listen to some favourite music and then, if appropriate allow your partner the same space to allow them to switch from being parent, working person, etc. – it will pay dividends to your relationship!

Learn and practise some simple breathing exercises which will help your relaxation process as well as providing a simple structure to allow you to release pressure during the day in any spare moments. Become aware where you are breathing from. When you are under pressure you tend to breathe shallowly and quickly, using the top of the lungs only. To release pressure, it is helpful to learn how to release the pressure from the muscles of the shoulders and to use the whole of the lungs to enable breathing to become more effective again.

A simple breathing exercise

Lie on the floor and place your hand on your waist. Practise pushing out the stomach muscles until you can inflate the bottom of your lungs using these muscles rather than breathing from the top of your lungs. Now using these muscles, inflate the whole of your lungs slowly to a count of four, hold for a count of four and then release slowly, through your mouth, to a count of four. When you are comfortable with the exercise, stand in front of a mirror and see if you can do it standing up without raising your shoulders at all (this takes a little practice). Once you have mastered the technique, you can use it anywhere, at any time. Repeating the process three times will allow you to release pressure and regain your composure. Try it before important meetings, presentations, when you are angry or upset, when you arrive home and before you go to sleep.

Deep relaxation

Formal deep relaxation lasting 20 minutes can leave you feeling completely refreshed as if you had slept well for several hours. Choose a time and place where you will not be disturbed. Consider muffling the phone and putting up a 'do not disturb' sign. Sit or lie with a straight spine – sitting upright on a straight backed chair or lying on your back on the floor (with a cushion under your head and/or thighs) are recommended. Take a few abdominal breaths. Then slowly in turn focus on each section of your body, clench it, hold the tension for a few seconds and then relax it, saying to yourself in sequence 'my ... is/are now completely relaxed'.

- Take your attention to your feet and toes. Clench, hold, relax and say to yourself 'My feet and toes are now completely relaxed'.
- Take your attention to your calves – clench etc.
- Take your attention to your thighs – clench etc.
- Take your attention to your buttocks – clench etc
- Take your attention to the abdomen and internal organs – clench etc.
- Take your attention to the rib cage and internal organs – clench etc.
- Take your attention to your hands – clench etc.
- Take your attention to your shoulders – clench etc
- Take your attention to your neck and jaw – clench etc.
- Take your attention to your face – clench etc
- Take your attention to your hair and scalp – raise your eyebrows as high as they will go, clench etc.
- Pause for a few minutes.
- Take two or more controlled abdominal breaths, breathing out tension and tiredness, breathing in peace and clarity.
- Pause for a few minutes.
- Scan your body for tensions and repeat the clench, hold and relax section as required.
- Imagine the inside of your brain being painted pure white. Feel the issues of the day drifting away.
- Pause for a few minutes.
- Slowly imagine yourself at the top of a tall building. Turn your attention to an escalator that is going to take you, at your own speed, down to the basement. Imagine yourself descending very slowly.

- In the basement there is a perfect setting (a deserted beach, a beautiful garden, a cool quiet bedroom – you choose). As you enter the space, tell yourself that you are going to lie down for five minutes in perfect peace while you enjoy the equivalent of five hours sleep. Lie down and let go.

When you are ready to re-emerge, take a gentle breath, wriggle your toes and ascend the escalator to bring you back into the world, refreshed and relaxed. Always after a formal relaxation, take the first few minutes gently. Stretch, look around you and compose yourself before returning to action.

Beginners often find it difficult to regulate timings and rarely manage more than ten minutes. You may want to record the programme onto a 20 minute audio tape to play back which has the additional advantage of waking you if you do fall asleep.

Establish a good sleep routine. Avoid caffeine, alcohol and eating heavy meals in the evening. Eat as early as possible to allow time for your digestive system to work before going to bed. Set a regular going-to-bed time, relax before attempting sleep (a warm bath, a milk drink, a light book, etc).

Exercise: there are two forms of exercise: those that release pressure and those that build stamina. Both are equally important. Try to build in two 20-minute sessions of exercise each week after having checked with your doctor that you are fit enough and asking their advice as to what would be most appropriate for you. Build up your fitness slowly, undertaking hard physical exercise when you are unfit is likely to do more harm than good. Any exercise that involves hitting or kicking a ball is excellent to release tension; squash, golf, football, etc. all fall into this category but may involve a certain level of fitness before they should be undertaken.Some forms of exercise are easy to adapt to both pressure-releasing and stamina building. Swimming and walking are good examples and may be undertaken by anyone who is not particularly fit: start by working hard and building to a good speed to release the built-up pressures and then stop, breathe and continue at a much slower pace, stretching your body out and aiming to complete a distance that you can increase each week.

Laughter has often been called the best medicine and it really is an effective reliever of stress. Find time to watch your favourite television programme, video or book and allow yourself to really laugh and let go of tension. Laughter releases endorphins (a chemical in the brain and a natural anti-depressant) which will allow you to forget your difficulties and by pointing out the absurdities of life will encourage you not to take yourself or your problems quite so seriously in the future. Make time to laugh and enjoy yourself but remember that it must be in an appropriate setting: roaring with laughter at your boss is not a great idea, but laughing with your partner at a television programme will do you both the world of good.

Insight: one of the problems associated with pressure is that you are likely to develop tunnel vision and to see no way out of the current difficulty. Insight is to remind you that the world by its very nature keeps on turning and that even this difficult time will pass. It is often difficult to maintain an objective view of the situation and it helps to find someone you trust (a priest, doctor, friend) who is not directly involved in the situation to talk it through with. Often an outsider will be able to help you see it from a different perspective. It is worth considering the Chinese word for 'crisis' which is written with two ideograms: one that stands for severe danger and the other which stands for opportunity. Too often, in a crisis, we can only see the danger without being able to see the opportunity: talking to an outsider can help you find the key.

Engage in your relationships reminds you that when you are suffering from symptoms of distress, you are likely to feel isolated and alone. Making the effort to communicate deeply and genuinely with those you love will help you rebuild your links with the world and, almost certainly, make your loved ones feel more comfortable. Usually we don't speak about our troubles because we don't want to worry them, but they are almost certainly worried sick by our silence. When someone we love is in trouble but not talking about it, we all tend to panic and invent the most disastrous scenarios – it is always better to know the truth than to live with our fears. Tell them what is really going on for you, ask for their support, reassure them of your feelings for them and you are on your way to overcoming the problem – whatever it is. Debt counsellors, among many others, will confirm that as soon as you can begin to speak honestly about your situation, you are on your way to resolving it.

Fuel: when you are in a challenging situation, the body's resources which should be involved in digesting your food are diverted to trying to deal with the supposed external threat so you need to pay attention to helping your digestion function well rather than overloading it. Some useful guidelines are:

- Avoid heavy meals (a heavy lunch will leave you feeling lethargic in the afternoon, a heavy dinner will hinder good sleep).
- Eat a light breakfast (cereal or fruit are excellent) to start the day well.
- Reduce your intake of red meat (it is very complex to digest).
- Reduce the amount of processed food you eat (it generally contains added salt, sugar and fat).
- Increase the amount of raw fruit, vegetables and fibre you eat.
- Aim to eat at least one good balanced meal each day.
- Increase the amount of water you drink (it helps rid the body of toxins).

A healthy diet containing a balance of protein, vitamins and starch will help keep you healthy and fit. Current advice states that we should be aiming to eat SIX portions of fruit or vegetables per day as well as increasing our intake of starches (rice, pasta, bread and potatoes) and eating fish twice a week.

Reduce the amount of caffeine that you take each day; it raises anxiety levels and should be regarded with caution, particularly when you are under pressure. Try replacing some of your regular caffeine 'fixes' (coffee, tea and cola drinks) with fruit juice, herb and fruit teas or mineral water. Reduce your alcohol intake. One glass of wine per day is recommended for health but increasing your intake in order to relax is self-defeating as alcohol is a depressant and should therefore be regarded with great caution.

Finally, **one small action**. When you are under pressure, you are likely to feel as if the world is operating without your having any control over it. Taking one small step to looking after yourself has a major impact in allowing you to feel that you are back in control of your own life. Prepare for yourself a list of 'treats' that would make you feel better about yourself and when you are under pressure, take time out to indulge in some of them. The following are a menu of activities you might want to consider:

- take time out and go for a walk in the fresh air
- stand up and stretch slowly to release tension
- find a place where you can do your breathing exercises
- read the newspaper
- listen to your favourite music
- watch nature (birds feeding etc)
- go home on time
- take a bath with aromatherapy oils
- turn the lights out and watch a candle flame
- prepare a special healthy meal
- buy fresh out-of-season luxuries to eat

My action plan for increasing my resistance to stress:

_____

_____

_____

_____

_____

MANAGING THE PSYCHOLOGICAL ASPECTS OF STRESS

Earlier in this chapter we touched on the fact that a situation often causes distress when it does not live up to our expectations. Too often we get upset when something does not work out the way we want it to rather than to live with and manage the way it actually is. Living in and managing reality is the key to reducing a great deal of what we find stressful in our lives.

The following list of questions are useful for identifying the inner conflict you may be experiencing:

- **What would I have liked to happen?**
- **What was I telling myself about the situation or the other person?**
- **What would I have complained about to my best friend?**
- **How should I have been treated?**
- **What was the other person guilty of?**
- **What made the situation so upsetting?**
- **What would make me happy again?**

When you can see the gap between your 'what should have happened' and the reality, it is possible to recognise that some situations that are presently causing you distress are not worthy of such a reaction. A useful affirmation is the prayer for serenity (used by Alcoholics Anonymous among others):

> God grant me the serenity to accept
> The things I cannot change
> The courage to change the things I can,
> And the wisdom to know the difference.

How can I resolve some of the situations that cause me to suffer from stress?

_____

_____

_____

_____

_____

How your personality can reduce resistance to stress

One of the personality traits of the successful business person is a competitiveness which may lead to an increased vulnerability to stress.

This questionnaire will help you identify your competitiveness and specific guidance on how to balance it better will be given later in this chapter.

QUESTIONNAIRE

Mark your answers Often, Sometimes, Rarely, Never.

1.	Once I have started something, I like to finish it	O S R N
2.	I try to be on time for all appointments	O S R N
3.	I do not find time for personal errands and interests	O S R N
4.	I am hard-driving and competitive	O S R N
5.	I do not listen well and tend to interrupt others	O S R N
6.	I find it difficult to wait calmly	O S R N
7.	I am in a hurry to get things done	O S R N
8.	I find it difficult to relax	O S R N
9.	I find myself doing several things at once	O S R N
10.	I drive fast even if I have plenty of time	O S R N
11.	I finish eating before others	O S R N

12.	I want my value to be recognised	O S R N
13.	I jump traffic lights	O S R N
14.	I keep my feelings to myself	O S R N
15.	I get frustrated by situations beyond my control	O S R N
16.	I think others are hostile to me	O S R N
17.	I am ambitious and want job advancement	O S R N
18.	I set my own deadlines	O S R N
19.	I judge performance on quantity rather than quality	O S R N
20.	I give everything to my work including taking it home	O S R N
21.	I am precise about details	O S R N
22.	I like to be best	O S R N
23.	I get impatient when others slow me down	O S R N
24.	When I am tired, I keep pushing myself	O S R N
25.	I let others set standards for me	O S R N

Score: _____ 'Often' answers x 4 points   = _____

_____ 'Sometimes' answers x 3 points = _____

_____ 'Rarely' answers x 2 points   = _____

_____ 'Never' answers x 1 point   = _____

TOTAL SCORE: = _____

It is likely that managers working in a business environment will have scores of 70 and above, while those in a more caring profession (teaching, health, etc.) may be in the 50s. Any score above 75 shows an increased vulnerability to stress and any scores over 85 probably indicate that their owners are already suffering from some degree of distress.

These scores are surprisingly easy to reduce. Many people find that after a few months with an increased awareness of how much additional pressure a high score may be giving that they can reduce their scores by up to 15 points without too much difficulty and without affecting their performance or image at work.

Some guidelines to reducing a high score are:

Change your attitude to time. Practise time management, prioritise, build in buffer time and contingencies. Make time for yourself, create new interests and hobbies. Enjoy the present and worry less about the future. Ask yourself 'Will it matter in 10 years, 10 weeks, 10 minutes?'

Slow down in walking, eating, talking and driving. Practise queueing patiently. Do nothing for five minutes per day, watch a cloud, watch the grass grow.

Be less competitive when winning is not important. Take up non-competitive sport and play with children and social friends.

Say 'no' a little more often and be honest about why (*see page 106*).

Manage your emotions. Recognise suppressed anger and hostility and find ways of dealing with it (*see page 293*).

Check your fuel input. Reduce your caffeine intake. Reduce or stop smoking cigarettes altogether.

Action plan to reduce my inappropriate competitiveness ...

_____

_____

_____

_____

_____

_____

TIME MANAGEMENT

You can't do everything, so only do what is important.

Time is the one resource that people suffering symptoms of distress complain most about not having enough of. People spend a great time of time and trouble budgeting financial resources and yet very little on the other truly finite resource – time. Time does not magically expand itself to cover the amount of things that have to be done: the amount of things to be done has to be managed to make the most of the time that is available.

Planning: the first step in managing your time is to make a small investment of it into planning to achieve the longer term gain of implementing it most effectively. Planning involves listing all the things that have to be done and scheduling them into the time available.

Consider carefully which parts of the day you are at your most effective and why. If you are a 'lark' and achieve your best results first thing in the morning or an 'owl' who achieves most at the end of the day, build that information into your planning. Aim to do your most important tasks at the time of day at which you are likely to achieve the best results.

Build in time where you will not be disturbed wherever possible to achieve these important tasks. If you have a secretary, ask her to protect you from all but emergencies for a set time. If you work in a team consider taking turns to answer the phone so that you all get some uninterrupted time. If there is a spare office, book it out when you need some peace and quiet to work.

Prioritising: below is a box containing four headings.

In which order would you intend to work through them?

Urgent and important	Urgent and not important
Important and not urgent	Not urgent and not important

Obviously 'Urgent and important' come first and 'not urgent and not important' come last. How did you score the other two? 'Important and not urgent' is probably a higher priority than 'urgent and not important' because only importance has any real relevance. Too often we get carried away by the excitement of urgency and panic without considering the level of importance of the task and a great deal of time is spent with only limited value.

How do you assess importance? It should be part of your job description and objectives which should have been agreed when you took on the position and reviewed regularly in assessments and review sessions with your manager. If there is a conflict between your manager and yourself about importance, then at the first opportunity book a meeting to review the issue and agree a position that you can both work towards.

Once you have sorted out the tasks into the four categories of importance and urgency, re-sort them into:

- **Do (things that are important that only you can do).**
- **Delegate (things that are important that others can do).**
- **Delay (things that might or might not be important, hold until clear).**
- **Dump (things that are not important to do).**

The most helpful aspect of time management is to clear out as many items as possible so that you have enough time to do what you need to do. So the first thing to do is to weed out all the things that are not important. Too often in organisations there is a huge amount of paperwork that is circulated for information, file it if you think it will be of value later and throw it away if you do not. If you find a department is sending you huge amounts of information that has no value to you, ask them why they are sending it to you and unless you can both agree a good reason, ask them to take you off their distribution list. Similarly with trade journals, read what you think is important and ignore what you don't.

The second aspect is delay. This is a section for things that you are not sure about or when you are very busy, that are important but not urgent. What is vital is to reassess this section regularly (at least weekly). Do not fall into the trap of losing things in a vast pile so that nothing ever gets either done or thrown out.

You should now be left with a list of things that need to be done and are important. You can now begin to identify which of these need to be done by yourself and which can be delegated or at least shared with others. Part of the definition of a manager is that they 'achieve tasks through others'. Don't fall into the trap of thinking you must do everything yourself. Delegation can involve:

- subordinates
- colleagues
- other departments
- your manager

Work out which would be the most efficient way of achieving the best results and talk to the individuals you identify to see if they can help you with the task. (*See further on page 344.*)

- You may find it helpful to break large tasks down into their integral parts so that they are easier to work towards.
- When you have competed a task, cross it off with a sense of achievement and move on to the next one.
- Each day, rewrite your list so that it never looks so intimidating that you find it difficult to attempt anything!
- Balance your list with the easy and difficult items mixed up so that you don't leave all the difficult items until the end of the day – or avoid doing them at all.
- Make yourself deadlines or bribe yourself (no coffee until ...) to motivate you to at least start difficult items.

Creating and managing 'To do' lists. When you have created a list of all the things you have to do, make sure they are prioritised in terms of their importance and urgency and make a 'To do' list.

Reorganise your workspace. Does your desk look inviting at work at? Can you find everything you need in a matter of seconds? It really doesn't matter what other people think about it, but honestly does it truly help you work in the most efficient way? If the answers to any of the above are 'no', make some time to reorganise it so that you can save time in the future. Some guidelines that you may find useful:

- Only have what you are currently working on in view.
- Keep your 'In tray' empty, deal with it each day.
- Have stacking trays beside the desk containing all the other tasks you have planned for the day
- Have the waste bin within easy access – it will encourage you to throw away what you don't need.
- Have a simple filing system so that you can easily find what you need.
- File regularly: daily for preference, weekly at the most.
- Reorganise the desk drawers, throw out all the accumulated rubbish and keep what you use most often in the most accessible place.

Avoid wasting time: make a time inventory for a few days and list each activity, how long it took and whether it was worth it. Are you making the best use of all your time? Review your inventory and see what you can do to transform it. If you find yourself spending a lot of time in ineffective meetings, talk to the chairperson and see if you can improve the agenda or just attend the sections that are relevant to you. Avoid meetings wherever possible; one-to-one conversations, face-to-face or on the telephone are generally far more effective than meetings. (*More about meetings on page 313*). Travelling to and from the workplace can be dead time for many people: consider whether you could use it to relax formally, read useful material or think through longer term projects. Always carry a notebook and pen, pocket tape recorder or some other means of capturing good ideas.

Avoid putting things off. More time is wasted procrastinating and worrying about a task than it generally takes to achieve it. Plan the best way to do it and then simply get on with it. (If necessary bribe and bully yourself.)

Avoid doing more than one thing at once. Too often the phone rings while you are writing an important report and you answer it with half your mind on the report and the other half on the phone call. Generally this is a mistake as often both the phone call and that section of the report will have to be repeated later as neither has had your real attention. Try the STOP:CHANGE:START routine.

- **STOP what you are doing when you are interrupted**
- **CHANGE your attention to the interruption**
- **START dealing with the interruption**

and repeat when the interruption is dealt with. When you give your full attention to a task, it is much more likely to be completed effectively. Never imagine that you can do twice as much if you are doing two things at once, experience shows this is never the case.

What is the best use of your time right now? When you have too much or even too little to do, ask yourself 'what would be the very best use of my time right now?'. It is very helpful for getting you out of panic feelings in a crisis as it leads you into action of some sort. And action is always much better than worrying. The best use of your time might well be to think through the consequences and plan – don't fall into the trap of believing that thinking isn't doing anything.

Talk rather than write. If you have information to transfer or to request, have a conversation rather than writing a memo. The amount of time spent in preparing what you want to say, dictating it, signing it and sending it are enormously wasteful. Wherever possible pick up the phone or go and see them. If the information is complicated, write it down yourself as a note rather than a formal memo. Always speak clearly and use the assertiveness skills (*see Stage 3*) so that both parties in the conversation know exactly what is being discussed and decided.

Treat time with respect. Remember that other people's view of time may be different from your own. If someone you have regular meetings with is often late, check with them what would be the most convenient time for them and ring before you leave your office to check they are on schedule. Don't fall into the trap for saying 'Have you got a minute to discuss ...' when it is obvious to both of you that you will want at least 15 minutes. Ask for what you want in terms of time and ask others to be clear about how much time they need for a conversation. If someone asks for ten minutes and then overruns, point out that the time has elapsed and suggest they book another time to complete the discussion. This may surprise them at first but very soon they will book an appropriate length of time. Creating time boundaries shows that you respect your time and that of others and will encourage them to do the same.

A final word: don't feel that it is impossible to sort out all your time difficulties. Start with a small and easy objective and save a few minutes each day: they soon add up. Five minutes saved each hour will give you more than three hours over a week. You might want to rewrite the old motto and make 'Look after the minutes and the hours will look after themselves'.

My action plan to improve the way I manage my time:

_____

_____

_____

_____

_____

Further reading

Living with Stress (C. L. Cooper/R. D. Cooper/L. H. Eaker) (1988) Penguin

The Creative Manager (R. Evans and P. Russel) Allen & Unwin

First Things First (P. Forsyth) Pitman Publishing

DEVELOPING EMOTIONAL MATURITY

Emotional maturity or 'character' has been recognised as valuable in organisations for many years but, because it is almost impossible to measure, has been largely left to chance in the recruitment procedures

Have you ever regretted taking a decision in the heat of the
moment?   *Yes/No*

Do you find yourself becoming paranoid about the actions
of others?   *Yes/No*

Are you uncomfortable living with change?   *Yes/No*

Do you find it difficult to manage your anger appropriately?   *Yes/No*

Do you sometimes wonder why others are promoted above you?   *Yes/No*

If you answer 'yes' to any of the above questions, it is likely that you
will benefit from considering your relationship with your emotions. It is often difficult to balance how you express and manage
your emotions. Bottling up and not expressing emotions is just as
negative to your career prospects as being seen as someone who
cannot control their emotions as we will see in the next section.

This chapter will explore:

- **understanding your emotions**
- **why emotions are important to your future success**
- **how emotions relate to interpersonal skills**
- **how they relate to your reactions in difficult situations**
- **how you can develop your Emotional Quotient**
- **how to manage uncomfortable emotions**
- **how to live more comfortably with change**

WHAT IS EMOTIONAL MATURITY?

'In the corporate world, say personnel executives, IQ gets you hired
but EQ gets you promoted'
(Time Magazine, 1995)

285

Emotional maturity or 'character' has been recognised as valuable in organisations for many years but, because it is almost impossible to measure, has been largely left to chance in recruitment procedures. A new book *Emotional Intelligence* by Daniel Goleman is likely to refocus attention on the subject as it explores the benefits to organisations and individuals alike.

Emotional intelligence is the phrase coined by a psychologists to cover the qualities that determine success in life and explain why often the most intellectually gifted aren't necessarily the highest achievers. These include:

- understanding one's feelings
- empathy for the feelings of others
- the regulation of feelings in a way that enhances life
- the ability to respond optimistically to setbacks

EQ is not the opposite of IQ, rather they complement each other. Some people are blessed with lots of both, some with little of either. What researchers have been trying to understand is how they complement each other; how one's ability to handle stress, for instance, affects the ability to concentrate and put intellectual ability to use. Among the ingredients for success, researchers now agree that IQ only counts for about 20%; the rest depends on a range of other factors they call Emotional Quotient.

WHY YOUR EMOTIONS ARE IMPORTANT TO YOUR FUTURE SUCCESS

It is likely that you can think of an intellectually gifted scholar at your school or college who seems to have disappeared from view in their career. What makes Richard Branson and many others who dropped out of school early more successful in their careers than some scholars with a first class degree?

It is worth considering what is required for success in today's world:

- the ability to understand people (customers, suppliers and colleagues)
- the ability to take the strategic view
- the ability to lead
- the ability to be resilient to setbacks
- the ability to be self-motivated
- the ability to be self-disciplined
- the ability to be positive and confident
- the ability to take personal responsibility for your life and career

The ability to understand people is the key to getting things done. Any organisation is a collection of individuals working together to achieve common goals and an individual with highly developed people skills can make an enormous contribution to this process. Understanding people will involve the use of empathy so that each individual feels understood and valued in their own right. Empathy includes the ability to read and respond to body language, highly developed listening skills so that the individual feels comfortable about talking and well developed communication skills so that people understand clearly what is expected of them. (*See Stage 3.*)

Research shows that the output of a group (or its collective IQ) is based not on the average IQ of the group but on the group's social harmony.

The **ability to take a strategic view** allows small irritations to be set aside in favour of achieving the longer term goal. A team where any one member needs to be 'right' all the time and to 'win' in every situation will rarely achieve its potential and the individual concerned is very unlikely to achieve personal success. It can often be very difficult to put aside uncomfortable emotions when one feels 'put down' or disagreed with but it is worth considering a more strategic view to life (*see Stage 5*).

The **ability to lead** is also based in emotional maturity as it may involve a high degree of courage to step out and offer direction and confidence to a group of people unsure what to do or where to go. It is common regret that there are not enough leaders in our world;

the ability to demonstrate leadership potential is a highly sought after commodity. (*See Stage 12*)

Self-motivation, a positive outlook and taking personal responsibility for one's own career and success. Organisations are becoming less and less likely to employ people for life, so it is more important than ever for you to take responsibility for yourself and your future. You need to do things on your own behalf if you want to be successful.

The **ability to bounce back after setbacks** has been studied for many years in the sporting world. If a first jump/dive, etc. is poor, what makes one athlete give up and virtually withdraw from the competition while another is spurred on to personal best results in their next attempt and so win a medal? The answer appears to lie in an optimistic outlook on life. Many organisations are now recognising the relevance of this in their interviewing procedures as salespeople etc. are inevitably going to face disappointments and need to be able to remotivate themselves to achieve better results in the future. One of the signs of an emotionally mature person is that they tend to build network systems before they need them so that they are well supported should a set-back occur. The emotionally undeveloped person often has a face a crisis on their own and therefore takes longer to recover from it.

A US insurance company concerned about why so many of its salesmen were failing in their objectives after having passed with flying colours all its recruitment tests, asked a University of Pennsylvania psychologist to design a test to help them assess how well candidates respond to set-backs.

Try it for yourself: Imagine the following scenarios and then choose the response ('a' or 'b') that most closely resembles your own:

You forgot your spouse's (girlfriend's/boyfriend's) birthday.
a. I'm not good at remembering things.
b. I was preoccupied with other things.

You owe the library £5 for an overdue book.
a. When I am really involved in reading something, I often forget when it is due to be returned.
b. I was so involved in writing the report, I forgot to return the book.

You lose your temper with a friend.
a. He or she is always nagging me.
b. He or she was in a hostile mood.

You are penalised for returning your income tax forms late.
a. I always put off doing my taxes.
b. I was lazy about getting my taxes done this year.

You are feeling run-down.
a. I never get a chance to relax.
b. I was exceptionally busy this week.

A friend says something that hurts your feelings.
a. He/she always blurts things out without thinking of others.
b. My friend was in a bad mood and took it out on me.

You fall down a lot while skiing   .
a. Skiing is difficult.
b. The trails were icy.

You gain weight on holiday and can't seem to lose it.
a. Diets don't work in the long run.
b. The diet I tried didn't work.

Score: 'a' answers = _____
               'b' answers = _____

It has been observed that those who answer with more 'b's than 'a's are more likely to overcome bad days, recover more easily from rejection and be less likely to give up on projects. People with an optimistic view of life tend to treat obstacles and set-backs as temporary (and therefore surmountable). Pessimists take them personally; what others see as fleeting, localised impediments, they view as pervasive and permanent.

DEVELOPING YOUR OPTIMISM

If you found yourself answering the above situations with mostly 'a' responses, take some time now to consider how to view at least some of the situations in your life from another, more positive, point of view. When you are faced with a set-back, find yourself a coach (someone you trust to help you) and explore whether it is possible to see the situation as temporary, something from which you may well have some lessons to learn but which does not mark you down as a failure.

Look back over your life and think about whether you have ever felt similarly to this before and what was the outcome in that situation. For example: if you ever failed an important exam, how did you feel at the time? What happened next? Did you in fact repeat it and succeed at the second attempt? Has failing that exam had as large an impact on your life as you thought it might?

Experience can be a great help. If you can find a similar situation or experience in your past that you not only survived but actually benefited from, it is very helpful in supporting you with a current problem. When you are young and a set-back occurs, it is difficult sometimes to understand that it will pass and possibly have no long-term effects. As you grow older, you have more experience to help you pick yourself up more quickly and with confidence.

Patrick had recently taken a new managerial position in the industry where he had a successful track record. His new boss was helpful but they had very different expectations of each other and after five months, Patrick was asked to resign. He was very shocked. He went back to his office, cleared his desk and took a taxi home where the full impact of what had happened began to sink in. His new appointment had received wide trade magazine coverage and he felt very vulnerable. That first weekend passed slowly, Patrick found it difficult to eat, sleep or do very much at all. By Monday morning, he had spoken to several friends who advised him on his legal entitlements and he returned to the office to negotiate and collect his settlement cheque. As the news began to spread around the industry, several of his friends called to commiserate, offer support and many of them said that they were not surprised, that the boss had a reputation for being difficult to work for and that Patrick was well out of it.

By the Monday evening, Patrick was surprised to recognise that his feelings had changed. He no longer felt so shocked and humiliated, he noticed a sense of relief that he was free and with a moderately large cheque in the bank, he decided to take a month off before taking any action to find another job. He saw friends, spent time with relatives, took a holiday and generally built up his confidence and physical reserves before deciding to change direction and become self-employed. Eight years later he reports that being asked to resign was probably the best thing that ever happened to him as it gave him the opportunity to think about what he really wanted from his life. He believes that it was the conversations with friends and family that helped him turn what might have been a catastrophe into an opportunity and recommends talking through difficulties with people you trust to help you through them.

My action plan to help me be more positive

_____

_____

_____

_____

_____

MANAGING YOUR EMOTIONS APPROPRIATELY

In our society we are conditioned to think rather than feel. One of the keys to emotional intelligence is the ability to be aware of our emotions and what we are feeling.

Try completing the following list:

During last week at work, I sometimes felt ...

under-utilised	confident	undervalued	jaded
imaginative	mechanical	powerless	anticipative
pessimistic	expectant	trapped	apprehensive
tired	ignored	important	appreciative
creative	purposeful	fulfilled	fearful
disgusted	hateful	cynical	supportive
generous	despised	needed	hurt
sharp	despairing	alive	aimless
inspired	loyal	protective	warm
approving	valued	challenged	recognised
baulked	frightened	insecure	betrayed
respectful	interested	ignorant	perplexed
reluctant	escapist	rewarded	optimistic
insignificant	happy	safe	lazy
enthusiastic	important	bright	powerful
desired	angry	joyful	fraudulent
frustrated	detached	authoritarian	caring
sense of achievement	irritated	suppressed	manipulated
rejected	sceptical	exposed	stimulated
serene	energetic	aggressive	satisfied
attractive	elated	bored	exploited
affectionate	alone	disapproving	vengeful
involved	tense	misunderstood	mean

Taking responsibility for your emotions

How often do you find yourself saying 'He/she/it made me angry'? It simply isn't true. There are times when we all feel like that but ultimately you are the only person responsible for your emotions. You allow yourself to become angry or frightened and different people making the same comment will be likely to evoke quite a different response. The more you can understand that it is you who has the power over your emotions, the more likely it is that you will be able to manage them more effectively. There is nothing wrong with any emotion; they are there to trigger a response for your own safety and survival. The question is just why does this particular situation feel so uncomfortable to you at this time?

Uncomfortable emotions

Emotional maturity does not mean that you will no longer feel any uncomfortable emotions. It means that you will be able to recognise them more quickly and clearly and so be able to handle them appropriately rather than your actions being ruled by them. It may be seen as a balance between emotion and reason.

When something happens and you feel, for example, very angry or frightened, you are unlikely to be able to respond appropriately in the moment. If you are able to recognise the emotion and take some time to think about just why you feel so strongly, it will often begin to dissipate. If you discover that you feel perfectly justified in your emotion because something is happening that you feel is unacceptable, taking this time out will give you the space to be able to assess how to take action in a rational and reasoned way.

Once you are aware of your emotional state, how can you manage it?

ANGER

How do you currently manage your anger? _____

What makes you angry?

injustice	waste	stupidity
cruelty	incompetence	hypocrisy
lies	insensitivity	being taken for granted
snobbery	being ignored	not being listened to
untidiness	being excluded	being told you are wrong

others: _____

Who makes you angry? _____

What signs does your body give when you are angry?

feeling hot	breathlessness/need air or space
heart pounding	a rush of adrenalin
sweating	tension in stomach
tension in jaw	tension in shoulders
sinking feeling	clenched fists

others: _____

How do you feel when you are angry?

powerful	destructive
frightened	like grabbing something and hitting out
like screaming	like stamping on something (or someone)
like running away	like hurting someone
like crying	other: _____

How do you express these feelings?

Do you usually keep quiet when you are angry?
Often   Sometimes   Rarely   Never

Do you usually walk away?
Often   Sometimes   Rarely   Never

Do you store it up and explode later?
Often   Sometimes   Rarely   Never

Do you appear to feel hurt when you are angry?
Often   Sometimes   Rarely   Never

Some guidelines for managing anger in a more constructive manner:

Walk away until you can respond assertively: speaking in anger rarely has a constructive outcome so wherever possible take time out until you can think more clearly. If it is not possible, try not to speak at all until the anger has subsided.

Declare assertively how you are feeling: remind yourself of the structure for effective communication (*Stage 3*) and speak in 'I' statements. (Telling the other person that it was them who made you angry is likely to have a very confrontational reaction!) 'I am angry and need to take a few minutes to think clearly again' is much better than 'You are making me really angry'. If you declare how you are feeling in an assertive way, it can often help dissipate the feeling almost immediately. Attempting to control the emotion often allows it to grow and become unmanageable. Recognising it and declaring it gives it no freedom to fester. If possible, discuss assertively with the other person why you think you are angry and see if you can resolve the issue.

'I am angry because I felt that I was being excluded from this morning's meeting, I didn't feel that I was being asked to contribute anything.'
'I am sorry you feel like that, it wasn't my intention at all. What exactly ...

If you feel unable to resolve the issue through communication or because the feeling is simply so strong that you can't think, you need to **find a way to dissipate your anger**. There are many helpful ways of doing this but you need to find the ones that work for you:

- breathing exercises, breathing out the anger and breathing in calm (*page 265*)
- going for a walk and observing nature
- a formal relaxation (*page 266*)
- taking physical exercise to release tension, running up and down stairs, etc.
- hitting a ball, a soft cushion, etc.
- shouting or singing (in a car with the windows shut is excellent)
- writing down all the reasons why you are angry and then burning the list (in a safe environment)

Expressing your anger appropriately: the trouble with anger is that often if it is not expressed, it builds up and then explodes all over the wrong person or in the wrong situation – the final straw syndrome. Try and keep your anger in compartments that you deal with rather than let it build up until you shout at your family or friends in the evening – the result of tension at work. Deal with any anger at work before you return home and vice versa so that you do not allow it to infect other relationships.

How can you deal with your own anger more effectively?

_____

_____

_____

_____

_____

FEAR

Everyone feels fearful at some time or another but it may be difficult to express and may hold you back from attempting something really important. Fear is an emotion designed to protect us from danger and as such is crucial to our survival but without careful consideration it may stop you from doing what you might benefit from.

The key to managing fear appropriately is to:

- recognise it
- acknowledge it appropriately
- assess the risk
- decide what action you are going to take

Recognising fear can often be difficult at work. Fear is the great unmentionable and you don't want to be thought of as a wimp. The culture in your organisation may verge on the high-risk but unless you can recognise what you are feeling, you will be unlikely to be able to manage it.

What are your symptoms of fear:

panic	breathlessness	muscle tension
dread	knotted stomach	feeling cold
go white	sinking feeling	frozen to the spot
tone of voice changes	others:	....

Acknowledging the emotion: as soon as you can acknowledge the emotion to yourself, it is likely that it will begin to dissipate just enough for you to be able to think clearly. Find someone that you trust to discuss it with (a friend or a colleague may be helpful) tell them how you are feeling and begin to assess it.

297

Assessing the risk: ask your trusted friend to help you by exploring:

- What are you really afraid of?
- What is the worst thing that could happen?
- Would you be able to survive it?
- Is there anything you can do to minimise the risk?

If the answer is that you are afraid of failing or making a fool of yourself, you may be able to take action to minimise the risk until it becomes acceptable. If you discover that you would be able to survive whatever happens, you will find that the fear will dissipate.

Deciding whether to be brave or not involves assessing the risks involved. In any challenge there is a risk and it is probable that you will need to weigh up the advantages or disadvantages before you can make your decision. But be aware that under the personal rights in Stage 3, you do have the right to say no. For example, if your organisation is suggesting that you undertake an outward bound course, a bungee jump or any activity that you genuinely feel is dangerous to your physical or mental health, they cannot (and certainly shouldn't try to) force you to agree. Re-read the section on how to say 'no' assertively and consider your options. It is your well-being that is at stake and you need to be responsible for yourself.

How can you deal with your own fear more effectively?

_____

_____

_____

_____

_____

_____

LIVING MORE COMFORTABLY WITH CHANGE

Most people have some concerns about change. It seems as if while we believe that we can just about cope with the status quo, there is a genuine fear that we might not be able to survive a new and unknown situation. The trouble is that in our fast-changing world, there is no chance of avoiding change.

Managers may have to manage change in many different situations (for example: personnel, location, procedure, profitability, as well as customers and their requirements) and manage their staff's reactions as well as their own. It is simply not effective to proclaim that change is inevitable and therefore everyone should just settle down and get on with it. Sometimes it is important to consider what people are losing

The trouble is that in our fast-changing world, there is no chance of avoiding change.

and allow a period of 'grief'. This is particularly worth considering in times of redundancies where it has been found that productivity will drop alarmingly among those left behind if they are not allowed time to come to terms with the change.

It is common for people to want everything to remain as it was. 'When on earth will things go back to normal' is an often-heard cry around organisations in times of change. And the answer is, of course, that they won't, that there is no such state as 'normal', that there is only how things were and how things are now. And people tend to look back with rose-tinted glasses on how things were.

What you can do is to remember that every change opens up possibilities of improvement for the future. Remember the Chinese ideogram for crisis where it contains two separate words: one for danger and one for opportunity. Rather than concentrating always on the dangers implicit in change, it is helpful to also consider the possibilities it presents.

In their book *Winning at Change* George Blair and Sandy Meadows suggest that a change winner is someone who:

- has a strong self-image
- possesses a high level of self-knowledge
- is flexible
- looks for feedback
- has good interpersonal skills
- looks beyond the short term
- sees life as a learning opportunity
- can take calculated risks
- sees feedback where others see mistakes and failure
- focuses internally for security (rather than externally)
- does not seek approval from others

Perhaps a commitment to personal development is one of the fundamental steps to living more comfortably with change as every item on the above list is covered in this book. Look through the list and assess yourself as fairly as possible against each item. Which areas do you still need to focus on?

How do you perceive change?

_____

_____

_____

How could you view it more positively?

_____

_____

_____

What changes are you likely to have to face?

_____

_____

_____

How could you handle them more positively?

_____

_____

_____

Further reading

Feel the Fear and Do It Anyway (S. Jeffers) (1987) Rider

Emotional Intelligence (D. Goleman) (1996) Bloomsbury

Winning at Change (Blair and Meadows) Pitman Publishing

DEVELOPING YOUR SKILLS FOR WORKING WITH OTHERS

One of the simplest definitions of management is 'achieving tasks through others'

LEADERSHIP QUALITIES AND HOW TO DEVELOP THEM

Do you often think you could run your organisation better than the present senior management team? *Yes/No*

Do you get frustrated waiting for decisions? *Yes/No*

Do you know where the organisation is going? *Yes/No*

Do you know how you are expected to get there? *Yes/No*

Do you feel you get inspirational leadership? *Yes/No*

Leadership is a topic which seems to be at the top of the agenda at the moment. Maybe this is because you feel that you are not receiving the sort of leadership you expect, that the leaders of your organisation seem to behave in a way that does not meet your expectations.

In his book *Key Management Ideas*, Stuart Crainer says 'Leadership is one of the great intangibles of the business world. It is a skill most people would love to possess, but one which defies close definition. Ask people which leaders they admire and you are as likely to be told Gandhi as J.F.Kennedy and Jack Welch (Chief Executive of General Electric) as Richard Branson. Yet most agree that leadership is a vital ingredient in business success and that great leaders make for great organisations.'

This section will cover:

- **what leadership involves**
- **what leadership qualities might include**
- **how to develop them**
- **how and when to use them**

What leadership involves

There are many definitions of leadership but one that seems to sum up many of the others is that of Sir John Harvey Jones. Writing about his experiences of chairing ICI, he suggests that: 'leadership is the ability to enable ordinary people to do extraordinary things.' If you think for a moment about some of the people you consider great leaders, this may be their unifying bond.

Is leadership the same as management? Not according to the many writers on the subject. The consensus is that there are plenty of managers and too few leaders in the business world. The differences have been charted by US management guru Warren Bennis in his book *On Becoming a Leader*:

- the manager administers, the leader innovates
- the manager is a copy, the leader is an original
- the manager maintains, the leader develops
- the manager focuses on systems and structure, the leader focuses on people
- the manager relies on control, the leader inspires trust
- the manager has a short-range view, the leader has a long-term perspective
- the manager asks how and when, the leader asks what and why
- the manager has his eye always on the bottom line, the leader has his eye on the horizon
- the manager imitates, the leader originates
- the manager accepts the status quo, the leader challenges it
- the manager is the classic good soldier, the leader is his own person
- the manager does things right, the leader does the right thing

Leadership is not necessarily linked to authority. Many world leaders have been given authority and status because they displayed leadership qualities rather than displaying them because they have been given the authority. Many leaders have not sought status or authority; they acted in a leadership role simply because they were clear about what they thought was required and were prepared to act to enable more positive movement forward. In organisations, those promoted to senior roles may or may not display leadership qualities but those doing so will probably achieve success.

Leadership qualities

'There are times when a leader must move out ahead of the flock, confident that he is leading his people the right way.'
(Nelson Mandela)

What are the qualities you think are important for leader to possess or develop? Make your own list:

_____

_____

_____

_____

_____

_____

Your list will probably contain many different ideas but after using this exercise with many groups of people, it is likely that it contains at least some of the following: courage, vision, confidence, commitment, dedication and initiative.

Courage: defined by Webster's dictionary as the 'mental or moral strength to venture, persevere and withstand danger, fear or difficulty', which enables you to fight for or defend what you believe is right. Courage is required to move ahead of the flock. Leadership is not the easy option. Courage, along with confidence, gives the leader the boldness to promote new ideas and ventures, as well as make the decisions that may be difficult but necessary.

Vision: this is the most commonly quoted quality of leadership. It is the ability to see possibilities for the future that others cannot. Vision and the ability to communicate it effectively hold the key to inspiring others to follow you to the future you believe possible. Vision endows the leader with inspiration, discernment, foresight and a well-developed imagination which generates the creativity that allows new and original possibilities.

Confidence: is having the faith or belief that you will act in a right, proper, or effective way. It stresses faith in yourself and your powers without any suggestion of arrogance or conceit. Confidence is the key to communicating your vision, after all, if you do not have belief in yourself and your ideas, how can anyone else? Confidence is often linked to courage as it is these two qualities that will help support you when times are difficult.

Judgement: there are two aspects to this quality. First, judgement can be seen in the ability to balance up options, the confidence to trust your instincts and the ability to be decisive – if you like, to make good decisions. Second, good judgement includes integrity. For a leader to be respected and therefore followed, they need to be seen as trustworthy, incorruptible and acting for the best rather than for themselves.

Commitment: is the devoting or setting aside of your time, your life even and your efforts in your determination to achieve a particular purpose. Any lack of commitment by a potential leader at work will have a demotivating effect on the rest of the team while a demonstrated commitment will be likely to create an atmosphere that encourages others to show the same dedication to the goal.

Initiative: is the showing of originality and the energy or aptitude to step forward and take on the mantle of leadership as well as the commitment to beginning any new process or direction. Initiative includes proposing new ideas and suggestions as well as demonstrating enthusiasm in everything you do. A leader needs to be seen as dynamic, setting new direction for the group and continually moving forward. A leader understands that standing still achieves little and takes the responsibility for the success of their group.

Developing your own leadership qualities

Francis McLeod, former Chief Executive of the Leadership Trust, has said 'Broadly speaking there are two approaches to leadership. You can theorise about it or you can get on and do it. Theorising about it is great fun, hugely indulgent and largely useless. Doing it – or doing it better – is demanding, frequently frustrating and of immense value. Learning to lead oneself better is the only way to lead others better.'

First, you need to consider and come to terms with the responsibilities of leadership. It can be a lonely isolated role, always being expected to provide the vision and direction for others so you need to develop a network of support for yourself. Family, friends, colleagues, coaches, mentors may all be part of this network but you will need to develop a strong sense of self-belief which includes high self-esteem, self-confidence and self-motivation (*see Stage 4*).

Remember always that you have a choice as to whether you take on the mantle of leadership or not. Many leaders in different types of organisation have had to face their concern that they were not the right person to take on this role – that they were not good enough. What is helpful to remember is that, of course, you are not good enough and certainly not perfect but what will make you the ideal candidate is if you genuinely believe that you have something to contribute and are prepared to take it on, to do your best and make a difference to the current situation. It has been said many times that the most important aspect to success is the doing it – unless you are there and prepared to begin, it is impossible to succeed. **So you have the choice – are you prepared to make a contribution or not?**

Always act with integrity. If you don't believe the task is worthwhile or that you have a contribution to make to it, you will be very unlikely to inspire or motivate others. Check the task carefully against your own values and beliefs because if it doesn't match, you will face difficulties in the future. Assess the task in its largest sense – if you can see your job as making a positive contribution to your organisation, its staff and, for example, the manufacturing base of the country, you will develop your commitment to the achievement and your self-belief.

Doing something important better than it has been done before always entails a risk.

Once you have made the decision to undertake the purpose, it is important that you operate from the constructive and positive rather than the negative. Encourage your team to develop their qualities, give them constructive acknowledgement as well as appropriate criticism (*see Stage 3*). Acknowledge the team's successes and review them to learn from them at least as much as you do from failures. Identify what you may have said or done to create the successes so that you can recreate the conditions again in the future. Building a positive outlook will improve your own as well as others' confidence.

Develop a positive relationship with risk-taking. Remember that if you play so safe that nothing is ever risked, the chances are that you will never achieve anything worthwhile. Doing something important better than it has been done before always entails a risk. Balance up the advantages and disadvantages carefully before taking a decision and take action to limit the risks. Ask yourself 'What is the worst that could possibly happen?' and whether you could take responsibility for it. Believing there is little to lose if it fails is one of the most powerful motivators to achieving extraordinary results. Remember how often in sport the underdog beats the favourites because they have little to lose and therefore can go out and enjoy themselves.

Also, if you do make a mistake, always take responsibility for it as soon as possible and begin to put it right. This will encourage subordinates to do the same, saving the time that is too often spent covering up problems resulting in no opportunity to learn from them and remedial action being delayed, causing even more damage.

The leader has the responsibility of continually evaluating the strategies so keep your focus on the long-term goal. Use creative visualisation (*see Stage 5*) to give you confidence that it is achievable.

Communicate the vision as clearly as you can so that the group can believe in it too. The more you can focus on the achievement of the goal, the easier it will be to look back, as it were, to identify the steps it will be necessary to take. Encourage strategies so that everyone is clear about where they are going and can plan to get there in measurable stages. Clear plans will add to the confidence with which the team perform their tasks and the measurable stages will give you confidence about whether you are on course.

There may be times when you feel that you have lost some of your confidence and self-belief begins to falter. Then you have to go back to your original commitment to the task and re-examine it. No one is ever totally confident, but what marks out a true leader is that they project confidence because the more you can behave confidently, the more you will begin to believe it yourself. Also your team will respond to your confidence and begin to deliver the results.

How are you going to develop your leadership qualities?

- Courage: _____
  _____

- Vision: _____
  _____

- Confidence: _____
  _____

- Judgement:_____
  _____

- Commitment: _____
  _____

- Initiative:_____
  _____

- Any others from your personal list: _____

Beginning to demonstrate leadership qualities

It may be that you feel it would be inappropriate to volunteer for a leadership role in your current position or that you would benefit from developing confidence in your own ability before doing so. There are many different ways you can do this.

You can support your current leader. It is not a requirement of leadership that it takes place from the front; you can demonstrate leadership from any position within a group. You may choose to lead a sub-group who are currently disunited and likely to move in different directions. If you can unite them behind the vision and strategy of the group and motivate them to support the goal, you can help the whole group achieve its objective more effectively and gain a lot of respect and satisfaction in the process.

You can offer ideas and solutions to potential problems whenever they occur. Good ideas and potential solutions are vital to the success of any group and volunteering them will help it move forward. Even if your original idea is not accepted by the group, it will probably encourage them to find the best one.

You can keep 'your eyes on the hills and your feet on the ground'. Keeping a long-term perspective will encourage the rest of the group to do the same. Difficulties within a group often occur because the short-term problems stop the members taking the bold step into the future.

What can you do to demonstrate your leadership ability?

_____

_____

_____

_____

_____

Further reading

On Becoming a Leader (W. Bennis) (1989) Century Business

Key Management Ideas (S. Crainer) Pitman Publishing

Effective Leadership (J. Adair) (1988) Pan

and biographies of people you admire as leaders, for example: John Harvey Jones, Nelson Mandela, Lee Iacocca of Chrysler

DEVELOPING YOUR TEAM

Do you feel others don't work as hard as you do?	*Yes/No*
Do you feel the people working for you are the best?	*Yes/No*
Do you feel you have to check everything they do?	*Yes/No*
Do you have to come up with all the ideas?	*Yes/No*
Is it hard to find good people?	*Yes/No*
Do people not seem to work together properly?	*Yes/No*

One of the simplest definitions of management is 'achieving tasks through others' and this chapter will focus on many of the issues about finding the right people to achieve the task with you and how to enable them to do so most effectively.

- **teams, why and how to build them**
- **developing team spirit**
- **empowerment**
- **motivation**
- **delegation**
- **coaching and counselling skills for managers**
- **conflict resolution**
- **interviewing**
- **appraisal**
- **training and development**

Teams: why and how to build them

The purpose of building a team is to create what is known as synergy where the sum of the whole is larger than the sum of the individual parts. In other words, a team of six people working together effectively will achieve more than the output of the six people working individually.

If the purpose of any manager is to achieve tasks through other people then the concept of good teamworking is crucial to the department's success because it will achieve more than any other way of working. And people like being in teams; they like the sense of belonging to a group of people small enough for them to feel comfortable in and to communicate with without having to raise their voices.

Building a team

One of the easiest ways to look at putting teams together is to relate it to sports teams of which you will probably have some experience. It is generally recognised that the ideal size for a team is somewhere between four and 15 (the same range as that of a sports team). It ensures that it is small enough for everyone to be able to meet together comfortably and be able to have their say. It is worth considering breaking up a group of more than 15 people into separate teams according to their role in the task to enable each to work as effectively as possible.

Balance is important in a team.

What sort of people make up a team? Everyone who is necessary to the task at hand and this will include different functions and specialisations. Balance is important in a team. One danger to creating a team for the first time is to try and put very similar people together – remember always that creativity and dynamism tends to be generated from differences rather than similarities. A successful sports team generally contains both attackers and defenders, tall and short players and players with flair or reliability. A work team needs to be based on the same principles, that each has their own part to play and that their strengths complement and support each other, rather than the team being a group of individuals each doing their own thing.

According to John Adair who has written widely on management and teambuilding there are two strands to creating an effective team. The first is complementary contributions (which we have already touched on) and the second is that they share a common task. Without a clearly understood purpose, people have no goal to strive for, so a clear objective is needed. The team need to understand exactly what their task is so that they can achieve it as effectively as possible. It is the responsibility of the manager to communicate the objective and ensure that it is understood clearly. (*See also the section on empowerment page 326.*)

Meetings are an integral part of teamworking and should be encouraged to deal with short-term scheduling as well as longer-term problem solving and improvement programmes. Some teams meet daily for a short periods and others once a week for an hour; the frequency should reflect the needs of the team and, possibly, at what stage they are in the achievement of the task.

R. Meredith Belbin has produced fascinating research in his book *Management Teams – why they succeed or fail* to show why some teams succeed or fail and details some of the core types it is valuable to have in any team.

Implementer or company worker (conservative, dutiful, predictable)

Qualities: organising abilities, practical common sense, hard-working, self-discipline.

Allowable weaknesses: lack of flexibility, slow to respond to new ideas, resistant to change

Co-ordinator or chair (calm, self-confident, controlled)

Qualities: a capacity for treating and welcoming all potential contributions on their merits, without prejudice. A strong sense of objectives.

Allowable weaknesses: not of exceptional intellect or creative ability

Shaper (highly strung, outgoing, dynamic)

Qualities: drive and a readiness to challenge inertia, ineffectiveness, complacency or self-deception.

Allowable weaknesses: prone to provocation, irritation and impatience. A tendency to hurt people's feelings.

Plant (individualistic, serious-minded, unorthodox)

Qualities: genius, imagination, intellect, knowledge. Solves difficult problems.

Allowable weaknesses: up in the clouds, inclined to disregard practical details or protocol

Resource investigator (extroverted, enthusiastic, curious, communicative)

Qualities: a capacity for contacting people and exploring anything new. An ability to respond to challenge.

Allowable weaknesses: liable to lose interest once the initial fascination has passed. Can be over-optimistic and uncritical

Motivator/evaluator (sober, unemotional, prudent)

Qualities: judgement, discretion, hard-headedness.

Allowable weaknesses: lack of enthusiasm or the ability to motivate other people – can be uninspired and uninspiring, a bit of a cold fish

Team worker (socially-orientated, rather mild, sensitive)

Qualities: an ability to respond to people and situations and to promote team spirit. A good diplomat.

Allowable weaknesses: indecisive in moments of crisis; they are adapters rather than changers

Specialist (single-minded, self-starting, dedicated)

Qualities: provides knowledge and skills in rare supply

Allowable weaknesses: contributes only on a narrow front. Tends not to see the big picture

Completer/finisher (painstaking, orderly, conscientious, anxious)

Qualities: a capacity for follow-through. Perfectionism.

Allowable weaknesses: inclined to worry unduly, reluctant to delegate. Can be a nit-picker

Some of the types can be seen as being similar to others. For example, plants and research investigators can be seen as the two most creative team roles, research investigators and co-ordinators are both good at liaising with others and motivating the team, co-ordinators and shapers are both strong leaders, plants and monitor/evaluators are both intelligent thinkers, co-ordinators and team workers act to promote team spirit and harmony, implementers and completers are the doers on the team and specialists and completers are both dedicated to achieving an extremely high standard.

Finding the right mix is important to creating an effective team. Some useful guidelines are:

- **Find a good chair.** It needn't be the team leader but they should be able to act with authority and their profile should closely match that of the co-ordinator.
- **Have one good plant.** More than one plant is likely to prove ineffective as they tend to pick holes in each others ideas rather than develop their own
- **Have a good spread of mental abilities.** The wider the spread, the more each will stimulate the others. A team without at least one clever member will rarely produce good ideas
- **Have a wide range of team roles** to encourage everyone to contribute effectively.

> • **Have a good match between attributes and their responsibilities.** A plant in charge of a detailed task is not likely to achieve the desired result
>
> • **Recognise any imbalances** and be prepared to make changes in roles or responsibilities.

In a small team you need to balance the roles and types in wider bands. It might be said that the co-ordinator, plant, resource investigator and the shaper are all outward-looking; while the implementer, monitor/evaluator, team worker, completer and specialist are inward-looking. If you can balance the number of individuals between outward- and inward-looking, you may find that many of the roles are able to be doubled up or, in a very small group, may not be required at all.

Developing team spirit

It is easy to recognise team spirit when it exists – people are enjoying working together, they are having fun, often they have team jokes and inoffensive nicknames, they all understand what they have to do and, more importantly, how they are going to do it, their communication is so effective that they tend to use a form of verbal shorthand to send messages to each other, they have empathy for each other and if anyone needs support or help, it is immediately available.

How can you help foster it? The answer in many ways is related to understanding the relationship between task (what has to be done) and process (how it can be most effectively completed). The task needs to be clear. The team needs to understand exactly what is involved, when it needs to be completed, what the criteria (standards and quality) of successful completion are and, where possible, have an understanding of the purpose of the task. When people can see the whole picture and where what they are doing fits, they are most likely to be committed to doing the best job possible.

In the 1960s, the Swedish car manufacturer, Volvo, created a breakthrough in manufacturing. They broke up their staff of specialists who each did their own jobs and created multi-disciplined teams of six people who together built an entire car. Suddenly productivity and quality increased dramatically as individuals became responsible for the final product.

The team should be involved in breaking down the task into the steps necessary for its achievement which will include how to best use everyone's strengths and skills, how to keep everyone busy and involved. This leads us into the process, or how the team will operate. The way we do things is an aspect of teamwork that is all too often forgotten. Perhaps we should remember that sports teams spend at least five times as long practising as actually playing (their task). It is worth considering allowing at least part of the team meeting for process or improving the way in which they work together to achieve the task. Some organisations are now holding monthly process-only meetings which have had very beneficial results.

Ian, the manager responsible for three teams in an insurance company, was unsure as to how to manage them effectively. He suggested splitting each team meeting into two 30-minute segments. The first dealt with any task difficulties and the second was reserved for process. The process meetings became so productive that they have now become commonplace within the organisation because productivity and team morale have risen dramatically. Because team members now have a forum to debate how they can work together more effectively, they have taken responsibility for thinking in advance of ideas to improve working practices and the quality of the final product.

Process includes the team knowing each individual's strengths and skills so that they can be utilised effectively, developing additional strengths and skills to enhance those that the team already possesses and developing ways of working together to produce optimum results. The more each individual feels that the team appreciates and uses their strengths and skills, the more valued and motivated they feel and the more likely they are to make a valuable contribution.

How do you identify the strengths, skills and potential of the members of the team? Some of them may be written in their original application form, some may be apparent at work, but it is very likely that each and every one of them has more to offer than is being utilised at the moment.

John, a manager in a large pharmaceutical company, arranged a series of 'away-days' where he took his team to a hotel and arranged 'getting to know each other' sessions. He asked everyone to prepare a 15-minute presentation on one of their passions in life. The results were amazing, the team proved to be made up of multi-faceted individuals who suddenly became real people to each other. Team spirit dramatically increased as they began to build a relationship together and when they returned to work, the benefits in productivity were a clear justification of the time and expense incurred.

Other managers in similar situations have discovered new skills among the team that had not been offered because it was thought they weren't required. Often finding out what people do outside work will reveal hidden strengths that the team can benefit from. Discovering more about each member of the team has the additional benefit of encouraging the bonding together of the team. Bonding may be regarded as the building of personal and working relationships between the members of the group so that they are able to act in unity when required.

If the team is able to share the same physical location at work, it will encourage the group to bond together. However, this may not always be possible, in which case regular team meetings will become even more important. Any shared events are a powerful bond for a group of individuals. The more important the shared event is, the stronger the bond will be among the individuals. The more history the group has, the more good and difficult situations it has been through together, the stronger the bonds will be. It is, therefore, a wise leader who encourages the team to tell stories of what they have achieved and learned together.

Training can offer a bonding experience to a team. Learning together, whether within the workplace or externally will usually accelerate the bonding process as well as improving the skills with which the task is to be achieved.

In the workplace, the leader can provide material evidence that the team is special and so build team spirit. This might include buying the team lunch on special occasions or cakes for the team meeting.

Susan, a manager in the National Health Service, created instant team recognition when she suggested that her team consider pink venetian blinds for their office (at the same price as the standard cream ones). Her team were delighted, felt different and special and, began to call themselves 'the pink team' which had a real impact on their team spirit.

The leader can also encourage an element of fun in working together which might include

Success is highly contagious.

wearing informal clothes one day each week or celebrating each achievement in a way that the team chooses. Encouraging the team to celebrate and learn from successes as well as failures is very healthy. Many sales departments give a whoop of joy when they achieve a telephone order and this encourages a climate of success among the rest of the team. We all want to be successful and the more each success can be celebrated, the more it will spread – success is highly contagious.

The team leader can also encourage the informal bonding that will take place in social activities. Many groups have found that socialising together creates a useful opportunity for building relationships as removing the structure of 'work' can open new possibilities for discovering new strengths and qualities about each other. You might consider spending a social weekend together with a particular focus that the group chooses. Common social activities include visiting theatres, sports events or the pub together and even taking part in charity fundraising events. The team leader can encourage these activities formally by suggesting ideas or even subsidising some of them from the team budget, but even more important will be the way in which they regard them. A team leader who only takes part in social events under sufferance or appears bored will destroy all the good efforts of bonds that they may verbally encourage in the workplace.

A good leader understands that they are responsible for the output of the team and that bonding has a real impact on this output and so allows the time for it to develop and genuinely participates to encourage its growth.

Managing a team's life cycle

The life of a team is a dynamic process that goes through different phases and the team leader needs to be aware of where their team is at any time and be prepared to meet the needs of each phase. This life cycle may be plotted on a Sigmoid curve and the stages given names to identify them:

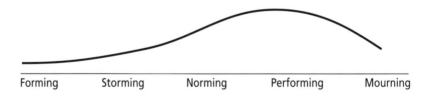

| Forming | Storming | Norming | Performing | Mourning |

The first stage in building any team is to bring a group of individuals together, decide its purpose, composition and terms of reference. The hierarchy of the team as well as individual responsibilities will be established. The members of the new team are likely to be slightly anxious as they try to get the measure of each other.

During the storming stage some conflict may appear as individuals begin to build relationships and establish their own identities. They may question many of the decisions made in the previous stage but a wise leader will help focus the energy into improvement and development rather than allow it to become negative. Well managed, this stage can be very useful and lay the foundations for a highly effective team.

Norming is when the team begins to set 'norms' for behaviour within the team. The leader needs to encourage this important stage as this is when the identity of the team is developed. How the group will operate, when they will hold their meetings, how they will behave towards each other and how they will communicate are just some of the issues that need to be resolved at this stage. Examples of 'norms' within teams include all the aspects of team spirit that we have already identified as well as working practices. This stage usually has a smooth, gently rising curve of productivity and the leader is responsible for setting the atmosphere of continual improvement through celebrating and learning from success as well as constructive debriefing of failures in order to move onto the next stage. The more thoroughly this stage is fulfilled, the higher the productivity will be in the next stage

Performing exists when the team is 'on a roll'. This can be seen in sports teams when they seem to be incapable of losing, everything is going their way and the team works for each other, smoothly and seamlessly with total confidence in their abilities. At work, this is the most productive time for any team, everything goes well, everyone is enjoying themselves and are likely to be achieving all their objectives with ease. There is comparatively little for the team leader to be doing during this stage apart from facilitating the process but they will need to keep a constant eye open for opportunities to avoid the next inevitable stage.

Mourning is the stage that follows storming unless the team leader has found an opportunity to re-start the whole cycle again. After any period of performing, a team will begin to find its output beginning to drop because the excitement of the challenge begins to fade as it becomes rather easy, complacency creeps in and it stops being fun. It is vital for the team leader to find an opportunity, a new member or perhaps a new challenge to restart the process again from the beginning rather than watch the team drop away in productivity and enthusiasm.

The task of the leader is to inject this new element into the team at a still rising stage of storming, remembering that the entire process of forming etc. has to begin again. Any new member of a team means an entirely new team; too often people try to slot new members into empty positions forgetting that a team is simply a collection of individuals and so each new individual creates an entirely different team. If this process is undertaken correctly and at the right time, it will allow the new team to begin performing at a higher level than the previous team and so allow a continually improving curve.

 As Charles Handy in his book *The Empty Raincoat* explains, there is unfortunately no guaranteed way of identifying time-scales against these phases. All you can be sure of is that each stage is occurring faster than previously. The team leader can only identify each stage by its results. The experience of consultants in asking teams where they are on the curve is enlightening – most teams see themselves further ahead in the early stages than they really are and will say they are performing even before norms have been set. At the other end of the curve, most teams will declare they are storming when their results are beginning to slip. The team leader needs to be as objective as possible and judge the results to avoid falling into the trap of wishing to be in performing and storming phases.

The team leader who can identify the stages correctly and act appropriately to fulfil the team's needs is well on their way to achieving its potential.

What can you do to enhance your teams?

_____

_____

_____

_____

_____

_____

_____

_____

_____

_____

_____

_____

_____

_____

_____

_____

_____

_____

Further reading

Build a great team! (R. Jay) Pitman Publishing

Kaizen Strategies for Winning Through People (S. Cane) Pitman Publishing

How to Lead a Winning Team (Morris, Willcocks and Knasel) Pitman Publishing

The Empty Raincoat (C. Handy) (1994) Hutchinson

Effective Teambuilding (J. Adair) (1986) Pan

Management Teams – why they succeed or fail (R. Meredith Belbin) (1992) Butterworth/Heinemann

EMPOWERMENT

Empowerment is a word that is currently on many people's lips as a desirable option and yet is used to cover all sorts of disempowering practices. Some organisations in the midst of downsizing and making redundancies have claimed to their staff that it is part of an exercise in empowerment although it is unclear why, especially to the staff to which it is proclaimed!

Empowerment means giving staff the power to do their jobs well. There are many strands to empowering staff which may include:

- giving them the authority and resources they need
- delegating as much of the task as possible
- allowing staff to set their own objectives within the department's strategy
- allowing staff to set their own standards of performance
- allowing staff to have some control over new members
- sharing the credit and learning from mistakes

Giving staff the authority and resources they need. Too often tasks are delegated to teams or individuals but without the authority that is required to complete the job effectively so that they have to return to the manager regularly in order to clear blockages, raise purchase orders, etc. When people are given the authority and therefore the responsibility for completing a task, they are likely to do it much better than if they are not trusted to manage it effectively on their own.

Always ensure that they have everything they need to do a good job – the right equipment, the right training, the right support. Asking someone to do an important job without giving them the tools they need to do it well is demotivating and you are unlikely to achieve the desired end product.

How do you know what they need? Rather than deciding for yourself, ask them. People know what they need and if you prompt them, they are likely to tell you. The people actually doing the job are in a much better position to know what they need to do it well than someone in a warm head office.

Delegating as much of the task as possible. There is an enormous difference between being asked to do simple, unrelated tasks and at least part of a whole project that you understand. There is a classic management tale of a man who walks around a corner to see people doing things with bricks. He asks three different people what they are doing 'Cementing one brick on top of another' says the first, 'Building a wall' says the second and the third replies 'I am building a cathedral'. Who do you think is liable to be doing the best job?

Allowing staff to set their own objectives. Too often 'setting agreed objectives' has meant the manager telling the individual what they are and then asking for their agreement. The more you can set out the strategy and objectives of the organisation and the department and then allow the individual to plan out what they think their objectives should be, the more likely it is that the objectives will be challenging and that the individual will strive to achieve them. Individuals are likely to set their standards, given the opportunity, much higher than you would dare to. They know best what they can achieve and trusting them will pay you dividends in the future.

Allowing staff to set their own levels of performance. Generally, levels of performance are set down in job descriptions but they are rarely how individual staff members measure how well they are doing. Most people look at the example of others, including their managers, and follow it.

One manager reported that he once worked for a boss who demanded everyone stayed in their offices until 7pm in the evening and that anyone who didn't was regarded as a 'slacker'. What happened was that the staff all stayed, but they didn't work – they chatted, filled in their crosswords, etc. – and left at the approved time but with no additional work done and no respect for the boss. 'It was really stupid' he says ' We knew we were simply playing a game and I suspect our productivity was much lower than it need have been. Because we were being treated like children, we behaved like them.'

When individuals are asked to set their own objectives and levels of performance, they are much more likely to set them high and, in addition, to be committed to achieving their own standards. For example, most managers would be likely to hope (and expect) each phone call to be answered within four rings, but ask the individual what they will commit themselves to and the research for this book proves that many will set themselves a standard of two or three (and what is more, achieve it).

A garden centre in Cheshire set up project improvement groups and one of these was given the task of setting up a security system to cut down on pilferage. This group recommended a new system of security tagging which included checking employees' bags – something the staff were happy to agree to because their representatives had made the suggestion but management would never have dared to suggest for fear of a backlash.

The moral seems to be that the more you trust people and treat them as responsible, the more they will respond.

Keith, a manager with 22 years' experience in the Marine Service, Portsmouth (MoD) was given the opportunity to transform a very professional group of service personnel into a well-organised, motivated, communicative team able to respond to a more customer-led market. After a long discussion with the staff, it was decided to follow a step-by-step approach:

- develop the team
- open communication

- introduce empowerment
- become customer focused
- continuous development/improvement process
- review and monitor changes

In this case, the empowerment process involved identifying areas of work that could be undertaken and monitored by the staff more effectively than from the office. After further discussions with the staff, the authority and support required to undertake such tasks was given, along with a guideline of requirements.

Eighteen months later absenteeism is at an all time low, productivity is up to a level that the monthly survey reports over a year show a cumulative increase in satisfaction levels of the ten CSF (Critical Success Factors) to 86.33 per cent. The internal staff surveys show a cumulative total of 84.11 per cent of satisfaction on how management and staff work together.

Allowing staff to have some control over new members. Any team that has been a success is likely to resist any changes, whether it be to replace someone who has left or to expand its membership. Wherever possible include them in creating the job description, ideal profile and even include them in the interviewing process. Try and encourage them to find someone who will add to the team rather than being a clone, but help them to find someone they can include easily. It will pay enormous dividends rather than choosing someone you like and trying to impose them – you may destroy all the good work you have done to build team spirit.

Sharing the credit. A manager who delegates the work but takes all the credit is unlikely to have a department working to its full potential. A manager, however, who passes on the good news that senior management have noticed and acknowledged an individual achievement is much more likely to have highly motivated people. The manager, however, who ensures that the senior manager knows exactly who was responsible for the achievement is liable to gain hero status for life.

Sheila remembers as a junior member of staff that she was responsible for attending meetings between her boss and clients in order to take notes. After one particularly difficult meeting when neither side seemed to be able to agree on a particular project, she offered a possible solution on the journey back. 'Write it up' he said. The next morning, he read her proposal, changed a few phrases only and sent it to the client with a covering note explaining who had come up with the idea. He became a mentor to her and encouraged her to build her career. She claims she would have gone to the moon for him if required.

Learning from mistakes. Of course empowerment can be a high-risk strategy and mistakes are likely to occur along the way. It is important to remember that mistakes happen in any situation.

If employees are trying their best, there are likely to be fewer but when one does occur, it is likely to cause distress for the individual concerned and quite possibly disempower them unless it is treated with care. All managers should encourage their staff to own up to mistakes as soon as they identify them (partly by doing so themselves). Mistakes should never be unnecessarily castigated. Discuss immediately what can be done to rectify them and once things are back under control, debrief in order to learn from the problem. No one wants to encourage mistakes but it is important to remember that sadly most of our learning comes through getting things wrong, and that therefore we should welcome all learning opportunities while minimising their impact.

How can you empower your staff?

_____

_____

_____

_____

_____

Further reading

(All the books recommended in the section on teams)

Empowering People (M. Stewart) Pitman Publishing

Getting the Best Out of Yourself and Others (B. Rodgers and I. Levey) Fontana

MOTIVATION

Motivation might be defined as the providing of incentives to encourage effective performance and any manager needs to be able to motivate their staff and to understand how to do so effectively in order to be successful. It is helpful to consider your own motivators before moving on to what might motivate your staff.

What motivates you? Consider the last occasion you were motivated ('raring to go') and see if you can identify some of the reasons. Then consider the last time you were demotivated ('turned off') and see if you can identify some of the causes.

My motivators   **My demotivators**

_____   _____

_____   _____

_____   _____

_____   _____

_____   _____

There has been more research published and more theories advanced about motivation than about any other aspect of managing people so this chapter will open with some of the better known theories. The best way to assess them is to consider them from your own personal viewpoint. Are they relevant to you? Can you see where you fit in in each of them?

Douglas McGregor: Theory X and Theory Y

In the past motivation was often seen as a 'carrot and stick' principle; offer staff a reward and if that doesn't work then use discipline.

The best known theorist of this approach was Douglas McGregor (*The Human Side of Enterprise*, 1987, Penguin), who suggested that managers using the carrot and stick approach held a set of propositions he called Theory X:

- the average worker does as little as possible
- lacks ambition, dislikes responsibility and prefers to be led
- is inherently self-centred, indifferent to organisational needs
- is by nature resistant to change
- is gullible and not very bright

He commented that workers treated as if they fitted Theory X were unlikely to perform effectively and he suggested that a new set of propositions should be considered. He called these Theory Y:

- people enjoy work as naturally as they enjoy play
- most people are capable of exercising self-control and self-discipline if they are motivated to achieve a target
- the average person will not only accept but will actively seek responsibility
- many people have the imagination, ingenuity and creativity to help solve problems in an organisation
- the capacity of the average worker is only partially utilised

What do you think? Have you ever worked for a 'Theory X' manager? How did you feel?

_____

_____

_____

_____

_____

Maslow's hierarchy of human needs

Abraham Maslow worked in the USA in the 1950s and 60s and concluded that we are driven by our inner needs which form a series of steps and that people need to satisfy each before they can move onto the next one (*Motivation and Personality*, Harper Row).

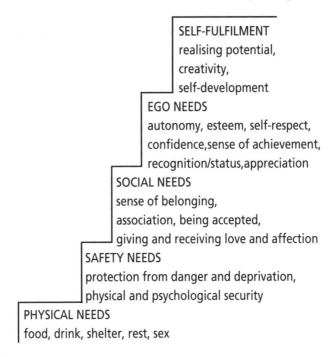

SELF-FULFILMENT
realising potential,
creativity,
self-development

EGO NEEDS
autonomy, esteem, self-respect,
confidence,sense of achievement,
recognition/status,appreciation

SOCIAL NEEDS
sense of belonging,
association, being accepted,
giving and receiving love and affection

SAFETY NEEDS
protection from danger and deprivation,
physical and psychological security

PHYSICAL NEEDS
food, drink, shelter, rest, sex

There are obviously exceptions to any rule and the artist starving in the garret is a good example of someone striving for self-expression while not having achieved all the steps Maslow quotes. What is interesting about this hierarchy is that people do not necessarily move in a continuous movement upwards. You may be in the ego stage at work looking for status and recognition when your home is burgled and you find yourself back in the second step re-establishing your security before you can consider your status needs again.

Maslow was working in the USA 40 years ago and whether his work still has any relevance to the current conditions is for you to decide. However, it is interesting to note that in the 1980s (perhaps one of the most materialistic decades) that many of the young high-earners in the City openly admitted to being motivated in the short term by money and status but, when questioned further, had plans to retire before the age of 40 to live in the country, start a family or do something completely different.

How do you relate to this hierarchy of human needs? Can you identify any unfulfilled needs in your life? What can you do to achieve them?

_____

_____

_____

_____

_____

Hertzberg's work needs

Frederick Hertzberg researched thousands of workers in the USA before publishing his results (_Work and the Nature of Man_, 1974, Granada Publishing). He identified the following true motivators as contributing to high morale and job satisfaction:

- achievement
- recognition
- responsibility
- promotion prospects
- nature of the job

as well as the below list of 'hygiene' factors whose absence or inadequacy in a job produces poor performance and dissatisfaction:

- head office policy
- pay
- type of management
- working conditions
- relations with colleagues
- fringe benefits

Hertzberg's research led him to the conclusion that the 'hygiene' factors were rarely high motivators. People tend to take fringe benefits and good working conditions for granted, but when they were removed (in a cost-cutting exercise, for example, or because they were inadequate) they had a highly demotivating effect. A salary increase had a short-term motivating effect when it was felt to be deserved but rarely did the effect last very long, while what was felt to be an unfair salary was a long-lasting demotivator.

How do you feel about this list? Do you relate to it? Does it help you understand your motivators/demotivators?

_____

_____

_____

_____

_____

McClelland's Motivation Model

David McClelland identified three types of people and suggests that each of us has a major motivational factor that fits into one of the following three types (*Human Motivation*, Cambridge University Press, 1988):

- **Achievement motivated:** desire for excellence, likes doing a good job, wants a sense of accomplishment, wants to advance in career, needs feedback.

- **Authority motivated:** likes to lead, to give advice, wants prestige and job status,enjoys influencing people and activities, likes his/her ideas to   predominate.

- **Affiliation motivated:** likes to be popular and well thought of, desires friendly relationships, interaction, dislikes being alone (at work or socially), likes to help other people, team player.

Do you agree? Which type are you primarily?

_____

_____

_____

_____

_____

Jacques' psychological equitability

Elliott Jacques' work draws a relationship between age, the capacity of the individual and their rewards (*Equitable Payment*, Wiley, 1961). He recognises that some are high-flyers who might burn themselves out in their middle age and some are steady, reliable performers who may not achieve such a high level of capacity but produce steadier levels. He also acknowledges that growth in capacity tends to be high in the early part of one's career and falls off as we approach retirement. He states that when capacity, what is expected of the worker and their rewards match, there is high motivation but when one is asked to produce either more or less than one's capacity or the salary doesn't match the task, then demotivation exists.

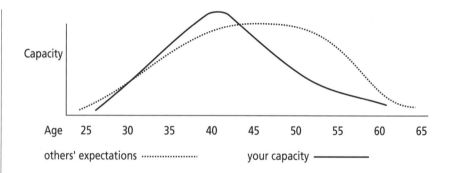

Although the capacity curve looks smooth, it is important to recognise that of course it does vary considerably over the short term. Illness, grief or any form of stress will reduce the capacity in the short term while a return to work after a holiday or a welcomed task or achievement may raise it considerably.

Can you recognise periods in your life when the capacity expected of you was incompatible with your expectations? How did you feel about it at the time?

_____

_____

_____

_____

_____

_____

_____

_____

Motivating other people

Robert Tannenbaum and Warren Schmidt identified a link between the way a leader uses authority and makes decisions, and the likely outcome of the behaviour of the group ('How to Choose a Leadership Pattern', _Harvard Business Review_, May/June 1973).

Tannenbaum and Schmidt's leader behaviour continuum

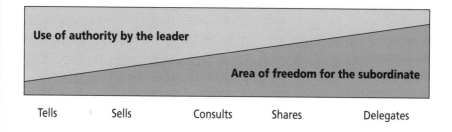

Tells   Sells   Consults   Shares   Delegates

It is interesting to note that even at either edge of the continuum, neither side completely gives up their power or authority. The manager will still be held accountable for the results of any delegation and subordinates always have the power to refuse to do what a managers tells them to.

Further discussion and research led to a conclusion that management styles at either edge of the continuum led to very different behaviours.

PUSH STYLE:
- works best with authority
- is high risk
- gets low commitment
- is win/lose
- needs enforcement
- is most effective in the short term

PULL STYLE:
- works without authority
- is low risk
- gets high commitment
- is win/win
- is self-enforcing
- is most effective in the long term

Neither style is 'wrong', the push style is highly effective in a crisis when a firm decision may need to be made swiftly without time for discussion while the pull style has obvious benefits when time is more flexible.

Which end of the continuum do you tend to operate from?

_____

_____

_____

_____

_____

Would it help to be able to operate equally well across the spectrum?

_____

_____

_____

_____

_____

How could you learn to do that?

_____

_____

_____

_____

_____

Motivating individuals

How can you motivate individuals? The first step is to get to know them well enough to discover what motivates them. Obviously motivation is an intensely personal thing; there are certain underlying principles, but it is generally the degree to which it is applied that varies from person to person. Providing a challenge to a team may result in one person being bored because it is too easy for them, another being terrified because it seems too difficult to achieve for them and it being just right for the rest.

How can you get it right for each person? Ask them. Don't assume that you know them well enough to be able to guess. Don't assume that because you have discovered what is right for you that it will be the same for everyone else. **Ask, don't assume**.

Remember that motivation is a dynamic process and may change over a period of time. Debriefing helps to discover how you might be able to motivate them more effectively. **The key question is 'How can I help you more?'**

The general guidelines are:

Fill staff in on the bigger picture: help them understand the task, the reason for it and its value. Arrange visits to other parts of the organisation and to customers wherever possible. Don't just do this in an induction process but as often as possible. The more people understand just what it is they are doing and why, the more likely it is that they will do their task as well as they can.

Set clear and achievable targets: make sure that they are clear about what it is they have to do and that they believe it is possible. Set targets together so that you are confident that they really are agreed and understood rather than being imposed. Make sure that there are measurable steps built in so that both you and they can regularly review whether progress is on target.

Involve people: let people know what is going on in the organisation. Where possible, talk to the team together. Giving important information to one person to pass around implies something that you may not be aware of – is one person more important than the rest? Always tell your team the truth (even if this means that you can only tell them part of the story). Once they know you have lied to them, they will never believe you again. Cut out the office grapevine wherever possible; it is generally highly distorted. Even bad news is better coming truthfully from the manager than rumours that cause worry and distress for months – the truth is nearly always better than rumour. Encourage the making of suggestions, offering of ideas and help in solving problems; they probably have more to offer you than you could dream of.

Build a supportive relationship within the team: resist showing favouritism where possible. Encourage each to ask advice from the other before coming to you. Encourage everyone to help out in a crisis. You might show the lead here by rolling up your sleeves and doing your bit as well. Discourage any 'not my job' syndrome. It may be worth considering team pay rises based on the achievements of the whole team rather than individual contributions.

Train the team together: group training sessions will help build team spirit as well as building understanding about the task.

Encourage flexibility of roles: the more everyone understands about each other's tasks, the more the team is likely to benefit and any leadership role can be rotated regularly so that everyone gets a chance to develop these skills.

Be positive. Remember to give praise and acknowledgement when it is appropriate. Build on successes and always look for a positive viewpoint. Encourage the team to do the same. Celebrate successes and learn from them at least as much as failures.

How can you motivate your team more? How can you find out what motivates each member?

_____

_____

_____

_____

_____

_____

Further reading

The Human Side of Enterprise (D. McGregor) (1987) Penguin

Motivation and Personality (A. Maslow) Harper Row

Work and the Nature of Man (F. Hertzberg) (1974) Granda Publishing

Human Motivation (D. McClelland) (1988) Cambridge University Press

Equitable Payment (E. Jacques) (1961) Wiley

'How to Choose a Leadership Pattern', *Harvard Business Review* (May/June 1973)

Build a Great Team (R. Jay) Pitman Publishing

How to Lead a Winning Team (Morris/Willcocks/Knasel) Pitman Publishing

Management and Motivation (various) (1985) Penguin

Any management book will contain a section on motivation, one highly recommended for theory is *Management and Organisational Behaviour* (L. J. Mullins) (1996) Pitman Publishing

DELEGATION

Yes/No/Sometimes

Do you take work home regularly? *Y/N/S*

Do you work longer hours than your subordinates? *Y/N/S*

Do you spend time doing what they could be doing themselves? *Y/N/S*

When you return from absence, is your In-tray overflowing? *Y/N/S*

Are you still doing tasks that you did before your promotion? *Y/N/S*

Are you interrupted with queries on ongoing projects? *Y/N/S*

Do you spend time on routine matters that others could do? *Y/N/S*

Do you like to keep a finger in every pie? *Y/N/S*

Do you rush to meet deadlines? *Y/N/S*

Are you unable to keep on top of priorities? *Y/N/S*

Give yourself one point for each yes answer and half a point for each sometimes answer and add them up. Points =_____

Two or less points indicates that you will probably only need to
read this chapter to help others around you. Three to five points
indicates that you would benefit from delegation and should give it
some serious consideration. If you have scored more than five
points, you don't need this book to tell you that you are trying to do
too much and unless you can begin to prioritise better and delegate
more, you are unlikely to achieve your objectives.

Delegation does not mean abdicating your responsibilities. It is
about achieving results, by empowering and motivating others to
carry out tasks, for which you are ultimately accountable, to a spec-
ified level of performance.

Do you have an opportunity to delegate more? For any specific task,
ask yourself:

- Is there someone who can do the task as well or better than you can? Are you really benefiting from the expertise of your staff?
- Is there someone who, while doing the task slightly differently from you or in slightly more time, can still achieve an acceptable level of performance?
- Is there someone who is paid less than you, who can do the task satisfactorily, thus lowering the cost?
- If you can't do the task until tomorrow, is there someone who can do it today?
- Is there someone who would benefit from doing the task, in terms of their personal development?

If you answer 'yes' to any of these questions, you have an opportunity for delegation.

Guidelines for effective delegation:
- choose the right person
- think ahead
- delegate whole tasks
- specify expected outcomes
- take your time
- delegate the good and the bad
- delegate, then trust

Choose the right person. This is crucial to the successful accomplishment of the task. It helps if they want to do the task so think back to the most recent appraisals to find a suitable candidate. The person you think most suitable may have a full work load, so you will need to re-plan and re-prioritise their current tasks. Are you delegating fairly across the team?

Think ahead. Any action, including delegation, has consequences so think it through carefully. Ideally the consequences will all be positive but you need to have considered them carefully. What will you do with your additional time? Is it possible that other, important, tasks will be overlooked if this member of staff takes over the delegated task? Delegation involves forming a contract with your subordinate so it is worth planning in advance:

- nature and scope of task involved
- results to be achieved
- methods to be used to assess performance
- time-scale involved
- nature and extent of authority required for task completion

Delegate whole tasks. This refers back to the motivation and empowerment section; a whole task, or at least a genuine understanding of how what you are doing fits into the whole objective, is much more satisfying to achieve.

Specify expected outcomes. This is where you set out the contract you have already planned and ask for their comments and input. Wherever possible you should aim to be flexible and incorporate their requests because if they feel the task is impossible in the way you have planned it, they will be unlikely to do a good job. This conversation links into the next.

Take your time. Don't rush the process. Delegation is a short-term investment of time for a longer term gain and often involves an element of negotiation. 'This is what I want you to do, how and when I want you to do it. What can I do to make it a satisfying and developmental process for you?' This is the time when you may want to involve your coaching skills (*see page 362*).

Delegate the good and the bad. In researching this book, one senior manager in the oil industry said, (only partly in jest) 'Oh I know about delegation. It's when you dump all the worst bits of your job to someone who can't say no, leaving you free to get on with the bits you like.' Sadly this is often our experience. It is possible that what you don't enjoy, someone else in the team will. That is why teams are made up of different sort of people and skills, but you will earn little respect if you are seen as always getting rid of the rotten jobs to subordinates. If you want to be a successful delegator who achieves high-quality results from your subordinates and develops them for future advancement in their careers, then you need to balance the good with the bad. Delegating a good job (with, perhaps, possibilities for recognition from senior management) will earn you respect and a growing reputation as someone it is good to work for as well as building your confidence in the ability of your team.

Delegate, then trust. If you have agreed measurable steps along the way of the completion of the task and agreed review sessions that you are both happy with, then there should be no need to breathe down the subordinate's neck or worry about whether they are going to let you down. If you are worrying, perhaps you did not choose the right person to delegate it to, but certainly the more you continually check or interfere, the less likely it is that the subordinate will do a good job. Think about how you would feel if a senior manager treated you as if they couldn't trust you to do a good job. If you would much prefer to agree review sessions and then be trusted to get on with it, then learn from the experience and do it to others. Motivation often contains an element of 'Do as you would be done by'. All the above guidelines are likely to lead to tasks being effectively delegated to subordinates, but still it is possible that you might run into difficulties. What are they and how can you overcome them?

Subordinates may put up barriers such as:

- 'I lack the experience or competence'.
- 'I have a work overload'.
- Avoidance of responsibility

All of these may be genuine in which case you can take action to resolve the problem, or simply may be excuses to avoid additional work. Some staff may genuinely not want to advance further in their career and continue in their present role which, if it is satisfactory, is their choice, but it may indicate a lack of confidence or even motivation. The way to discover the truth is to use the counselling skills (*see page 353*) to uncover the real problem before coming to a conclusion. Once the problem is clear, you may well be able to arrange training, reset priorities or arrange some coaching sessions.

Your own resistance to delegation may include:

- ' I like doing it myself'.
- 'I can do it better than anyone else.'
- ' I can't explain what I want.'
- 'I don't want to develop competition from my subordinates.'
- 'I can't take the risk of mistakes.'
- 'I don't trust them to do it properly.'

Many of these are linked to the issue of whether you are committed to be an empowering manager. Of course some mistakes may occur. They probably would if you were doing it too, but what can you do to minimise the risks? Training, regular reviews and clarifying of what is required and the quality of the final result should assist in minimising the risk of mistakes. Certainly the more you show that you trust them to do a good job, the chances are that they will achieve it. **The more you trust people, the more likely it is that they will prove to be trustworthy**. The resulting competition from developing your staff should be seen in the context of freeing you to develop yourself for the next step in your career path. If it is an issue of having to let go of something you particularly enjoy about your job, see if you can find another, equally satisfying, task that will lead to your own development.

Barriers within your organisation. There may be reservations from senior staff and within the culture of an organisation about delegating and developing junior staff including:

- **bosses won't tolerate mistakes**
- **no one to delegate to (lack of staff)**
- **unclear lines of authority and responsibility**
- **everything is too urgent – no time to plan**

If your bosses won't tolerate any mistakes, you probably need to have a conversation with them about human nature! However, of course no senior manager wants poor quality products/documents/services endangering the relationship with customers or consumers. What can you do to ensure that learning and development is balanced with the need for total quality? You can ensure that every individual has what they need to do a first-class job, including resources, time, training, support and, where appropriate, advice. Before delegating ensure that there is time for the person to prepare for the task as well as time for you to give a proper brief.

If everything in your organisation has to be done in a panic then you might want to consider whether you could coach them in time management techniques so that there is time to do things better in the future. Sometimes there is an attraction to crisis-management because it seems exciting. See if you can engineer a change in culture so that the future becomes exciting enough to replace the short-term crisis buzz. An organisation that has a clear strategy and knows where it is going is rarely sucked into the 'fire-fighting' mentality.

If there is a confusion about responsibility and authority, clear it up. Ask your manager exactly where the lines lie. Explain why you need to know – so that you can help them by achieving more. Always tell them what the benefits for them will be.

If you have no one to delegate to, start to keep a log of what tasks you are doing and how long you spend on each one. After a month or so, you ought to have a list that will contain many examples of tasks that are not very important or at least of limited value to the organisation and that are taking a considerable amount of your highly paid time. Research what it would cost to employ a junior member of staff and correlate the two. Meet your boss and put forward the proposition 'This is what it would cost to employ a junior who could free up x hours of my time in which I could support you better by ...' and sell them on the benefits. If there is a ban on employing new staff, you may be able to negotiate at least a temporary solution IF you can sell them on the benefits.

Delegation is a powerful tool for a successful manager; it:

- creates additional time for you to take on more satisfying work
- develops your staff to perform even better
- builds your reputation for getting things done
- attracts bright people to work for you
- is highly economical

Who could you additionally delegate to:

_____

_____

_____

_____

What tasks could you reasonably consider delegating?

_____

_____

_____

_____

How much time would this create and how will you use it constructively?

_____

_____

_____

_____

 Further reading

Most management books contain sections on delegation; try

Management and Organisational Behaviour (L. J. Mullins) 1996 Pitman Publishing

COACHING AND COUNSELLING SKILLS

Is it difficult to find out what a subordinate's problem really is?	*Yes/No*
Do you wish it were easier to teach people things?	*Yes/No*
Do you wish subordinates would solve their own problems?	*Yes/No*
Do you wish subordinates would answer their own questions?	*Yes/No*
Do you want to be an empowering manager?	*Yes/No*

Coaching and counselling are widely used terms within organisations but with their functions and boundaries very often misunderstood. For the purposes of this book, we will be only considering their work-related functions and uses.

Coaching skills are used to help a subordinate with work-related difficulties or to learn new skills and techniques, while counselling skills for managers are used to help you to discover what might be troubling the person and what prevents them from fulfilling their functions effectively.

This chapter will cover:
- clarification of counselling skills for managers
- what the appropriate uses of counselling at work are
- examples of how they might be used
- clarification of coaching skills
- appropriate uses of coaching skills at work
- examples of how to use them

Counselling skills for managers

It is surprisingly common at work for staff to present you with an excuse that actually isn't the whole truth (what is known in jargon as a 'presenting' problem). Examples include:

- 'I hate this computer' when they actually have a phobia about all technology.
- 'I want to leave because I can't manage the commuting' when they really dislike working for you.
- 'I'm ill – I've got flu' when they have a personal crisis at home.
- 'I'm late because the train was delayed' when they are unhappy with their job.

Too often the easy solution (such as computer training) doesn't solve the problem and their level of performance doesn't improve. One way you, as a manager, can help them be effective at work is by uncovering the real problem by using counselling skills.

There has been a huge upsurge in the popularity of counselling and many managers, not really understanding what it involves, have seen it as part of their job to attempt to solve subordinates' personal problems. It is NOT part of a manager's job to become involved in the lives or personal problems of their staff. If a working definition of management is to achieve results through people then it is the results that the manager is primarily concerned with and however much you care about your staff, it is simply not appropriate (either as a manager or as an untrained counsellor) to attempt to solve any personal difficulties.

Your staff's personal lives should concern you only in as much as their problems/difficulties interfere with their work. By using counselling skills appropriately you will almost certainly be able to get a clearer idea of what is going on for them. Then it may be appropriate to suggest that they seek professional help (you might even allow them time off work to gain this help) so long as you link it to their working effectiveness.

It is not appropriate to:

- force someone to undertake/receive professional help
- tell people what to do about their marriage/drinking/grief, etc.
- tell them to pull their socks up

Counselling skills: involve all the skills of effective communication with some additional questioning and listening techniques. The purpose of counselling could be described as to hold up a 'mirror' to the individual so that they can begin to see themselves more clearly. The focus should be almost totally on the other person and your part is to listen, to clarify and to encourage the individual to expand, rarely saying what you think, feel or believe and then only if appropriate.

The first requirement for the effective use of counselling skills is that you regard the individual concerned with **respect and empathy**. If you feel that you cannot do this, you might want to enrol the help of an appropriate outside person such as a member of the personnel department. There is no way you can fake empathy or respect so don't even try. If you don't have respect for them and/or don't particularly want to enable them to perform more effectively, you won't achieve the necessary openness from them – no matter how well-honed your counselling skills are.

The second requirement for the effective use of counselling skills is that of **boundaries of confidentiality**. If the individual suspects you might leave the office and tell everyone what you have heard, they are unlikely to be open with you, so explain your confidentiality boundaries at the beginning of the meeting. If you wish or feel the need to change them after hearing what they have to say, ask their permission, explain why and get their agreement. For example, if you discover an alcohol dependency which is a danger to clients, staff or the work of the department, you may need to report it and also help the individual find professional help. This may involve personnel who can recommend them to an organisation-sponsored programme. If you cannot get their agreement to internal assistance, you might recommend an external programme. Explain 'I would like to be able to help you because I need you to be able to regain the level of performance that you were previously reaching. Is there anything else I can do to help this happen?'

Questions: counselling involves the careful use of questions to keep the conversation on target and to encourage the individual to expand on the topic. All questions should be open, so that it is not possible to answer with simply a positive or a negative and should be phrased to encourage additional input, for example 'What happened next?' 'Tell me what you think the problem is?' 'How did you feel about …?'

Another very effective question technique is to repeat what the individual has just said in the form of a question (sometimes referred to as 'reflecting') to show that you are listening and to encourage them to clarify and expand on what they have said. For example:

- … and I was furious with them (followed by silence)
- *You were furious with them?*
- Yes, I was. I felt that they had …

It is terribly important to reflect back exactly the words they have used. Any change in wording here is likely to indicate that you haven't really been listening and, particularly if it is an emotion being discussed, really annoy the individual because you are changing what they are trying to communicate.

Listening is absolutely crucial to using counselling skills to discover the real problem in a situation. The elements of effective listening are worth repeating:

Look interested
Inquire with questions
Stay on target
Test understanding
Evaluate the message
Neutralise your feelings

Staying on target is crucial in uncovering the real problem as the individual is very likely to do all they can to avoid it. **Testing understanding** (paraphrasing and clarifying) are vital aids to making sure that you have understood clearly what they are telling you and **evaluating the message** (assessing the body language and tone of voice) will help you assess whether they are telling you the whole story and how they feel about it. But perhaps the most important quality of listening that a good manager using counselling skills needs to be aware of is **neutralising your own feelings**. Remind yourself that this is about them and not you, keep calm, keep your voice level and avoid reacting emotionally to anything they tell you. If you do react emotionally (perhaps because they tell you how they really feel about you or even because their problem is one that you share, for example: grief over the death of close friend) you may need to wrap up the session as carefully as possible explaining why you feel you are not the right person for them to be talking to at this time and asking them if they would like to talk to someone less involved within the organisation or a professional counsellor.

The following is a scenario with comments about what is happening to illustrate the process:

Hello David. Come in and sit down.'

'So we need to talk about this morning.'

'Mmm.'

'I'm really sorry, it's a real mess. I don't know what I am going to do about it though.'

'No, well I think we have to talk about it but I would prefer to do that this afternoon. Maybe we can arrange a time for later (**setting the scene and the boundaries**). What I'd really like to talk about now is you.'

'Me?'

'Mm, yes. I'm concerned about you. As you know I'm really pleased with your work and, as we discussed at your appraisal, I was hoping to put you up for promotion soon – everything you have been doing has been going really well but I have noticed in the past few weeks that you have been making a lot of mistakes – which is very unlike you. I have also noticed that you used to be in before me in the mornings and that recently you have been coming in quite a bit later. It seems to me that you are not really yourself at the moment and I am wondering if there is something that's distressing you or worrying you at the moment or just something that's not quite right.' (**reassuring and giving observations**)

'Yes, well, I'm looking after the children at the moment and I have to take John to school as usual but also take Caroline to her playgroup which starts later and is a bit out of my way – so that makes me late.'

'Ah, so you're looking after the children and you have to take Caroline to her playgroup and that's why you've been coming in later. Right.' (**reflecting**)

'Yes, it's because Pat's away.'

'Ah and how long has she been away for?' (**open question**)

'Er, exactly two weeks today.'

'So she's been away exactly two weeks today. When are you expecting her back?' (**reflecting and open question**)

'I really don't know. She's gone off with a neighbour a couple of doors down ...' (**lowering of voice and pace**)

'Oh, I see, so she's gone off with someone.' (**match his tone and pace. Silence – he fills it**)

'Mmm so it makes it pretty difficult you know to ...'

'Yes, I can see that it must be very difficult for you. (**reflecting and responding**)

'Anyway you know it's ... I get the kids organised in the morning and although I'm getting in a bit later I have been cracking on and trying to catch up at lunchtimes and things.' (**trying to make light of it**)

'Yes, I can see that you're working really hard but I'm very concerned about you. Now I can see why you haven't been yourself, it all makes sense. So it seems to me that you've got a really big problem at home at the moment.' (**reassurance and bringing him back to the issue**)

'Yes, I really don't know what to do about it. My mother might be able to help a bit but not for very long as Dad isn't too good.'

'Mm so in the short-term your mother might be able to help.' (**reflecting and clarifying**)

'Mm.' (**seems reluctant to move on**)

'What about the longer term? (**open question and moving on**)

'Well, I hope there isn't one.' (**non-specific**)

'So at the moment you are hoping Pat will come back.' (**putting it into words for him – clarifying**)

'Yes, I mean, we are talking.' (**he picks it up and moves on**)

'Mm, you're talking.' (**reflecting**)

'But its not very hopeful and the kids are very upset, they don't understand it, I don't either.'

'So you don't understand it, the kids don't understand it and they're upset. You are upset too? (**he hasn't mentioned his feelings**)

'Yes and then this mess with the client – it really is the last straw, I don't know what to do ...' (**pause, he fills it**) *'I really need some space to sort things out.'*

'So you really don't know what to do and you need some space.' (**reflecting and responding**) 'Could I help you in any way?'

'Well, I was going to ask you for some time off before this mess up.'

'Ah, I think that sounds like a really good idea to have some time off to sort out a few things at home.' (**summarising**). 'How much time do you think you would need?' (**open question**)

'Well, three, four, a week. A week I should think.'

'A week, OK, that sounds very reasonable. Do you think next week would be a good idea?' (**moving him on, focusing, closed question to encourage him to make the decision**)

'The session ends with arranging hand-overs of work, what he will tell the other staff, confidentiality and agreeing a follow-up meeting when he returns to work, arranging a debrief of the morning's problem (back to work issues) and looking forward to a resolving of the personal difficulties so that he can return to working at his previously high performance.

GUIDELINES FOR USING COUNSELLING SKILLS AT WORK

- Remember that your first objective is always to help the individual improve their level of performance.
- Use counselling skills to help uncover the real problem.
- Use counselling skills to help the individual take steps to solve their problem – don't try and solve it for them.
- Always begin with respect and empathy.
- Set confidentiality boundaries.
- Beware of the iceberg effect – it may be that the problem is a great deal bigger and more complicated than it first looks. Think carefully before taking the plunge.

How could you benefit from developing your counselling skills?

_____

_____

_____

_____

Further reading

There are a great many books on counselling but a good one for managers is *Counselling People at Work* (R. de Board) Gower

Coaching for managers

Coaching is an integral part of a good manager's toolkit of skills. Its purpose is:

- **to improve performance**
- **to teach new skills**
- **long-term development**

A definition of coaching might be:

A manager systematically improving the ability, experience and effective-ness of their staff/team on a one-to-one or small group basis, by providing planned, supervised tasks/projects with appraisal and advice. All this with the agreement of the individual and taking place at or in the workplace, during working hours, informally and as a continuing process.

Teaching new skills has often been seen as a process in which the subordinate is either sent on a training programme or told by another how to do the task. However, research undertaken with both IBM and the British Post Office shows a group of staff separated into three groups who were taught in very different ways and their recall measured after the event.

	Told	Told and shown	Told, shown and experienced
Recall after three weeks	70%	72%	85%
Recall after three months	10%	32%	65%

Obviously you will want your staff to be in the highest recall category and coaching can provide you with the skills to allow your staff to learn new skills in the most effective way possible.

It is worth remembering that there are three main ways that people learn:

- being taught
- joint exploration, a mixture of teaching and learning from experience
- self-learning or learning from experience

Being taught is perhaps the one we most regularly experience and are most likely to offer subordinates. It has many advantages in terms of time, clarity about what is required and confidence by the teacher that they know what they are doing. Its downside is likely to be that recall, understanding and motivation may be limited because there has been little involvement by the learner.

Joint exploration is one that is growing in popularity. It is part of the mentoring or job-shadowing process. A new member of staff (or new to the task) will be assigned an experienced person who will explain the process, demonstrate and then suggest that the learner try it for themselves. Notes may be taken and questions may be asked before the learner tries it out for themselves. This is widely popular in all organisations. It utilises the skills of experienced members of staff and is a good compromise between the two more radical options.

Learning from experience can be a high-risk/high-reward strategy and is ideally suited to those of a 'when all else fails, read the instructions' mentality. It is essential to limit any risks such as too high a wastage of materials in the learning process or damage to equipment or software! Its benefits are that once mastered, the skill is unlikely ever to be forgotten. The coach, in preparing for a session with a subordinate on a new skill, should consider which mode they prefer to operate and, even more important, remember to ask the subordinate which way they prefer to learn. Because the objective of the session is that the subordinate learns the new skill as easily as possible, it is more important that the session works for them than proves easy for the coach.

Coaching skills

'An expert coach does not tell, he questions; he does not give orders, he explains and listens carefully to other views; to him prejudgement is anathema; he is willing and able to change his mind in the light of new facts, however inconvenient they may be – he has little use for snap judgements or hasty decisions on important issues. Above all, he is relaxed and patient.'

Coaching involves all the communication skills with particular emphasis on:

- listening skills – especially empathy
- asking open questions
- paraphrasing
- responding – using 'I' statements
- clarifying
- summarising

GUIDELINES FOR COACHING
- agree the purpose of the session, its aims and objectives
- decide on the best learning approach (tell, tell and show, tell, show and experience) – ask them
- coach
- ask how they feel as often as what they think
- agree the action
- set a time for reviewing
- check that they are comfortable and confident

Coaching may be formal or informal. Informal coaching is rarely planned but the manager needs to be aware of every opportunity to help his/her staff learn and experience as much as possible for themselves. Informal coaching may take a little longer to achieve a result than simply telling the subordinate the answer or telling them exactly how to do the task. The purpose of coaching is, after all, to aim for a satisfactory result rather than to control exactly how to achieve it. Rarely will the constant improvement of results be achieved, though, by always following the same procedure; improvement in quality or productivity often requires a change in the way the task is achieved and often the person who is actually doing the task is the best person to judge what improvements are required.

An example of informal coaching:

'*Excuse me, have you got a minute?*'

'Yes, of course. What can I do for you?'

'*I've had a call from Perkins and I am not sure what to do about it.*'

'What is the problem?'

'*They supply most of the parts for the Brown fixed-price contract and because the costs of their raw materials have unexpectedly increased, they intend to raise their prices to us by 5 per cent as of today.*'

'Yes, I can see that it is a problem. What do you think the options are?'

'*Well, ... we could absorb the cost, we could try and find another supplier or we could try and renegotiate with Browns. I think those are the only options there are.*'

'OK. Can you take me through the likely implications of each of these options?'

'*Well, if we absorb the increased costs, we would be making reduced profits on the contract but we would be keeping Browns happy. Trying to find another supplier might take us quite a long time and there would be a risk about quality standards, but trying to renegotiate with Browns might upset them and possibly result in us losing future business.*'

'Hmm. How long before the Browns contract is due for review?'

'*I checked that, it's three months.*'

'Given that the raw materials have increased in price, what would be the best possible outcome from your point of view?'

'*Well, that Perkins absorb the costs until we renegotiate, at which time we could try and include a clause that includes a contingency for these unexpected difficulties.*'

'Do you think that might be possible?'

'Well, yes, I suppose it is. I hadn't thought of that. I was so surprised by the call that I didn't think.'

'Well that sounds like a really good idea, would you be the right person to go and see them?'

'Yes, I'm happy to do that. I'll call them and arrange to go over this after-noon.'

'I wonder if it might be a good idea to begin to cover a fall-back position. What do you think we should explore in case that doesn't succeed?'

'You're right. Maybe a fall back position with Perkins might be to consider sharing the increased costs with them – but I will put John onto ringing round other suppliers to begin to explore what our options are in that area as a safeguard.'

'OK, good. Can you come back first thing tomorrow and let me know what is happening?'

'Yes, of course. Thanks a lot. OK.'

We can see that by remaining calm and asking a lot of open questions to encourage the subordinate to think for themselves, the manager has created an atmosphere where the subordinate has begun to solve the problem for themselves. The manager, by being fully aware of the situation and supportive of the proposed action, has not abdicated his/her responsibility, but is building confidence in the subordinate to create possible solutions to the problem.

Formal coaching, whether the delegation of a task or the improvement in performance of a current one, allows time for preparation which should include the following:

- objective and fall back position
- state what you want them to do and why
- encourage them to respond with agreement or concern (using open questions such as 'How do you feel about taking this on?')
- explore any concerns (using counselling skills)

- investigate any benefits for the subordinate
- set clear performance targets and time-scales for the task
- explore options of how they will achieve the desired result (using open questions 'How do you think you will best do this?')
- ask them how you can help them (open questions 'How can I help you best to learn/improve this?')
- build in regular review sessions so that you can check progress and coach any difficulties
- check how they are feeling

Finally, there is a widely held view that a coach needs to be an expert in what they are coaching. Surely this is not the case, otherwise no one would be able to coach those who are expert to improve even further. In the sporting world even the world leaders in their game have coaches who are certainly nowhere near as good as they are. Their experience is that a coach needs to understand the process (the task or the game) but they do not have to be good at it themselves or even be able to do it at all. What a coach can bring to even an expert is an objectivity which someone deeply involved in a process can rarely achieve, a respect and empathy for the individual which builds confidence and trust and a firm belief in the possibility of continually improving even that which is good.

John, who is responsible for staff of 15 in a busy insurance company, comments: When I first heard about coaching at work, I assumed that I was already doing it and, what is more, doing it very successfully. However, the more I read and discussed it with my staff, the more I realised my shortcomings.

Far too often, I had focused on what had to be done in broad outlines – with a date for delivery and rather firm rigid instructions on how I expected it to be done. 'I want a report on the recent art thefts by Friday and I want you to go and talk to X,Y and Z. I want you to include our costs to date on claims set against premiums and I want you to find out what we can expect the level of risks to be over the next two years.'

What I **didn't** do was discuss what I expected the report to look like, how long it should be, whether tables, graphs, etc. should be included and who it should be designed for. Also, I certainly didn't motivate them by allowing them any real creative input of their own. They followed all my instructions and rarely included anything I had forgotten to mention! The results were usually that I didn't get what I wanted because I had been unclear about how the report should be but much too specific about what should be in it. I am working hard to improve my coaching skills and certainly the results are encouraging – both in terms of what I receive and how my staff feel about being delegated tasks. An additional, and unexpected, bonus is that I have discovered that two or three of them produce much, much better reports than I do.

How could I use coaching skills to improve performance?

_____

_____

_____

_____

Further reading

Coaching for performance (J. Whitmore) (1992) Nicholas Brearly Publishing

The Manager as Coach (Duncan and Oats) Pitman Publishing

The Mentoring Manager (G. Lewis) (1996) Pitman Publishing

MANAGING CONFLICT

Many people are extremely uncomfortable when those around them are in conflict and avoid it wherever possible. For a manager, particularly when conflict appears within their team, it is crucial to be able to manage it effectively so that the level of the performance of the whole group does not fall.

It is important to remember, at this stage, that conflict isn't necessarily a problem. If conflict can be managed at an early stage, it may prove to be a catalyst to creativity rather than a negative force.

CONSTRUCTIVE CONFLICTS:

- tend to be centred on interests rather than needs
- tend to be open and dealt with openly
- are capable of helping a relationship develop
- focus on flexible methods for solving disputes
- help both parties reach their objectives

DESTRUCTIVE CONFLICTS:

- tend to be centred on people's needs rather than interests or issues of fact
- focus on personalities, not action or behaviour. ('You are an awkward person' rather than 'You seem to have been awkward recently, what's been the matter?')
- involve face-saving and preservation of power
- attack relationships
- concentrate on 'quick-fix' solutions
- tend to repeat themselves

A constructive conflict may quickly evolve into a destructive one unless both sides can resolve the situation effectively and it is at this stage that the manager may have a vital role to play.

There is a dynamic to the way destructive conflicts evolve:

1. Harmony or perhaps the avoidance of conflict.

2. Silent concern when one party realises a difference but is unwilling (or unable) to express it.

3. Identifying the problem, expressing the concern out loud and being disagreed with.

4. Conflict where unrelated issues (often emotional or relational) are brought in by both sides.

5. Raising the alarm when other parties are appealed to for support

6. Fight or flight when it may lapse into physical or verbal abuse or flight (transfer or resignation).

7. The downwards spiral – at this stage it is likely to repeat itself regularly.

There are several points at which it is appropriate for the manager to intervene to facilitate and help the parties resolve the conflict.

The first, and easiest stage to act as peacemaker, is during **expressing the problem**. The guidelines for behaviour are similar to that of Madam Speaker of the House of Commons (an excellent role model). The aim is to allow both sides to express their views clearly but without engaging in any personal put-downs. You need to encourage the group to listen to other views without feeling threatened and helping the proposer to state them both unemotionally and without aggression. At all times you should be seen to be acting impartially; any suspicion that you have a preference will only add fuel to the potential fire. At this stage you may need to paraphrase and summarise in order to clarify and help people listen.

An example:

'I think that idea is stupid.'

'OK, Paul, I hear that you have some concern about this. Can you tell us exactly what the problem is for you?'

'Well, I think that what we ought to be doing is ...'

'OK. That's an option, certainly. Can you explain to us your reasons behind your view?'

The more the manager remains calm, the more probable it is that the rest of the group will remain calm and by using open questions to uncover the whole issue, it is more likely that the group will be able to listen to the proposal. The person with the problem is likely to diffuse their feelings if they feel that they are being listened to and taken seriously, even if their idea is democratically rejected at the end of the meeting.

However, very often the manager is not present when the conflict appears and may only discover it when one of the protagonists or another member of the group raises the alarm. At this point it is just as important to remain impartial, listen to what is said, acknowledge the problem and begin to find a way to resolve it. Some guidelines include:

- see both parties for equal amounts of time
- listen but remain completely impartial
- reassure them about your confidence in them both (only if this is the truth)
- ensure that each party tells you at least one good thing about the other (see following example)
- call both parties back together
- make it clear that the behaviour is unacceptable
- lead them to build bridges

EXAMPLE

(*Note:* this example has been included to show the process rather than reflect real life timings – resolving conflict can take some time to achieve).

You, the manager, return from a visit to a client to find that two of your staff (Peter and Paul) have had an abusive row in the office. In order to be seen as being impartial, call both together and explain that you are going to speak to each of them individually before speaking to both of them together later in the day. Decide which you are going to speak to first.

'Paul, I am extremely concerned to hear that there was an incident with Peter in the office while I was out this morning.'

'Well, it certainly wasn't my fault.'

'Right now I am not interested in whose fault it was or any excuses – shouting abuse in the office is unacceptable behaviour.' (**setting the boundaries**)

'I know, I shouldn't have shouted but he has been driving me mad for weeks now and I completely lost it when he said that I was being stupid.'

'If there is any misunderstanding about the task or if he is not doing his part effectively, you know that you should come to me with it rather than allow it to cause this sort of uproar. Is there any misunderstanding?' (**clarifying the problem**)

'No, except that he implies all the time that he is better than me.'

'Does he do his job properly?' (**still clarifying**)

'Well, yes. There's nothing actually wrong with what he does.'

'So, there is no misunderstanding and he does a good job, but I am I right in thinking that there is a personality clash between you?' (**still clarifying**)

'Absolutely. Ever since he joined, he's changed the whole atmosphere here.'

'Now, from my point of view, you both do an extremely good job. The team's results are extraordinarily good and I don't want to lose either of you. At your last appraisal, you were talking about building your career here and I agreed that I would support you in any way I could. Are you still committed to that course of action?' (**reassuring and clarifying**)

'Oh yes, he's the only problem. I love my job – apart from him.'

'I am really pleased to hear that (**reassuring**). I understand that you don't find him particularly easy to work with (**empathy**) and I am not expecting you to become best friends, my only concern is that I can help you find a way to work together effectively. You have already said that he does a good job – can you tell me what you think he is contributing to our success? (**moving on – this stage may take some time, use silence and your counselling skills**)

'Well ... he has improved the way we look at customers' needs, his knowledge and contacts has given us a new focus, etc., etc.'

'OK, so he ... (sum up). Now I would like you to go away and think about what we have been talking about while I talk to him. I won't discuss our conversation with anyone else and I don't expect you to either. I'll arrange to speak to you both together later on. How do you feel about that?' (**open question**)

The manager repeats the process with Peter and realises that each of them don't believe the other respects them or acknowledges their skills. He then calls both of them back to his office.

'Right. I am extremely disappointed about the situation this morning and want to make it clear that the behaviour was quite unacceptable and I am not going to tolerate it. You are both valuable members of the team and I want you to work together effectively. I am not necessarily expecting you to become best friends but what saddens me most is that I can see that you each add to and complement the other. What I want you each to do is to focus on the positives. Peter, can you tell Paul something that you can see he is bringing to the team?'

Peter: (**knowing that he has already told the manager several things**) *'Well, I have to say that since you joined you have helped us ...' (etc.)*

'OK, thank you Peter. Now Paul, can you tell Peter something that you admire about him?'

Paul: (**also having already told the manager several things**) 'Well, I must say when I joined I was impressed by ...' etc.

Once you have got them each to acknowledge each other, you may be able to repeat the process several times as they tell each other more of what they told you earlier. You can possibly ask them if there is anything they want to say to each other at this stage (they might even apologise for the morning's incident). You might leave them alone in the office for a few moments while they discuss how they are going to work together better – the equivalent of shaking hands and making up – and because you have persuaded them to acknowledge each other, you have almost certainly resolved the issue of each believing that the other doesn't respect them. Complete the meeting by restating what constitutes unacceptable behaviour and declaring (only if it is true) your confidence in them both.

Conflicts between departments. Resolving conflicts involving members of different departments can be a good deal more complicated.

Imagine you are John and Julian comes to tell you that he is having a problem with Sarah. You talk and discover that the problem seems to be a serious breakdown in communication which is causing your department delays in achieving their work. What do you do?

If you go and talk to Sarah (or ask her to come and see you) the chances are that Susan is going to be really upset about your interference in her department and also that Sarah probably won't take you very seriously either. The best course of action is to go and see Susan, explain the problem from her point of view and ask her to talk to Sarah to assess the situation before coming back to you to discuss how to handle it.

Susan talks to Sarah and rings you back to say that she agrees that there is a problem and it does need to be resolved. What course of action should you now take? In order to remain impartial, it is vital that you and Susan act in unity, agree which of you will take the lead but sit together at each of the following meetings and explain your unity to both Sarah and Julian. Then follow the previous order: see both individuals separately to gain the facts and encourage positive benefits to working better together and then see both together to break the deadlock and build a better relationship.

Now, suppose that Susan comes back to you and says that as far as she is concerned, Sarah is doing all the right things and that the problem seems to be with Julian to whom you should give new instructions – she proposes to take no more action. You disagree completely. What would you do then? Having a row with Susan will only lead to a conflict between the two of you when what you are trying to do is to resolve conflict! You need to explain why you feel this is unsatisfactory and, if she still refuses to reconsider, tell her that you intend to go and see Michael, preferably together, but on your own if necessary. You then need to coach Michael to sort out your potential conflict before you can even think about resolving that involving Sarah and Julian.

To summarise: acting effectively to help resolve conflict requires:

- complete impartiality
- remaining calm and in control at all times
- setting out clearly what and what is not acceptable behaviour
- using counselling and coaching skills where appropriate

Susan, a manager in a provider of community care, remembers 'I had real difficulties resolving problems when I first started. I thought I was doing well but the same difficulties kept arising between the same members of staff until I understood more clearly what was really unacceptable and said so. I think when I was trying to be terribly nice and understand everything from everyone's point of view, they simply weren't taking me seriously. Now I listen slightly less and spell out exactly what behaviour I require – and it seems to be working.'

Peter, a manager in an engineering company, comments 'The thing I found hardest was not to make judgements and get involved. It got so bad that I found myself sorting out one particular individual's difficulties for them so often that I became seen as some sort of special protector for them. Impartiality had gone out of the window and I was losing any respect I had built up. Once I began to help this individual sort the problems out for themselves by focusing on the positives, everything changed. He began to take responsibility for his own difficulties and in fact had far fewer than ever before. We all won through it – better relationships between the staff, more respect for me again and much better quality of final products.'

What will you do to deal with conflict more effectively?

_____

_____

_____

_____

Further reading

How to Solve Your People Problems (J. Allan) 1989 Kogan Page

Managing People for the First Time (Livewire) Pitman Publishing

RECRUITMENT – FINDING NEW MEMBERS OF YOUR TEAM

Your team has been performing really well, generating lots of great team spirit, everyone is working well together and then, suddenly, something changes. It may be that one of the members hands in their resignation, decides to take early retirement, is promoted or even transferred out of the department. But sooner or later you are going to have to face the difficulties involved in finding a new member of staff to replace one of the functions in your team.

It needn't be as difficult as you fear if you go about it in a systematic fashion.

- produce a job description
- produce a character description
- cast your net appropriately
- plan the selection process
- help the new member fit in as smoothly as possible.

Job description. You've quite possibly already got one in your filing system, but it almost certainly will benefit from adaption. Most job descriptions are very out of date and may well have been written by someone who isn't actually doing the job. It is worth producing three different job descriptions before you prepare the final one for publication. First, ask the person who is currently doing the job to do their own; you may be surprised how it differs from the one you hold in your file. Second, prepare one of your own containing what you would like the next holder of the post to be doing and third, ask the remainder of the team to create one with their views of what the new holder of the post should do.

Recruiting a new member of staff is an opportunity to move the whole team forward. Too often recruitment is aimed at finding a clone for the person who is leaving the post rather than to to find the ideal person to join the team to help it move forward. Because a team is a constantly growing and changing entity, it is quite likely that the previous occupant of the post was ideal for the time and stage that they were recruited, but now, partly because of his/her input, it has changed and the ideal candidate will be required to play an enhanced role.

Character description. What sort of person you require in terms of personality and character is just as important as what sort of qualifications and previous experience you expect them to have. It is likely that you have spent a considerable amount of time and energy in helping your team to blend together to produce the synergy that is the result of good teamworking; now is not the time to waste all that effort by choosing a square peg to fit in a round hole. Involve your team in this process as much as

Recruiting a new member of staff is an opportunity to move the whole team forward.

possible. They are the ones who are going to have to work with the new member of staff and their views are likely to be helpful in the development of a profile of the ideal candidate. Re-read the section on the roles people play in teams (*page 315*) and consider whether this recruitment might provide an opportunity to provide further balance or creative diversity.

The profile of the ideal candidate should include a character outline, a description of the qualifications and previous experience required. Ignore prejudicial views on age, gender and any other 'ism', most of which are in any case illegal under employment law. If you concentrate on what you want the ideal candidate to do and what sort of character they should be, it is quite possible that the perfect appointment may not look exactly how you imagined.

Casting the net. Your personnel or human resource department will have considerable experience in this area so discuss it fully with them. Your options will probably include:

- internal advertising
- local and/or national press advertising
- local employment agencies
- networking

Both internal advertising and networking have two great advantages. First, they cost you nothing and second, any responses are likely to have either some detailed knowledge of your organisation or a personal recommendation. Advertising (through the press or an employment agency) will involve you in some cost which needs to be carefully assessed, but is likely to provide a much broader range of applicants. An employment agency may even offer to screen candidates on your behalf against your profile.

Plan the selection process. Hopefully you will now receive a large quantity of applications who generally fit the requirements stated in the advertisement. How do you go about selecting one of them to fill the position?

- select the interviewing criteria
- decide who will do the interviewing, introduce them to the team and show them around
- write to each candidate to be interviewed, listing the time of the interview, who will be interviewing them and what the process will consist of. Ask them to ring back to confirm their availability

First, you need to have prepared and prioritised a list of criteria for the selection process. You have already produced a list of all the desirable qualities, characteristics, qualifications and experience that the position requires, but the likelihood is that none of the applicants will be a perfect match. You need to separate each topic and prioritise it. For example, you may decide that it is essential that the successful applicant is experienced on your particular model of equipment, it would be highly advantageous if they have a good broad education (i.e. specific exam qualifications), useful if they have experience in your particular industry and nice if they like to play football (to join the rest of your team). These criteria will help you go through the applications to choose a suitable number to interview.

It is worth remembering that interviewing is a tiring process and if you attempt to see too many candidates, it will take a great deal of time and may not produce the best result. An ideal number of candidates seems to be six, which allows you to complete the interviewing comfortably within one day.

You have now selected the six best applicants for interview. How do you go about it most effectively? You need to plan how to manage the interviews. It is always better if two people conduct the interview as it provides a more balanced outcome and helps both of you put any personal prejudices to one side and work together against a set list of criteria. It may be that one of your personnel department will want to take part in the process or another manager who is not necessarily connected to your department. Ideally you should set aside one hour for each applicant so that you have a chance to assess them in depth rather than on a first impression. You should plan at least the first half hour of the interview so that you have a list of questions and topics to help you assess them fairly against each other. The second half of the interview you may leave more flexible so that you can encourage them to interview you (after all, you want them to gain a commitment to wishing to join your team rather than just get a job) and to, if you wish, go further into any interesting topics that have come up.

The other aspect to arranging interviews is to think about how to introduce the applicants to your team so that they can gain at least some impression of them and so that the team too can be involved in the process. You may want to ask the applicant to arrive half an hour before so that one of the team can show them around the working area and introduce them to the rest of the team for a little while.

The day before the interviews, prepare a list of names of the applicants together with the time of their arrival and distribute it to everyone who might need to know: security, reception, personnel and the members of the team. Nothing gives a worse impression of an organisation than not being expected.

At the end of the formal interviews, gather your material together, debrief the sessions with your co-interviewer and compile your comments onto one list. Call the team together and ask them for their comments. It may be that one candidate immediately emerges as the leading contender or you may have a situation where two are equally good and you might need to consider holding a second interview to finally make a decision.

Avoid the temptation to compromise too much. Taking on a new member of staff is an expensive, time-consuming process and every attempt should be made to find the right person rather than picking the best of a poor bunch.

Taking on someone who is obviously not what you are looking for will prove to be damaging. Consider re-advertising while using temporary staff to cover the vacancy rather than being panicked into making a poor choice.

Where possible, let the candidates all know the outcome as soon as possible. This is professional and shows respect for them and their feelings. Always contact your first choice first and offer them the position, if you are authorised to do so. The danger of turning down the others before you contact your first choice is that it is always possible that they might turn you down.

Help the new member of staff fit into the team as smoothly as possible. The first few weeks of an employee in a new job need to be managed carefully to ensure that they begin to perform effectively as soon as possible. Remember that the first impression is all important. It is likely that your new recruit is quite nervous, they may have left a secure job to join your team and need to feel reassured that they have done the right thing. Plan to greet them when they arrive, make sure that everyone (including reception, security and personnel) are expecting them and plan their first day so that everything is efficient and smooth. Many organisations ask new members of staff to arrive half an hour after everyone else so that things are under control when they appear. Always remember that if they are skilled, experienced and exciting enough for you to want to employ them, others will as well, so look after them.

Your organisation may have a first-class induction programme but always plan for yourself how you can improve the introduction into your particular team. You might consider asking one member of the team to act as a 'buddy' to show them around, explain the culture and generally look after them. You might pay the bill for a team lunch so that the building of a relationship begins as quickly as possible.

You should also plan to spend a considerable amount of time with the new recruit – it is too late at the three-month appraisal to raise concerns about their performance. You need to be having regular sessions with them during the first three-month period so that you can confirm that they are up to speed and that you are happy with your choice at that stage.

A new member of staff gives you the opportunity to gain some objective feedback about the current processes and lead you to further improvement. A new pair of eyes will often notice anomalies and ask the question 'Why?' about the culture that has been taken for granted by those of you steeped in it. Encourage your team to welcome this objectivity and use the new member of staff to comment on what they observe so that you can benefit doubly from their joining; for the first three months you have your own objective consultant without the cost. Use their comments wisely.

How can you improve your recruitment procedures?

_____

_____

_____

_____

_____

_____

_____

_____

Further reading

There is much detailed advice in many of the books available on personnel management.

How to Solve Your People Problems (J. Allen) (1989) Kogan Page and *Managing People for the First Time* (Livewire) Pitman Publishing

Both contain useful sections on Recruitment and Selection

Finding & Keeping the Right People (J. Billsberry) Pitman Publishing

APPRAISALS

Sadly, appraisals are often taken less than seriously by both parties involved in them. Many managers dread having to do them (Oh, no, not that time of year again) and wonder whether they have any value at all, while the staff dread them nearly as much (It's ridiculous, they still haven't got round to doing what was agreed last year) and (My manager doesn't see enough of me to know how I am doing).

Perhaps one of the answers is to give them a new name in your department and rethink what their purpose is and how to make them relevant and valuable. Many organisations have decided to call their appraisals various names such as:

- personal development planning
- individual performance assessment
- progress and planning
- joint review and action planning
- performance improvement and development

What is the purpose of an appraisal? It should be to review the individual's progress to date and plan further development for the future.

It is a discussion between both parties, not an interview. It is an opportunity for coaching rather than for criticism or judgement. It is about performance and should not be linked to salary and disciplinary matters.

It has often been stated that if a manager is good, he or she will have a relationship with each member of staff where they are both continually working to help each other improve and develop their performance. This is perfectly true in practice but as human beings we often find that we become so involved in the everyday task that is often difficult to see 'the wood for the trees'. Most of us take time at the New Year or even on birthdays to review our lives, where we are going and what we would like to do to move forward. A formal appraisal system allows this need to take an objective look at progress in the workplace. Currently most appraisals are undertaken yearly and you may well decide that it would be helpful to have quarterly follow-up sessions to review progress and adapt, if necessary, the action plan.

Everyone in the organisation should be part of an appraisal system. Any organisation that claims to be committed to development and continuous improvement while allowing its staff to avoid being appraised is sending the wrong message to its employees. This book is aimed at the manager of a team, which raises the question 'Are you the right person to appraise them?' The answer is probably 'yes' but it is always worth considering how to obtain some feedback from the other members of the team. The most constructive feedback is likely to come from those working closely with the member of staff on a daily basis.

Most appraisal systems are based on a form that is copied to the manager and the subordinate. Many organisations are now asking several other staff to fill in the form to return to the manager for added feedback. So planning and allowing plenty of notice before an appraisal is essential.

PLANNING AN APPRAISAL

- give at least one week's notice
- plan the location and time carefully
- give thought and care to filling in your feedback form
- don't plan more than two each day
- start with the willing volunteers first

Give plenty of notice. You have to organise a convenient time for the meeting and fill in the appraisal forms which may take a considerable period of time to do properly. Any individual given only 24 hours to review their progress over the past year and preview the future is likely to produce a very narrow, superficial result. A week's notice is perhaps the absolute minimum to provide a good overview. Encourage them to take it seriously and fill in their form with care.

Consider carefully which location and time of day will suit both of you best. Neutral territory is often helpful – a meeting room is often ideal. Calling staff into your office may lead them to feel intimidated and put you in a dominant position, a situation which is not likely to lead to a balanced discussion. Since an appraisal is about work performance, it is generally best held on site, although, ideally, away from the daily workplace. There are stories of appraisals being held in the pub and in restaurants but luckily these are rare because it is unlikely that you will be able to hold a frank and open discussion surrounded by other people socialising. Try to match the location and timing to each person individually as what suits you may well not suit others. Allow plenty of time, at least two hours, and be prepared to give the session your full attention. Avoid booking another important meeting directly following an appraisal so that your attention doesn't wander towards the end. If the session looks as if it could run considerably longer than two hours, find an appropriate point to discuss adjournment until another day.

The appraisal form. Most organisations use forms to aid the preparation of an appraisal session. These forms generally consist of two sections: a review of the previous period and a preview of the future. You should fill in one form about the individual concerned and they should fill in their own about themselves. When they have completed their form, they should pass you a copy of it so that you can prepare for the session itself.

The questions that should be considered in preparing for an appraisal are:

REVIEW OF PAST PERFORMANCE

What are your hopes/aspirations for this appraisal?
What particularly do you want us to cover?
How do you feel about the past year?

Job

What do you see as the main purpose of your job?
How has the job developed over the last year/period?
Which aspects of your job do you find most/least interesting?
Which aspects of your job do you find most challenging?
Which aspects of your job do you feel happy about?
Which areas were most frustrating?
What has produced the successes?
What has caused the problems?

Relationships

Who are your main work contacts?
Who directly affects your performance most?
How do you feel about your work relationships?

Development

What do you think are the key skills you need to do your job?
How do you rate yourself in these?
Do you have skills that are not being fully used?

Personal

How do you feel about the problems we've identified?
What would you say you've learned from this?
Is there anything you would do differently, in hindsight?

Completion

Is there anything else you'd like to raise?

IMPROVING FUTURE PERFORMANCE

How do you think your job might develop in the next year?
How would you like to see your working relationships develop?
What can be done to improve things?
How would you prioritise the things you've identified?

Job/relationships

What can you do to help things happen?

How would you go about doing that?

What help would you need from others/me?

What do you see as appropriate objectives for the next year?

How could you measure success?

What might block success?

How could these blocks be overcome?

What alternatives do we have?

Developmental

What additional training/development/special projects would be useful?

What sort of responsibilities would you like to take on?

Personal

How do you see your future career progressing?

How do you see your future with this organisation?

What are the next steps in your personal development?

Conclusion

Is there anything else you would like to talk about?

How do you feel about what we have discussed?

What do you see as the main targets that we've discussed?

When should we meet again to review progress?

Give thought and care to filling in your section of the form. Look out the previous action plan and any objectives that have been agreed. Mark progress as specifically as you can (many appraisal forms ask for percentages) and prepare to give specific details about both successes and areas that you feel have not achieved their targets. Try to avoid any personal prejudices and focus on the output (the performance) of the individual concerned, that is their responsibilities, their working relationships and their career aspirations. Aim to concentrate on average performance rather than any extremes that may have occurred during the period under review. It is worth planning to spend three-quarters of the session on what is going well but could still be improved rather than focusing on what is not going well.

An effective appraisal session takes both time and concentration so don't try to appraise the whole department in one day – you will be exhausted and those in the afternoon will suffer badly. Ideally plan one in the morning and another in the afternoon and give both your full attention. You will gain far more by taking your time and doing them well rather than rushing through them. Perhaps this is one reason why appraisals have such a poor reputation in many organisations.

Start with the willing volunteers first. If there is a reluctance to take appraisals seriously in your department, always aim to begin with someone who is at least willing. The success you achieve together will help to change the attitudes of the rest of the team. If you try to crack the toughest nut first, you are likely to spend a great deal of time and attention for very little reward.

The appraisal session: the time has arrived, you have the room booked, everything you might both need available, the phones are redirected, you each have your forms filled in – now what?

- set the scene
- allow at least equal time for each of you to speak
- encourage them to give their views before you do
- ask open questions and listen carefully
- be positive, approving, and specific
- try not to discuss other people
- complete each section before moving on
- create an action plan
- encourage feedback for yourself

Set the scene: avoid diving straight into the process. Allow yourself a few minutes to help them relax and focus on the objectives for the session. A short introduction period will help you both relate to each other and set the scene for genuine communication. It might be helpful to ask them how they are feeling about the session and what their objectives are.

Allow equal time for speaking and encourage them to give their views first. Always remember that this is their appraisal and not yours. Of course it is an opportunity for you to give them acknowledgement and good constructive feedback, but you will both gain far more from it if you can encourage them to speak first. Each section might begin by you discussing what they have written. Discuss that in detail before you add anything you feel has been missed and then discuss that. See your role as adding an additional viewpoint as well as facilitating the session. Be aware that some people will be very hard on themselves and find it difficult to acknowledge any successes while others find it hard to admit any failings and claim full achievement of each and every objective. Treat each appraisal session individually and respond to each member of staff appropriately.

Use all your communication skills. A good appraisal requires the use of all the effective communication skills (*page 66*), listening skills (*page 93*), coaching (*page 360*) and counselling skills (*page 353*). Open questions are useful to help you encourage them to speak and to develop their point. Before the session re-read the section on giving constructive feedback (*page 99*) and remember to give praise where appropriate as this may prove more motivating than the most constructive criticism. Always be specific and descriptive about any feedback you give and keep it in 'I' statements. 'I noticed ...' rather than 'Everyone says you ...'

Avoid discussing other people. Because many people find being appraised an uncomfortable process, beware of red herrings being introduced to divert your attention away from the individual concerned. One of the most common red herrings in appraisals is that of other people. The individual being appraised may well raise an issue they are having with another member of staff and if you are not careful, you will spend the session discussing the wrong person. Stay on target.

Complete each section before moving on. It is important to summarise and clarify what you have agreed about each section before you move onto the next because, at the end of the session, you will be expected to write up the conclusions. If you can agree together what the balanced view is, there will be less chance of disagreement after the session about the report. If while you are discussing the achievement of this year's objectives, a point is raised about how it could have been better, make a note and bring it back into the preparation of next year's objectives. Try and separate the review from the preview of the future so that you don't get into a muddle.

Planning the next year: creating action plans and objectives for the next year are a crucial part of an appraisal session. Many training consultants suggest that you write the employees' objectives before the meeting but this may result in conflict or lack of motivation. Of course, you need to prepare and consider some goals and objectives, but if you can set and agree them together you will have involved the member of staff and it is much more likely that they will be committed to achieving them.

Encourage feedback for yourself. No manager can manage a subordinate effectively unless they ask for feedback. 'How can I help you?', 'What could I do to help you achieve these objectives?' 'How would you like me to support you?' are just some of the open questions that will give you the information you need to help the individual achieve their objectives and manage them more effectively in the future. An appraisal session should be as much a learning experience for you as for the member of staff being appraised. Listen as carefully as you can to what they have to tell you – it may surprise you.

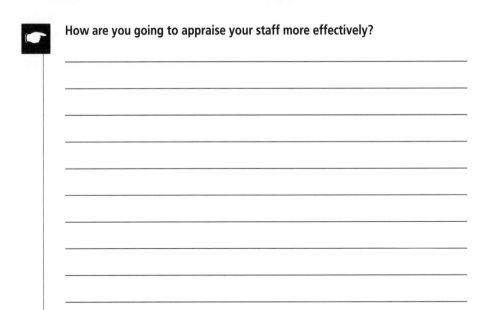

How are you going to appraise your staff more effectively?

_____

_____

_____

_____

_____

_____

_____

_____

_____

_____

Further reading

The Perfect Appraisal (H. Hudson) 1992 Century Business

TRAINING AND DEVELOPMENT

Every single organisation pledges its commitment to the training and development of its staff but, sadly, the results suggest that still comparatively little is being done. If you want the very best team, you will need to do all you can to ensure that your staff are trained and developed to help them achieve both their personal potential and the potential of the team.

Some organisations believe that an individual who is learning anything, related to work or not, is more likely to be able to embrace change willingly and is more open to learning new work skills. Rover Cars, for example, contribute to the cost of employees learning skills such as ballroom dancing, brick-laying and pottery as well as more work-related skills including foreign language courses.

There are two main obstacles to training and development programmes within organisations: the cost and time involved. There is no easy solution to these obstacles: each organisation needs to assess for itself whether the short-term investment is worthwhile in terms of the longer-term benefits. But you, as the manager of a department or team, have some responsibility for the training and development of your own staff and even with restrictions on budgeting imposed on you, there are options that can be considered.

One organisation on Tyneside wanted its managers to attend training on time management and found that all the managers identified claimed that they did not have enough time available to attend! The solution of the training manager was to design a 'Ten Minute Idiot's Guide to Time Management' which contains only two elements – taking 'Time Out': and keeping a 'Clean Diary'. 'This course has proved to be effective immediately and is employed keenly by its adherents' claims its inventor.

Any training or development needs to be as effective as possible. Just sending people on a course is not likely by itself to achieve the desired result. Training needs to be carefully tailored to the individual concerned and the benefits to both parties explored in some detail. For a member of staff to get the most out of a course, they may need to know that acquiring this skill will lead to promotion or be part of their personal development plan created in the appraisal session. A manager's responsibility does not end with signing the purchase order for training; he or she needs to discuss with the individual what the objectives, for both parties, of the training are and debrief the learning on return to work as well as supporting and coaching the resulting action plan. After all, knowing what to do is rarely the same as putting it into action and the manager has responsibility for the implementation of newly acquired skills and techniques.

Training needs to be carefully tailored to the individual concerned

Training and development takes many forms and this chapter will consider the costs and benefits of some of the options:

- external courses
- internal training with an external consultant
- internal training with an in-house trainer
- internal training with an experienced operative
- coaching
- training within working hours
- training outside working hours
- shared cost of training
- using Open University, evening classes and other community education opportunities

External courses. There are a great many providers of courses and programmes open to members of any organisation which cover a wide variety of topics. The advantages are that the trainer will be both experienced in delivering training and an expert in their particular field. Because the training is taking place away from the working environment, the participant is able to concentrate on the task in hand without interruption, given an opportunity to reassess their own particular role at work and how it can be improved, as well as to gain enormously from learning alongside people doing similar work in other organisations. The networking opportunities and insight gained from this mixing of people should not be underestimated. The disadvantage, however, is that this form of training is quite costly to the organisation.

Internal training with an external consultant. One way to reduce the cost per head of training is to employ the experienced and expert trainer to work with a group of people within your organisation. Because you will be supplying the venue, the participants and most of the administration, the cost will be considerably lower. Another advantage is that your team can all learn together, building team spirit, sharing the experience and be able to support each other in the implementation. The disadvantage is that there is no input from external participants, no network-building and less chance to look at the whole situation from an objective point of view.

Internal training with an in-house trainer. Many organisations employ trainers within their personnel (or other) departments. The advantages are that the training can be very clearly focused on the particular issues involved and the cost is greatly reduced (sometimes no charge is made to the department at all). The potential disadvantages are that the trainer may not be perceived as an expert in the subject and may not have the credibility of an external consultant.

Internal training with an experienced member of staff. More and more organisations are beginning to take this option seriously. It is likely that your Finance Department contains at least one member who could probably run a programme on accounting for non-accountants at least as well as an external trainer. Similarly, if you want to provide specialised training on a piece of equipment, you may benefit from considering one of the present operators of the equipment rather than call on the manufacturer. This form of internal training tends to be immensely practical rather than theoretical. The advantages are that it is very realistic, is focused on exactly what the organisation wants and develops the individual who is delivering it. You might also ask a member of your staff who has attended an external training programme to share, formally, what they have learned with the rest of the team, thus paying for one person to attend but ensuring that valuable material to spread to the remaining members of staff. You may well discover a new star in your ranks. The disadvantages are that the individual may not be particularly gifted at teaching or communicating and that those learning may not take it quite as seriously as they would if an external 'expert' were delivering it.

Coaching (*refer back to section on page 360*). Coaching is very often the most effective way of teaching and learning new skills and works best in a one-to-one situation allowing plenty of hands-on experience. This is the oldest form of training. One individual learns (or discovers) a new skill and then spreads the skill by explaining how it works, showing their partner and then allowing them to try it out for themselves. Coaching can be used for work-related technical skills as well as the personal development aspects that are increasingly valuable in the workplace such as communication skills etc. Coaching helps build relationships between individuals, is highly cost-effective and ensures a high degree of learning and understanding (because of the aspect of experience that is built in). The only disadvantages are that it takes a little longer than simply telling someone what to do (but this is outweighed by its advantages) and that occasionally you might find that an experienced operator does not want to share their skills for fear of losing their powerful position within the team (this would require some coaching from you to resolve the issue).

How do you find the time for training? Finding the time for formal training programmes can be particularly difficult in the current climate of stretched resources. There are two options – training within working hours and training outside working hours.

Training within working hours is the common expectation of both managers and staff and has many advantages. Staff understand that they are being paid to learn and therefore take it seriously, they are likely to be alert and in the right frame of mind to concentrate and, because training is often a change from day-to-day tasks, are prepared to be enthusiastic and positive. The disadvantages are that while they are attending training, their work is not being done. It generally takes a serious commitment from senior management to build in training time to the productivity forecasts.

Training outside working hours is a concept that is growing, particularly in smaller and service organisations. It has many advantages: teams are able to learn together, no time is taken away from the tasks that have to be completed, there are likely to be no interruptions and some social aspect may be built in (leisure clothing may be worn, refreshments supplied, etc.).

The disadvantages are that staff may be tired in the evenings or loath to give up their weekends or leisure time for the organisation. You really can't insist that staff train in their own time unless it has been built into their contracts of employment and it is possible that there will be several empty spaces or, perhaps even worse, resentful attendees who are there in person only. If you consider that this way of training is the answer for you and your team, you will need to consider carefully how to present it to them; for it to be successful you need to gain their willing agreement.

Shared cost of training. One way organisations have found to build commitment to learning is to pay either part of the cost of training or part of the time required. If, for example, a member of staff expresses an interest in undertaking an MBA course which is likely to cost a great deal of both time and money with no guarantee that they will continue working for you when it is completed, you might negotiate that they take an Open University course with a certain number of hours a week allowed by the organisation for study.

Many smaller organisations offer either time off to study or to pay part of the fee for the course. It is certainly true that if a member of staff is expected to pay part of the cost themselves or to give up a certain amount of their own time, it is likely that they will be highly committed to what they choose to take on. In an ideal world, every organisation would make both time and money available to enable its staff to develop the skills necessary both to do a good job and to equip themselves for advancement in their career. Realistically, many smaller organisations simply cannot do this and sharing the input of money and time for development is a great deal better than refusing any training to its staff.

Using community education opportunities. There are an enormous amount of education possibilities available at very little cost within the community. The Open University and evening classes are just two examples which both offer a surprisingly wide range of subjects and levels of study. It is well worth getting hold of the programme each year to check that you know exactly what is available, both for yourself and your staff. The Open University produce some fascinating programmes which you may want to watch – even though you are not doing the course.

Self-discovery: always remember that the business and personnel development sections of your local bookshop can be a valuable resource for the development of skills and knowledge. Reading other people's ideas can be an inspiring experience as you may discover all sorts of potential answers to some of the areas that you have been finding a challenge. Encourage your staff to read widely on the topics that are associated with their work, lend them books and suggest titles that they may find helpful.

What skills have you got that you could share with your team?

_____

_____

_____

_____

_____

What skills are there available within your team that could be shared?

_____

_____

_____

_____

_____

Further reading

Most management books contain a section on training and development. Pitman produce a series of **Ready Made Activity** books which provide material useful for anyone considering running a training programme on a variety of topics (including _communication, negotiation, presentation skills_, etc.)

UNDERSTANDING THE VALUE OF EXPERIENCE

Reviewing each day, or week, is a powerful aid to your development

This is the last chapter of the book and you have worked your way through all the aspects of personal management development that the sources for this book felt were the most important for success. So, now what? Do you sit back and just wait for the success to roll in? No, unfortunately it isn't that simple.

First, you need to be implementing whatever you have learned from this book and decided would be of value to you. As we said earlier, **knowing what to do and actually doing it are quite separate things**. You, and only you, can actually become a better manager and a more effective performer of your tasks at work if you take responsibility for your own development. There are plenty of people who may be able to help you but, ultimately, only you can make yourself both more effective and more successful. However committed other people are to your success and however gifted they are as a coach or a mentor, they can't make you do anything about it.

You have to consider and answer truthfully the following questions:

- Do you really want to achieve your potential for your career?
- Are you prepared to do what is necessary to achieve it?

And then you have to carefully work out what, for you, are the necessary steps to achieving your personal potential. When you have done this, then it helps enormously to find yourself a coach and/or mentor to help you work through some of what may be difficult learning processes.

IMPLEMENTING YOUR OWN PERSONAL DEVELOPMENT PLANS

Before we move onto reviewing your experiences, it is worth just reminding you of some simple guidelines to implementation:

- start with easy situations
- make small changes in your behaviour
- don't put things off
- work with what is rather than what you think it should be

Start with easy situations. Don't immediately try to dive into the deep end and solve all your most difficult situations first. Build up gently, starting with the easy situations so that as you resolve them, you build up your confidence and learn from your own experiences. The temptation is always to think 'Ah, now I have a handle on how to deal with the most difficult person in the department, or situation that I dread, so now I can solve them for once and all'. The danger with acting on this impulse is that it may not be resolved at the first attempt and it is likely that you will lose confidence and decide to give up and implement nothing that you have learned.

Make small changes in your behaviour. Even if you only adapt your behaviour by 1 per cent it may have a major impact on your effectiveness. You may remember people who have returned from courses determined to change dramatically the way they operated and the reaction on those around them. 'What on earth is going on? Oh, yes, that course. Well, if we don't react then soon everything will return to normal.' People are used to you as you have been and it will scare them to death if you suddenly try and change yourself and the way you operate. Make small changes so that they can relate to you and respond to any new openings you are giving them. Tell them, if appropriate, that you want to help them more and that is why you are intending to make some changes in your relationship. Remember 'How do you eat an elephant? In bite-sized chunks' and avoid attempting to swallow the whole thing in one gulp.

Don't put it off. Putting new plans into operation can be a challenging process. If you start with small changes, that will help by reducing the elephant into something more manageable. But the only way to achieve anything worthwhile is to actually begin to do it. Make a commitment to beginning at least one small step of your plan and tell someone to ensure that you don't manage to avoid it!

Work with what is. Avoid getting caught in the trap of thinking that before you can do anything, you need to change organisations because this one is impossible. We are very clever at coming up with all sorts of reasons why we shouldn't do things. Don't put off the implementation of your development plan just because things aren't the way you think they should be. One interesting by-product of changing the way you operate is that you may well find that the people and culture around you appear to change as well. Always begin by working with what currently exists rather than complain about why it shouldn't be that way.

And when you have learned all you set out to do, look out for more development opportunities.

Personal development is a never-ending journey. There is no final goal to be reached. Using the analogy of a car journey, you may have started at Brighton and plan to get to Birmingham, but once there you will realise that there are many more places, some in different directions, that you could aim for. **Your personal potential has no limit** – there is no final destination. And every single thing that you do, however successfully, could always be improved. It is this continual striving for improvement that is the final stage on the journey to success.

REVIEWING SKILLS

One of the most valuable experiences that the sources for this book acknowledged was that of reviewing each and every experience of the day to learn from it. Too often people either forget what they have done as soon as they have completed it or worry about it in case something goes wrong even after it is all over. A helpful process is to find a time each day to review – this might be on your journey home or before you go to sleep each night.

REVIEWING PROCESS

- Go through each section of the day in your head.
- What went well and what did you do that helped it work out?
- What didn't go quite so well?
- What could you, with the value of hindsight, have done differently to improve the quality of the outcomes
- Make a note of what you learn.
- Decide whether you need to revise anything from the day – if so, make a note of it.
- You have now completed the day, so forget it and relax.

It is important to continue to remember to learn at least as much from your success as your difficulties. Similar to the experience of praise rather than criticism, often when you try to do more of what you do well, you hardly have to think about how to improve what you aren't doing so well. Review everything that has gone well to see if you can identify any trends that helped you achieve it and then consider whether it would be appropriate to use the same techniques in a more difficult situation.

When reviewing a situation that hasn't gone particularly well, it is important not to carry it around with you like a boulder on your back: 'I really really messed up over that one, what a fool I am'. Consider if there is anything you need to do the next day that will either put it right or repair a damaged relationship. For example, if you have been short with someone rather than listen, you could go back and apologise and ask if you can have the conversation again. If there seems to be nothing you can do to change the situation, learn all you can from it and then move on, forget about it. Feeling guilty about a past situation is a complete waste of energy and doesn't do anything to resolve it – so put it behind you and resolve to learn whatever lessons you can so that it is unlikely to be repeated.

Reviewing each day, or each week, is a powerful aid to your development. As human beings we tend to gain much more from our own experience than any other form of learning. Sadly we seem even to need to go through it ourselves rather than learn from other people's experience.

A coach or a mentor can be very valuable in helping you review your performance and identifying any learning opportunities. They will also help you to implement the lessons, if you allow them to.

Richard, a senior IT manager, finds that reviewing each day on his journey home has provided benefits that he hadn't expected. As well as giving him pointers to learning that he can then use in his own personal development plan, he has learned to stop worrying so much and relax better. By the time he has completed his review and made notes about what he is going to do the next day and pulled out anything he wants to consider with his coach, he finds that the working day is then complete for him. When he gets home, he is relaxed and more able to enjoy his social life, he sleeps better and arrives at work ready to put his notes into operation, confident that nothing has been missed or forgotten.

How are you going to review your day in order to learn from your own experiences?

_____

_____

_____

_____

_____

_____

_____

_____

_____

_____

_____

_____

_____

_____

_____

_____

_____

_____

_____

_____

_____

_____

_____

_____

_____

_____

A FINAL WORD

There is not a single person on the planet who can stop you doing what you really want to – except you

If you have worked you way through this programme of self-development, you will have done a great deal of work and may be feeling a little intimidated about the future. This short, final, section is to encourage you to take the bold step of making the greatest contribution you can to the field of work that you choose.

Too often people feel that they do not have enough to offer and so hold back from making the contribution that they are capable of. The world needs each and every one of us to be the very best we can be and make our own unique contribution to its future. It is up to you to decide what and where your particular career lies and then to move ahead to take your rightful place within it.

This book has aimed to guide you through your journey of development so that you are equipped to take on your own particular challenges. There is a wonderful story that God needed someone to do something about the famine in Africa in 1984 so he came down to earth and knocked on a door which finally opened to reveal a dishevelled Bob Geldof 'Oh dear', God said, 'You weren't really what I had in mind – but nevertheless – you'll do.' Perhaps it is the same for us – none of us is quite perfect, but nevertheless we are in the right place at the right time and we'll do.

You have to decide what it is that you want to make a contribution to, build the support networks and coaches to help you, learn from your experiences and do the best you can. And when the going gets difficult, remember:

- failure isn't when you fall down,
- failure only exists when you don't get up again.

So pick yourself up, dust yourself down, learn from the experience and start again.

Everything you say and everything you do makes a difference.

INDEX